Children and the Law in Texas

Ramona
Freeman
John

Children and
the Law in Texas

What Parents Should Know

University of Texas Press
Austin

Requests for permission to reproduce material from this work should be sent
to Permissions, University of Texas Press, Box 7819, Austin, TX 78713-7819.

∞ The paper used in this book meets the minimum requirements of
ANSI/NISO Z39.48-1992 (R1997) (Permanence of Paper).

Library of Congress Cataloging-in-Publication Data

John, Ramona Freeman, 1932–
    Children and the law in Texas : what parents should know / Ramona
Freeman John. — 1st ed.
      p.   cm.
    Includes index.
    ISBN 0-292-74050-6 (cloth : alk. paper). — ISBN 0-292-74051-4 (pbk. : alk.
paper)
    1. Children—Legal status, laws, etc.—Texas—Popular works. 2. Parent
and child (Law)—Texas—Popular works. I. Title.
KFT1291.M5J64 1999
986.76401'35—dc21   98-36496

Dedication

To my husband, Dick.
Love of my life, best friend,
And the patient partner
Who typed this whole Thing.
Many times.

Contents

Preface   **ix**

1. Judges, Lawyers, Ad Litems, and Witnesses   **1**

2. The Parent-Child Relationship   **9**

3. Establishing Paternity   **15**

4. Adoption   **22**

5. Liability of Parents for Their Children's Acts   **36**

6. Children and Divorce   **38**

7. Managing and Possessory Conservatorship   **41**

8. Visitation   **50**

9. Child Support   **56**

10. Modification of Custody, Visitation, Support, and the Rights of Parents   **66**

11. Interference with the Possession of Children   **71**

12. Termination of the Parent-Child Relationship   **79**

13. Removal of a Child from the Home   **87**

14. Children Who Are Victims of Abuse, Neglect, and Crime   **101**

15. Rights of Grandparents and Other Non-Parents   **117**

16. Children Who Run Away from Home   **125**

17. Children and Marriage   **128**

18. Changing a Child's Name   **134**

19. Removing Disabilities of Minority   **137**

20. Children and Health   **141**

21. Children with Disabilities   **150**

22. Children and Drugs   **162**

23. Children and School   **173**

24. Children Who Work   **188**

25. Children and Their Property   **191**

26. Benefits Available to Children   **198**

27. Children and Driving   **201**

28. Children Suspected of Breaking the Law   **205**

29. The Child in Juvenile Court   **229**

30. Certification: Children in Adult Criminal Court   **247**

31. Keeping Your Child out of Trouble   **254**

32. Victims of Juvenile Crime   **259**

33. Rights of Unborn Children   **262**

Index   **267**

Preface

This is a book about the law and how it affects the lives of Texas children and their parents, and they are the people for whom it was written. It isn't for lawyers. They already have whole libraries, filled with books, to tell them about the law, and they may know all of this anyway.

I wrote this book because I love children, just as you do. And I believe that the more you know about how our law affects them, and your relationship with them, the better their lives and yours will be.

The law hasn't always protected children. There was a time when a ten-year-old could be hanged for stealing a loaf of bread. In the early days of our country, children were mere possessions of their parents with no rights of their own. The first juvenile court was established about one hundred years ago.

Recently, we've become more aware that one of society's most cherished assets is our children. They are the fabric of our tomorrows. They will define our nation in years to come. We've passed special laws dealing with children, to provide them additional protection and assure them the greatest opportunity to develop into productive, happy adults. As you'll see, many laws are different where children are involved.

While I'm a lawyer, I'm not your lawyer, and this book is not meant to give you advice regarding your case. It's meant only as a starting point, to help you understand how the laws of Texas affect you and your children. If you have a legal problem, please discuss it with your attorney. Don't try to make a decision that will affect the rest of your life based on what you read here. It's impossible to cover in this or any book every set of circumstances that might arise. And besides, the law changes; what is accurate information now may not be later. Existing federal law makes enactment of new legislation by the state legislature concerning paternity establishment, for example, a virtual certainty. When I have mentioned specific laws I have tried only to give you a general idea of what they require. Courts look at each word of a statute to decide what it means. Ask your attorney how a particular law applies in your case.

Also, don't assume that your case is just like your friend's. It isn't; the facts and circumstances are never exactly the same. Talk to an attorney.

If you don't have an attorney, contact your local bar association, or speak with friends who've been represented by someone in a similar case to see if they suggest hiring that person as your lawyer.

If you can't afford to hire an attorney, check with the bar association for the names of agencies that provide low-cost or even no-cost legal assistance. Some bar associations also have their own program to provide private attorneys in certain cases for people who need help but can't pay legal fees.

Almost always in Texas law "the child" means both the male and the female child. Rather than constantly using the cumbersome "he or she" in referring to "the child," I alternate between "he" in one chapter and "she" in the next. The same is true of personal pronouns that refer to "the judge," "the caseworker," "the police officer," "the lawyer," "the parent," and other persons who could be of either gender. Of course, in some places the legal issue discussed (pregnancy), the nature of a relationship (father), or a proper name (Lisa) dictates which pronoun is used.

I've tried in this book to help you become more familiar with Texas law. I've also expressed an occasional opinion. What I've said is what I believe. Not everyone will agree with me. No problem. Anyone who wants can write a book of his own.

Texas laws aren't perfect. Some things happen which aren't fair, but our law provides the means of making changes when they're needed. Throughout history, people have dedicated their lives to making our law more just for everyone. Many people, especially young people, have literally given their lives to protect and preserve what we have gained so far.

We've come a long way, but we have a long way to go. Obey the law as you work for change in those areas where the law falls short of our ideals. This is the only way we can defend the great body of our law which is fair and just, and which exists for the protection of us all.

By your living example, preserve the legal heritage of young Texans, which is:

- To know their rights and the rights of others;
- To exercise their rights, with gratitude and pride;
- To respect the rights of others without exception;
- To speak out clearly for change where change is needed;
- To never give up until we reach our goal of equal treatment, for all people, under fair laws, justly administered.

Children and the Law in Texas

Judges, Lawyers, Ad Litems, and Witnesses

What's the story on judges?

Most could make more money practicing law. Most work very hard and care deeply about making the right decisions.

When a judge enters or leaves a courtroom, you stand. The reason you do is to show respect for the office the judge holds and the law he enforces. I hope it also reminds the judge of the responsibility he bears.

The robe the judge wears is a symbol of the authority he represents.

Most importantly, judges are human. Some are wiser, fairer, more reasonable than others. But in their courtrooms, they rule supreme. If you challenge them, you lose. So see the next question.

What is proper courtroom behavior?

To make a favorable impression on a judge or jury:

- Show up. If you have an emergency and can't come to court, call as soon as you know and ask what the judge wants you to do. (We're talking about a major problem here, not the sniffles or a headache.) Be prepared to prove what you told the judge (a written doctor's excuse, for example).

- Be on time. If you're late, you'll probably delay other cases as well as your own. Your tardiness tells the judge you don't consider your case important. Besides, you will reduce your attorney to jelly, bobbing in and out of the courtroom, desperately trying to find you, while smiling confidently and assuring the judge that you'll be right along. When you do finally arrive, everyone will be out of sorts with you, and who needs that? At the very least, call if you'll be late.

- Don't chew gum, eat, drink, or read a newspaper in the courtroom.

- Don't talk while the judge is in the courtroom. If you must, make it short, and whisper. Otherwise the judge can't hear the testimony and the bailiff will tell you to be quiet. If you have to say more than a few words, step into the hallway.

- Dress appropriately. This means being clean and well groomed. Remember, many judges tend to be conservative, perhaps more so than you, and court is a formal setting where serious business is conducted. If you want to make a good impression, here are some general rules about dress:

  For women and girls, a skirt is best, slacks are okay, but forget about shorts. Jewelry and makeup should be inconspicuous; less is better. If anyone could believe a woman or girl needs a bra, she should wear one. Ask yourself if your grandmother would consider that skirt too short or that neckline too low. If so, they're too short and too low for court.

  Men should probably choose a coat and tie, although for men as well as boys they aren't absolutely necessary. Slacks or jeans and a shirt are fine for boys. Sleeveless undershirts are absolutely out and so are cutoffs. This is not a day at the beach.

  Don't wear a hat or sunglasses in the courtroom.

- Get your drink of water and go to the bathroom before you enter the courtroom. If you're off taking care of such matters when your case is called, everyone has to wait.

- Don't make faces, sigh deeply, or interrupt when the other side is talking. I know that's difficult when they're twisting the truth, but resist the urge.

- Be courteous to the court staff. Bailiffs, clerks, and court reporters wield influence in subtle ways.

- Never get into an argument, verbal or physical, with others involved in the case. You shouldn't even speak to those involved on the other side of the case. If something must be communicated to them, let your lawyer do the talking.

What are the rules a good witness should follow?

Here they are:

- Never lie under oath. Never.
- If you don't understand a question, ask the attorney to repeat or rephrase it.
- If you don't know the answer to a question, or don't remember, say so. Don't try to come up with an answer when you have none.
- Always be polite to the attorneys and the judge. Call the judge "your honor" and attorneys "sir" or "ma'am."
- Never be sarcastic. Few things are more likely to arouse a judge's anger.

- Never lose your temper.
- Never argue with an attorney. Sometimes an attorney will try to provoke you into being sarcastic or angry or argumentative, because that creates an unfavorable impression with the judge. Don't let it happen.
- Don't guess. If you're asked for exact dates, distances, or figures, and you aren't sure, say so. Tell the attorney "It was about as far as from here to that door" rather than trying to guess the exact distance in feet.
- Listen carefully and answer only the questions asked. If your attorney wants more information, he'll ask more questions. Don't rattle on.
- Take your time. Think before you answer.
- If you realize later your answer was wrong, correct it.
- If an attorney objects to a question, don't say another word unless the judge overrules the objection.
- Remember that you're a witness from the moment you enter the courthouse. The judge and jury may be observing your behavior. Never do anything anywhere in the courthouse you'd hate for them to see or hear.
- Discuss your testimony with your attorney in detail before the trial. Tell him everything you know which could be relevant to the case. Good and bad.
- Everyone is nervous on the witness stand. Judges know that. So don't worry about looking scared, or your voice shaking. It happens all the time. And don't worry if you can't help crying. The judge will usually give you time to compose yourself.
- Look at the attorney asking the question. If you avoid eye contact with him, you seem evasive. If you look to the other attorney before you answer, it appears as if you are asking him to supply or approve your answer.

What does your lawyer owe you?

He should tell you the truth, answer all questions concerning his professional experience fully, and disclose anything which might interfere with his wholehearted efforts as your lawyer. He should share relevant information with you as soon as it's received, together with any offer for settlement. He should provide a candid evaluation of your case and its probable outcome, but should never pressure you to act against your wishes.

His attorney's fees should be fair. Discuss those fees and other charges at your first meeting, and ask for a written contract covering all financial matters.

Legal fees typically include only payment for the attorney's time and legal advice. You're responsible for payment, as they arise, of other expenses, such as filing fees, court costs, depositions, and fees for experts or attorneys appointed by the court. Sometimes, the judge may order the other side to refund part or all of these costs to you.

Legal fees are often based on hourly rates. To get an idea of what's reasonable, check what attorneys in your area with similar experience charge for such services.

Your local Perry Mason will charge more than a young lawyer with a year's experience handling traffic tickets, and he should, because he has more finely honed legal skills. However, unless you have a serious custody battle or other major problem, you may not need the fastest gun in the West. Being competent doesn't require being the best.

If your attorney charges by the hour, ask how time sheets are kept and request monthly billing, with that month's time sheet.

Sometimes an attorney asks for a retainer in advance, against which fees are drawn as earned. That's okay if the amount is reasonable. If part of it is unearned when his work is finished, that should be returned to you.

Don't sign the attorney's contract if you don't understand it completely. Take it with you to study, and if you have questions, show it to another lawyer before you make a commitment.

Your attorney should know something about the law that applies in your case.

Hey, that's why they go to law school and why you pay them the big bucks. If what your lawyer doesn't know hurts your case, you haven't received what you bargained for, and you may have the basis for a malpractice suit. This doesn't mean your attorney has to know all there is to know about the law applicable to your situation. He is held only to the standard of most competent lawyers in your community.

He should work hard for you.

You deserve your lawyer's best effort. He should move your case as quickly as possible toward the most favorable outcome achievable for you. But be reasonable. You aren't the only client your attorney is representing. If you are, look elsewhere quickly. If you haven't paid legal fees as your contract requires, your attorney may ask the court for permission to withdraw, but may not neglect or delay your case in order to be paid before trial or settlement.

He shouldn't reveal anything you tell him without your permission. Rules of ethics forbid your attorney to reveal information you provide unless you agree, and his staff is bound by the same code. An attorney who can't keep his mouth shut doesn't belong in practice.

Reasonably often, your lawyer should give you updates on your case, and copies of all papers received or filed. He should listen to your questions and suggestions and discuss them with you. It's patronizing for a lawyer to tell a client not to worry because the attorney will take care of everything.

Your lawyer should return nonemergency phone calls by the following day. If that's not possible, someone from his office should call to let you know when your lawyer will contact you.

Never tolerate rudeness from your attorney. You're paying the bills, and he isn't doing you a favor by representing you. Courtesy is basic to any satisfactory relationship, and this one is no different.

Your lawyer should be on time for your appointments. If there's an unavoidable delay, his staff should explain and try to minimize your inconvenience.

For an attorney to walk into court, depositions, or negotiation without being ready to do his best is unacceptable. Your attorney can't change the facts in your case, but there's one factor which he controls completely, and that's preparation. It can make the difference in whether you win or lose. But don't give him information at the last moment and then wonder why he isn't prepared.

Before taking a significant step in your case, your lawyer should discuss it with you, especially if costs are involved.

Your attorney may want to call particular witnesses, retain certain experts, or take specific depositions, but if you disagree, you're the boss.

Remember, though, the reason you hired an attorney is for professional legal advice, and you may be tying your attorney's hands by your decisions. Nevertheless, they're yours to make.

You must be able to rely upon your lawyer. If he misses hearings, doesn't return phone calls, or behaves in any way that raises questions in your mind, find another attorney.

What's the difference between a guardian ad litem and an attorney ad litem?

"Ad litem" means "pending litigation." Both guardians ad litem and attorneys ad litem are appointed by the court to serve only during a particular case, and their duties almost always relate to just that case.

A guardian ad litem is appointed to protect the best interest of a child or other person whose physical or mental condition makes him incapable of looking after his own best interests.

An attorney ad litem is appointed to represent the child or other party as his attorney.

Who can be appointed guardian ad litem?

A volunteer advocate, such as a Court-appointed Special Advocate (CASA), or any other adult the court decides has the competence, training, and expertise to protect the party. An attorney may be appointed guardian ad litem, even if he has already been appointed that person's attorney ad litem.

The problem with that is that the guardian's role is to protect the child's best interest, and the attorney's role is to fight for the child's wishes. When what the child wants is not in his best interest, the attorney can't fulfill his responsibility to both roles. If that happens, he must continue to serve as attorney ad litem and ask the judge to appoint someone else as guardian ad litem.

The child's managing conservator can be appointed if he isn't the child's parent, isn't asking for adoption of the child, and has no personal interest at stake in the suit.

When must a guardian ad litem be appointed for a child?

If the Department of Protective and Regulatory Services (PRS) files a termination suit, or asks to be appointed managing conservator, the child must be given a guardian ad litem as soon as the case is filed.

If anyone else files a termination suit, a guardian ad litem must be appointed immediately, unless the child himself is a petitioner, an attorney ad litem has already been appointed for the child, or the court specifically finds that the child's interest will be protected adequately by another party whose own interest doesn't conflict with the child's.

The court may appoint a guardian ad litem in any other Suit to Affect the Parent-Child Relationship.

What is the guardian ad litem of a child supposed to do?

The guardian must interview the child if the child is at least four years old. Additionally, the guardian must interview everyone he thinks is likely to have significant knowledge of the child's history and condition. Tell the guardian if there's someone you feel he should interview.

The guardian may investigate as much as he feels is necessary to determine the child's best interest, and may obtain copies of the child's medical, psychological, and school records.

The guardian has the right to receive copies of all papers filed in the case, to participate in agency staffing of the case, to attend hearings, and to review orders to which the parties have agreed.

A guardian who isn't also the child's attorney may testify in court. A guardian who is also the attorney can't. That is because attorneys can't be witnesses, except regarding their attorney's fees, in cases where they represent one of the parties.

Who can be appointed as an attorney ad litem?

A licensed attorney in good standing. In some parts of the state the attorney must belong to a pool of attorneys who have met training and other requirements set by law and the judges.

Who has the right to receive an appointed attorney ad litem?

If PRS files a termination suit, or asks to be named managing conservator, the child must be appointed an attorney ad litem immediately.

In a termination suit, regardless of who files it, these people have the right to an attorney ad litem:

- An indigent parent who opposes the termination (the judge decides who is indigent);
- A parent served by publication;
- An alleged father who didn't register with the paternity registry and whose identity or location is unknown; or
- An alleged father who did register with the paternity registry but can't be found.

What is an attorney ad litem supposed to do?

The duties are the same as those an attorney has toward any other client, unless he's appointed attorney ad litem for a child. In that case, the law requires the attorney to do what a good lawyer would do anyway:

- Investigate the facts of the case;
- Obtain and review the child's medical, psychological, and school records;
- Interview the child if the child is four or older; and
- Interview all parties to the suit and all individuals with significant knowledge of the child's history and condition. I'm not sure how an attorney can literally be expected to interview all parties who may have significant knowledge of the child's history and condition, but he should try to talk with those most likely to have knowledge of the facts relevant to the case.

What if a party to the suit thinks the guardian ad litem or attorney ad litem is biased or not meeting his responsibilities?

A party can file a written motion objecting to the ad litem and stating specific reasons for his objections. The court must rule on the motion and remove the ad litem if the objections are justified.

Who pays the attorney ad litem's fee?

The county, if a judge decides the parents can't pay, and one or both of the parents if the judge decides they can.

2

The Parent-Child Relationship

You probably think you have a pretty good idea of what the words "child" and "parent" mean. So did I, until I became a lawyer and started reading the Texas Family Code.

Under the law in Texas, a "child" is a person under eighteen years of age who has never been married and who has not had her disabilities of minority removed for general purposes. More about that last part in Chapter 19.

Of course, that definition just tells us who a "child" is under usual circumstances. The legal definition of a child may be different in certain instances. For example, if a child breaks the law, whether she is a "child" for the purpose of dealing with her in the juvenile courts is entirely different. If you want to know who is a child in that situation, see Chapter 29.

In relation to child support, a "child" may be someone over eighteen to whom someone else is ordered to pay child support.

At least, so far as I know, there is still only one legal definition of a "parent."

You are a parent if:

- You are a birth mother; or
- You are a man or woman who adopted the child; or
- You are a "presumed" father (which will take some explaining); or
- Although you weren't married to the mother, a judge has decided you are the biological father and has named you the legal father as well.

You are not a legal parent anymore if a court has terminated your relationship with your child.

Unless a judge orders otherwise, as sometimes happens in divorce, custody, or termination of parent-child relationship cases, the parents of a child have certain rights, duties, and powers.

Probably the simplest statement in the Family Code is this definition, which I love, "Adult means a person who is not a child."

What legal rights do parents have regarding their child?

The right to:

- Physical possession of the child;
- Direct the child's moral and religious training;
- Decide where the child lives;
- The child's services and earnings;
- Inherit from the child;
- Consent to the marriage of a child fourteen through seventeen years old;
- Consent to the child's enlistment in the armed forces of the United States;
- Consent to the child's medical, dental, psychiatric, psychological, and surgical treatment;
- Represent the child in legal actions and make other significant legal decisions concerning the child;
- Receive payments and use them for the child; and
- Make decisions about a child's education.

What legal duties do parents have toward their children?

The duty to:

- Take care of, control, and protect the child;
- Provide reasonable discipline for the child;
- Support the child, which includes providing the child with food, clothing, shelter, medical and dental care, and education; and
- Manage the child's property.

What are the rights, duties, and powers of children relative to their parents?

It's interesting that Texas law doesn't name the rights, powers, and duties of children in relationship to their parents, except as they are reflected in the rights, powers, and duties set forth for parents.

It does state that a child born alive after abortion or premature birth is entitled to the same powers and privileges granted by our laws to any other child. Whatever those may be.

How does a mother show she is a child's parent for legal purposes?

If she is the biological mother, by showing proof that she gave birth to the child. Usually, with a birth certificate. If she is the adoptive mother, by showing proof of the adoption. Usually, by a document called a Decree of Adoption received at the time of adoption; sometimes by a new birth certificate issued after the adoption.

Do a mother's parental rights, duties, privileges, and powers regarding a child differ from those of a father?

No.

Is a husband whose wife is artificially inseminated the child's legal father?

Yes. He must consent in writing, and the statement must be signed before a notary public. Even without that consent, his conduct may be enough if it ratifies the artificial insemination.

What are the rights of a man who's the biological father of the child that results from artificial insemination?

He has no rights, unless he's married to the mother. The child is the child of the mother and her husband.

If a husband's sperm fertilizes another woman's egg, which is then implanted in the wife's uterus, or a donated embryo is implanted in the wife's uterus, what then?

Same rules apply. The spouses must give their consent, and the child is theirs, not the donor's.

Is the legal relationship of a child and his birth parents different from the legal relationship of a child and his adoptive parents?

No.

Is the legal parent-child relationship any different for a man whose paternity was established in court, but who never married the mother?

No. The marital status of the parents doesn't matter.

What is a "presumed biological father"?

Get comfortable. This will take a while. A man is a "presumed biological father" if:

- He and the child's biological mother were married, and the child was born during that marriage, or within three hundred days after the marriage was ended by divorce, annulment, or his death; or

- Before the child's birth he and the child's biological mother tried to get married and thought that they were (even if the marriage is, or could be found to be, void), and if the child was born during the time they thought they were married or within three hundred days of the time their attempt at marriage ended for any reason; or

- After the child's birth, he and the biological mother married or tried to marry each other and thought they had (even if their marriage could have been found to be void). In this case, he must also:

  + *Have filed a written acknowledgment of his paternity, or*

  + *Have consented in writing to be, and actually been, named, the child's father on the birth certificate, or*

  + *Have been obligated to pay child support for the child because he made a voluntary written promise to do so, or because a court had ordered him to do so; or*

- He never tried to marry the mother, but he consented in writing to be named the child's father on the birth certificate; or

- Before the child turns eighteen he takes the child into his home and holds the child out as his biological child.

What does it mean to be a "presumed biological father"?

It means that you are considered the biological father of the child. A presumption is something that is accepted as true, unless and until someone goes to court and proves it isn't.

Can a child have more than one "presumed biological father"?

Yes. You can't believe how complicated things can get.

If a child does have more than one such "presumed biological father," what then?

If the mother, or any man claiming to be the child's father, wants a legal father named, he or she must go to court and ask a judge to decide. Each man claiming to be the one true father has his own presumption going for him. As guidance for the judge, the state legislature has said "the presumption that is founded on the weightier considerations of policy and logic controls."

I translate that to mean judges should use their heads and do what's right.

If a child is born while a man and woman are married, can either the husband or wife go to court and deny that the man is the child's biological father?

Yes. If a judge finds he's the biological father, he becomes the child's legal parent, with all the rights, duties, privileges, and powers of a parent. If a court finds he isn't the biological father, he has no further rights, duties, privileges, or powers regarding the child. If this question arises, it's usually during a divorce.

Can a child have more than one living legal father at the same time?

No.

What are the differences between a legal father, a biological father, and a presumed father?

A biological father is the one who impregnated the mother. A biological father has no rights to a child unless a court establishes them, unless he is also a presumed father or the legal father.

A legal father is either a man who adopted the child or a man whom a judge found to be the biological father of the child. He is a legal parent, with all the parental rights, duties, privileges, and powers relative to the child.

A presumed father was defined earlier. He has the rights, duties, privileges, and powers of a parent toward a child unless or until a judge finds he isn't the biological father.

What are the differences between guardians and managing conservators?

Conservatorship is established under the rules of the Texas Family Code, while guardianship is the creation of the Texas Probate Code.

There are guardians of the person, and guardians of the estate. Parents are the natural guardians of the person of their children. If one parent dies, the other becomes guardian of the child's person.

Parents have the right to appoint guardians of the person and estate of their children in their wills. The last surviving parent's will controls who will be guardian of the child's personal estate, subject to court approval.

The guardian of the person of the child is much like the managing conservator. The guardian of the child's estate has the duty to take care of and manage the child's estate in the same manner that a prudent woman would manage her own. She is entitled to possess and manage the child's property.

Only one parent can be appointed guardian of the child's estate. Which parent is to be appointed is determined on the basis of the child's best interest.

Usually, a parent manages a child's estate, unless no parent is able to do so or the child has no living parent. If a guardian of a child's estate has been appointed by a probate court, that person will manage the estate.

For more about managing conservators, see Chapter 7.

3

Establishing Paternity

For many years, a child whose parents had not married suffered the outrage of being labeled "illegitimate," as if the child himself was somehow tainted because of his parents' actions. The law has changed. No longer does such a child bear that stigma. Today, the law refers to him as a "child with no presumed father." I'm not sure how much progress that represents, but at least it's an attempt to recognize the equality of all children.

Today, a number of laws exist to protect children from discrimination because their parents weren't married.

There's now a way to establish legal paternity of a child, and to hold the child's father responsible as a parent, just as if he had been married to the child's mother. The other side of that coin is that a father whose paternity is established may no longer be denied his rights as a parent because he wasn't married to the child's mother.

Does naming a man on a child's birth certificate make him the legal father?

No. The man named on the birth certificate is the child's presumed father. That means he's considered the child's father until someone goes to court and proves he isn't.

Identity of the father is to be filled in on a child's birth certificate only if:

- The child's mother was married to the father when the child was conceived, born, or after the child's birth; or
- A judge has named a legal father; or
- The father has signed the birth certificate or a legal written consent to be named the father on the birth certificate.

If a child has no presumed father, the indication that no father has been named may be removed from his birth certificate by applying to the state registrar.

If a child has no presumed father at the time of birth, but later his father's paternity is established, a new birth certificate may be issued which includes information about his father. The Social Security numbers of the child's mother and father must be listed, but they aren't part of the legal birth certificate and can't ever be used for any purpose other than establishment and enforcement of child support orders.

Why are judges asked to decide who is a child's biological father, and to name that man the child's legal father as well?

Some of the reasons are:

- A biological father may want the chance to visit with and know his child, the right to be a father to him;
- A mother may want to be able to collect child support from the father;
- A father may want to seek custody of the child;
- Either party may want the child to have the biological father's name; and
- Either party may recognize that it would be an act of love to encourage the child to have a relationship with both parents.

How does a mother or biological father go about having a judge decide who is the child's legal father?

By filing a lawsuit to determine parentage. The other parties involved must be given legal notice and copies of the papers filed.

Who can file such a suit?

- The child's mother;
- A man claiming he may be the child's father;
- The child, through a representative the court selects;
- The child's guardian;
- A person who has had actual care and physical possession of the child for at least the preceding six months;
- Authorized agencies, or a licensed child placement agency;
- Certain government entities (the attorney general files on request, or when public assistance has been paid for the child);
- A person named as a managing conservator in an Affidavit of Relinquishment or consent to adoption regarding the child; and
- A person who has visitation or custody rights granted in another state or country.

Does a man who thinks he's a child's biological father have the right to file a suit to establish his paternity if the mother is married and she and her husband claim her husband is the child's father?

The Texas Supreme Court said in the case styled *In the Interest of J.W.T.* (872 S.W. 2d 189, 198 [Tex. 1994]) that a man believing himself to be a child's biological father could file an action to establish his paternity, even if the child's mother and her husband claimed the husband was the father, provided that the man did so "expeditiously." I think the court in that case just meant "make up your mind and claim the child quickly if you're going to."

What if a child has more than one presumed father?

Anyone seeking to establish paternity should file a suit and name every possible candidate for father as parties. I don't see what else could be done if there's more than one presumed father. Let the paternity tests that would be ordered sort the whole thing out.

Can a suit to determine parentage be filed before a child is born?

Yes.

How long after a child is born can a suit to determine paternity be filed?

At any time up to and including the day the child turns twenty years old. However, if the suit is brought in the probate court in order to permit the child to inherit from a deceased parent, the child may be able to bring the suit after he turns twenty if he didn't have a chance to do so earlier.

If a court has named a man the legal father of a child, can anyone else file a paternity suit later, claiming another man is the child's biological father?

No. If the child is adopted, or paternity is established in a paternity suit, that's the end of it. No one can ever come in later seeking to establish his own paternity. However, if the legal determination of paternity occurs in a divorce, without a paternity suit, another man can challenge paternity later.

If a paternity suit is filed, and the mother and the man who is the alleged father in the suit both agree he is the father, what happens?

The case can be contested by a presumed father, another man claiming to be the biological father, a government entity, an authorized agency, or a licensed child placement agency. Usually, that doesn't happen, and a judge will find the man named in the paternity suit is the biological father, name him the child's legal father, and decide the issues of custody, child support, and other matters relating to the child.

If a suit to determine parentage is filed, and any party to the suit or anyone else with the right to do so denies that the man named in the suit is the child's biological father, what happens?

The judge will order parentage testing of the mother, any man alleged to be the father, and the child, to establish by physical evidence who is the child's biological father.

What kinds of tests will be ordered?

Almost always, just a special kind of blood test which determines the likelihood of parentage by examining DNA of the child, the mother, and the man who's the alleged father. But the whole field of scientific testing is undergoing change. New, and perhaps even more accurate, types of genetic testing are appearing on the horizon. It's awesome.

What degree of certainty does blood testing provide in determining paternity?

In order for the judge to consider the test results, they must show that at least 99 percent of the male population couldn't be this child's father, and this man is among the 1 percent or less who could.

Because these tests are so close to conclusive, most lawsuits are settled when the results are in. They make it far more difficult for a man to deny his child, or a woman to falsely accuse a man of fathering her baby.

A judge can order further tests if the blood tests were inconclusive, or if, even though the particular man is within the 1 percent of those who could be the father, one of the parties still isn't convinced. Sufficient evidence to determine parentage can even be collected by brushing a swab inside the mouth between the cheek and gums.

A judge can also order that no more tests are necessary if they're becoming too expensive, or if they show the man alleged to be the child's father is not.

Who pays for the tests?

The judge decides that. The tests are expensive and not all doctors perform them, so it's a good idea to check on what hospitals or laboratories in the area do, and how much they charge.

What if the tests show the man named as the father in the lawsuit is not?

The case will be dismissed, and can't be filed again, unless it's proven later that the person who came to take the test wasn't the person the suit claimed was the father, or some other kind of fraud occurred.

When anyone who has been ordered to have parentage tests refuses to do so, what happens?

If the person who filed the case refuses, the case can be dismissed. If anyone else refuses, a judge may decide the paternity question against that person if there's other evidence of paternity. Additionally, the fact that the person refused to submit to testing can be disclosed at trial.

If the party against whom the suit was filed doesn't show up in court, what will the judge do?

If a judge decides the missing party received legal notice and a copy of the papers filed in the lawsuit, the judge can rule in favor of the party who is present if there's evidence to support that person's position.

What if the tests show the man claimed in the suit to be the biological father is among the 1 percent of the male population who could be the child's father?

The court will hold a hearing called a pretrial conference. At that time, evidence about the paternity tests is presented. If the court finds at least 99 percent of the male population was excluded as the biological father, and the man alleged to be the child's biological father is among the remaining 1 percent who could be the father, the court can issue temporary orders regarding temporary custody, visitation, and child support. The court will also set a date for the full trial of the case.

What is the legal effect of a judge finding at the pretrial conference that the man claimed to be the biological father was among the 1 percent of males who could be the child's father?

In addition to allowing the judge to issue temporary orders, it changes who has the burden to prove his side of the case. At the beginning, whoever files the lawsuit is required to prove whatever that party is claiming to be true about paternity of the child. But, once those "ninety-nines" have been excluded, and the man named in the lawsuit was not among them, whoever claims in the suit that the man is not the father must prove it.

What issues are decided in the trial of a paternity suit?

Paternity, custody, child support, including possible child support going back to the time the child was born, possible reimbursement to the state for public assistance paid to support the child, health care coverage for the child, visitation, rights and duties of the parents, payment of prior medical expenses, possible name change of the child, and attorney's fees.

Can you have a jury trial in a paternity case?

Yes, on the issues of paternity and custody. On issues of child support and visitation, the jury usually isn't asked to make a decision, and if it is, that decision is only a suggestion to the judge, who may or may not follow it.

A federal law was recently passed that says states can't grant the right to a jury trial in paternity cases. But Texas won't have to comply with that law before the legislature meets in 1999, and a constitutional amendment may be necessary. For now, there's still the right to a jury trial.

Once a judge or jury has decided that a man is the child's biological father, what happens?

A decree is issued, declaring him the legal father of the child, and establishing the parent-child relationship. There is no legal difference in the parent-child relationship thus established than if the child had been born during his parents' marriage.

Can a man protect his rights if he isn't a presumed father but may well be the biological father of a child?

He can file a notarized Notice of Intent to claim paternity with the paternity registry established by the Bureau of Vital Statistics. The form is available at district, county, or municipal clerks' offices, hospitals, and prisons. The information is kept on file. If the mother petitions to terminate his parental rights, and says his identity or whereabouts are unknown, provided he filed the Notice of Intent, he must be served and given notice of the termination hearing so that he can contest it.

He must file the form before or within thirty days of the child's birth or his rights to the child can be terminated without his knowledge.

If the mother does know the father's identity and whereabouts, he has the right to be served with the petition, and his rights can only be terminated as described in Chapter 12.

Of course, if a man qualifies as a presumed father as described earlier, he doesn't have to file any notice with the paternity registry to be entitled to service and notice.

This is a strange statute. It protects the rights of a biological father when the mother neglects to tell him about the child, or honestly doesn't know who or where he is. But most men don't rush down to register after a brief encounter, on the outside chance a child may result, though I was surprised to learn that several thousand have done so in other states with similar laws.

The main reason the legislature passed this law was to make it easier to free a child for adoption by simplifying the termination of parental rights of a man who has disappeared and done nothing to claim his child.

4

Adoption

One of the happiest things that happens in a courtroom, where many things happen that aren't happy at all, is an adoption.

It's natural for people to long for children of their own. We all need others as a focus of our love, and to love a child is one of life's richest rewards. It gives a sense of continuity with the past, joy in the present, and hope for the future.

Just as deep is a child's need for parents who will love and nurture her, and whom she can grow to love in return. Not to have such parents is surely one of childhood's greatest tragedies.

An adoption reaches out to join children and parents who choose to fulfill those needs for one another.

As with most things, adoptions do have their problems. Sometimes an adoptive child has experienced physical or emotional trauma which will affect her all of her life, and adoptive parents aren't always prepared to provide for the special needs of such children. Adoptive children often experience difficulties with their sense of identity, or with deeply held feelings of rejection. It would be strange if a child whose parents gave her up for adoption never wondered why, or whether there was something wrong with her that made them leave her behind.

Bonding, that process by which children and parents become emotionally attached to one another, is more complicated and takes longer in adoptive families.

Any time problems arise, it's normal for adopted children to idealize their birth parents, and how they might have treated them. Any time adoptive parents experience negative feelings toward an adopted child, it's common for them to wonder if a birth parent would have the same feelings.

Of course, there are always problems to solve as you raise natural children, too.

No one ever said parenting would be easy.

Nevertheless, there are so many special circumstances surrounding an adoption that anyone considering it should seek adoption counseling before taking the big step. Be sure that you understand exactly what's involved, and that your expectations are realistic.

Finally, there are those other persons who are affected by an adoption, the birth parents. Sometimes a child becomes free for adoption because both birth parents are dead. More often, it's because their rights to the child have been terminated. And there are many reasons for such termination. Perhaps the parents were abusive, or abandoned the child. However, there are many instances where birth parents genuinely love their child, but simply can't raise her. They decide to place her needs above their own by releasing her for adoption. Such sacrifice deserves our respect.

In every adoption, there must be an end to one relationship before another can begin. And often that end has brought heartbreak, not only to the birth parents, but to the child who has lost them as well. Whatever you may think of the birth parents, whatever they were or were not, and whatever the child herself may feel about them, now or in the future, she has suffered a loss. Even if that loss, and the adoption that follows, are in her best interest, and even if she is grateful to you and eager for the adoption to proceed, in some deep and secret place she has lost something of herself, a basic part of her heritage and identity.

Sensitivity and compassion should be as much a part of adoption as joy.

What is adoption?

Establishment of the legal parent-child relationship between a child and an adult who isn't the child's birth parent.

Who may be adopted?

Any child who lives in Texas when the petition is filed and who has no legal parent, or whose only legal parent is joining the child's stepparent's request for adoption.

A child at least two years old may be adopted by a former stepparent if the child's only legal parent consents and the former stepparent has had actual possession of the child for the prior six months.

Even without the legal parent's consent, such a child may be adopted by a former stepparent who has had actual possession of a child two or older for the prior year.

When does a child have no legal parents?

When her parents are dead, or her legal relationship with them has been terminated by a judge.

Who may adopt a child in Texas?

Any adult is eligible to adopt a child who's available for adoption.

May single people adopt a child?

Yes.

If two people are married, must they both request the adoption or may only one spouse adopt a child?

Both must request the adoption.

A parent married to a person requesting adoption must join in the stepparent's suit.

Is there any age requirement for persons seeking to adopt a child?

You must be at least eighteen. There's no maximum age limit. However, some adoption agencies won't accept applications from people who are older or younger than their guidelines specify. A ninety-eight-year-old trying to adopt a two-year-old, or an eighteen-year-old trying to adopt a sixteen-year-old, just wouldn't make sense. The age of the parties may be one factor a judge will consider in deciding whether the adoption is in the child's best interest.

Is there any legal financial requirement in order to adopt a child?

No. However, financial ability to provide for a child's basic needs may be another factor a judge considers in deciding whether adoption is in the child's best interest. A parent doesn't have to be able to send the child to a private school, but she should be able to see that the child is fed.

Is there any legal limit to the number of children people may already have if they are seeking to adopt another?

No. Once again, this is a factor a judge may consider in deciding whether to grant the adoption. Some adoption agencies limit the number of children parents may have.

Must parents be of the same race or ethnic background as the child they seek to adopt?

No. In fact, the law doesn't allow child placement agencies to decide where to place a child based on the child's or parent's race.

Is there a legal prohibition against a homosexual adopting a child?

No. The court will decide whether to grant the adoption based solely upon the best interest of the child.

How do people go about finding a child to adopt?

In one of three ways:

- By making application to a private, licensed child placement agency;
- By making application to the Texas Department of Protective and Regulatory Services, which is also a child placement agency; or
- Through placement of the child with them directly by the child's parent, or any other person having the legal right to do so, such as the child's managing conservator if the child has no parent.

Can a doctor or lawyer find a child for a couple who want to adopt, and place the child with them?

No. It's a crime for anyone to do that except the child's own parent, or managing conservator if the child has no parent, or a child placement agency licensed by the state.

No one else can even serve as a go-between between the parent and the person seeking to adopt without breaking the law.

Can a licensed child placement agency charge a fee for placing a child in an adoptive home?

Yes.

Are prospective adoptive homes screened before a child may be placed in a home for adoption?

Yes, except in adoption by close relatives. The court will appoint an investigator, and those seeking to adopt must pay the bill.

Is it legal to pay anyone other than a licensed child placement agency for delivering a child to a person for adoption?

No. Anyone who buys or sells a child for money or anything else of value commits a very serious crime.

Can any payments legally be made in connection with an adoption?

Yes, but only these:

- A fee to a licensed child placement agency;
- Attorney's fees for legal services provided in the usual course of practice (for example, fees for preparing and filing the adoption papers, and representing the parties seeking adoption in the suit, or fees for representing parties to the adoption who are given notice by publication);
- Fees to doctors for medical services provided in the usual course of their practice (for example, prenatal care); and
- Reimbursement to any person who paid medical or legal expenses for the child's benefit.

Is it legal to advertise or to answer an advertisement seeking to place a child for adoption?

Yes. But only if the advertiser doesn't ask for anything of value to be paid in exchange for the child, the person who responds to the ad doesn't offer to pay anything of value for the child, and no payment of anything of value is actually made for the child.

What are the advantages and disadvantages of the different means of securing placement of a child for adoption?

The advantages of going to the Texas Department of Protective and Regulatory Services or another licensed child placement agency are:

- It's more likely that a thorough investigation has been made concerning the history of the child and her biological parents;
- It's more likely that all legal requirements have been met to free the child for adoption before the child is placed in the adoptive home;
- It's usually more difficult for a birth parent to change his or her mind about the adoption later than it is if the child was placed privately by a birth parent; and
- Often such agencies provide the legal services of an attorney to handle the adoption, and the adoptive parents don't have to hire one.

The disadvantages of using a child placement agency are:

- The costs of adoption through a private agency may be more than the adoptive parents can afford, though this is not true with adoptions arranged through the Texas Department of Protective and Regulatory Services;
- There may be a considerable wait for a child; and
- A couple may not meet an agency's requirements for placement.

The advantages of having a child placed in the adoptive home by the mother or a managing conservator with the authority to do so are:

- There's no fee to pay;
- There's no wait for placement; and
- There are no conditions such as age or number of other children which licensed agencies sometimes impose on adoptive parents.

The disadvantages of a private placement are:

- There's no investigation regarding the background of the child or her biological parents, as is required when an agency places the child. Often, there's no verification of information provided by the individual placing the child;
- The legal requirements are less likely to be met before the child is placed in the adoptive home. The adoptive parent must hire an attorney to make certain the entire process is handled according to the law; and
- There's a far greater likelihood of a birth parent changing his or her mind before the adoption has become final, and a greater chance that he or she will be legally able to do so.

I can't emphasize enough how important it is to seek legal advice before considering an adoption. The possibilities for heartbreak are just too great if everything isn't done according to law.

Are there any special requirements if the agency placing the child for adoption is located in another state?

Yes. In addition to complying with Texas law, prior to placing a child from another state in Texas, the agency must obey the Interstate Compact on the Placement of Children. This law requires giving the proper Texas authorities written notice of the intention to place a child here, including detailed information about the child, her parents, and the person with whom she is to be placed. Texas authorities must then investigate and notify the placement agency that the placement doesn't appear to be contrary to the child's best interest.

Also, of course, the person with whom the child is to be placed must agree to the placement.

Who is required to follow this law?

Any state, court of another state, person, charitable agency, or any other entity which places a child in Texas.

This law doesn't apply to a parent, stepparent, grandparent, adult brother or sister, adult uncle or aunt, or the child's guardian bringing or sending the child into Texas, or when the child is left in Texas with any such person. It's a criminal offense for anyone required to follow this law not to do so.

When such an agency places the child in Texas, who has the authority to decide issues concerning custody, treatment and disposition, and care and supervision of the child?

The sending agency, until the child is removed from the home or adopted.

Can the placing agency require the persons with whom the child has been placed to return the child?

Yes. Until the child is adopted.

Who is financially responsible for a child who has been placed in Texas by an out-of-state agency?

The placement agency and the adoptive parents are responsible for support and maintenance of the child until the adoption is granted.

Once a child is placed in your home for adoption, what must you do to adopt her?

File a Petition for Adoption with the court, asking the judge for permission to adopt the child. It may also request that the child's name be changed.

Who files the petition?

If the child came to you through a child placement agency, it will probably be filed by that agency. If the child was placed in your home through private placement, you'll have to hire an attorney to file it for you.

What effect does the status of a child's parents have on whether a Petition for Adoption of a Child may be filed?

An adoption petition may not be heard unless:

- The child has no living parent; or
- A judge has terminated the child-parent relationship with each living parent; or

- A Petition to Terminate the Parent-Child Relationship is joined with the Petition for Adoption. Obviously, if the person seeking adoption is married to a parent of the child, that parent's rights don't have to be terminated for the adoption to be granted.

What is meant by the statement that a Petition for Adoption can't be considered unless a child has no living parent?

"Parent" here means a birth mother, a man or woman who has previously adopted the child, a legal father, or a presumed father. If any of these persons is living, the adoptive petition can't be heard until the parental rights of each such person have been terminated.

What does it mean to "legally terminate" a parent's rights?

It means that a petition has been filed, asking a judge to terminate, or end, the parent-child relationship between the child and the parent, and a judge has done so. After termination of the parent-child relationship, the former parent no longer has any legal relationship whatsoever to the child, and has no rights, privileges, duties, or powers regarding the child. For additional information, see Chapter 12.

If a child has a living parent whose rights have not been terminated, the only way a judge will consider a Petition for Adoption is if the persons seeking to adopt also file a petition to terminate the rights of the child's parent or parents at the same time. In that instance, the judge hears the termination petition first. Only if the judge decides to terminate the parent's rights can the adoption petition be heard.

If the child has no living parent, but does have a person or agency who's been appointed her managing conservator with the right to consent to adoption, what then?

Legal notice and a copy of the petition must be given to the managing conservator, who may then sign a written consent to the adoption and file it with the court, or oppose the adoption at the time of the hearing. If the managing conservator does oppose the adoption, there will be a trial, and the judge will decide whether or not to grant the adoption.

If the child has a managing conservator, must that managing conservator consent to the adoption?

Yes. A written consent is necessary. A judge can waive this requirement if there's no good cause for refusal to consent. If a petition is filed, and the managing conservator won't consent to the adoption, the judge will hold a hearing to decide whether to proceed without that consent.

Must a child consent before she can be adopted?

Yes, if she's at least twelve years old. The consent must be in writing, or given in person by the child in court. However, the judge may waive this requirement if she feels it's in the child's best interest to do so. The consent of children under twelve isn't a legal requirement. Nevertheless, I think a child's wishes should at least be considered in deciding a matter so vitally important to her. Allowing the child to have a role in the process is a good thing for everyone.

Must a child have lived in the adoptive parents' home for any specific length of time before an adoption petition can be filed?

No, not before the petition is filed. But the child must have lived with the adoptive parents at least six months before the adoption can be granted. However, if there's a reason to proceed with the adoption sooner, the adoptive parents can ask the court to waive the six-month requirement, and the judge has the power to do so.

After a Petition for Adoption is filed, what happens?

Those people with rights concerning the child must be given notice of the petition because their own rights may be affected. They receive notice through a legal procedure called "service of citation," which means an authorized person gives them a copy of the petition. Those who have a right to this notice are:

- Any managing conservator of the child;
- Any possessory conservator of the child;
- Any person having access to the child by court order;
- Anyone who's been ordered by the court to pay child support;
- Any legal guardian of the person or estate of the child;
- Every parent whose rights to the child haven't been terminated (there are legal papers that can be signed by such parents that make giving them citation and notice unnecessary);
- Any man the petition claims is the biological father or probable biological father of the child (there are legal papers which can be signed by such men which make giving them citation and notice unnecessary); and
- The state attorney general's office, in cases where a child support right that may be affected by the granting of the adoption has been assigned to the attorney general.

What is the next step after a Petition for Adoption has been filed and all the parties have been served with citations?

All of the necessary documents must be obtained, including:

- Death certificates of any deceased parents. If you don't have them, people with personal knowledge of their deaths can be called as witnesses to confirm the fact the parents are dead. It's just easier if you bring the certificates;

- A certified copy of any court order terminating the parent-child relationship between the child and her parents;

- The managing conservator's written consent to the adoption, unless the managing conservator is one of the petitioners;

- The child's written consent to the adoption if she's at least twelve years old;

- Waivers of Citation by any persons who have a right to service of citation in the case but wish to give up that right; and

- Any Affidavits of Relinquishment, Affidavits of Status, or Waivers of Interest from parties connected with a termination suit which was filed at the same time as the adoption petition.

What action will the judge take after the Petition for Adoption is filed?

The judge will order a "social study" of the circumstances and conditions of the child and adoptive parents. The judge will appoint the Texas Department of Protective and Regulatory Services to conduct the study if the adoptive child is being placed by that agency. Private social workers will be appointed to prepare the social study for a fee in other cases.

There are minimum qualifications for a person to be permitted to conduct such social studies, as well as minimum standards, guidelines, and procedures for such social studies. Most district clerks keep a list of private social workers who do social studies.

The social study must contain a history of any known physical, sexual, or emotional abuse of the child.

A copy of the social study must be made available to the adoptive parents before the adoption is final. The judge will set a date by which it must be completed.

If the adoption is contested, the attorneys must be furnished with copies of the social study by the seventh day after its completion, or the fifth day before the trial begins, whichever is earlier.

Does the judge have to grant the adoption if the social study recommends it, or deny the adoption if the social study opposes?

No. The decision is up to the judge. The social study's recommendations are not binding on the court.

Is a criminal background check of the adoptive parents required?

Yes.

How soon after the petition is filed will the trial be held?

The trial date must be set forty to sixty days after the social study was ordered, or the date the criminal history was requested, whichever is later.

It isn't at all unusual for a trial to be delayed considerably beyond that time because of difficulty in getting service of citation, or obtaining all the necessary documents, or the busy schedules of attorneys, or the crowded court dockets. A judge may, for good cause, set the trial for any date after the social study has been filed and the court has received the criminal histories of the parties involved.

Does a child who is to be adopted have a right to have her own attorney appointed by the judge to represent her in the proceedings?

No. In a case where only adoption is sought, there's no such requirement. A judge may appoint either a guardian ad litem or an attorney for the child, but it's up to the judge to decide if that's necessary to protect the child's interest.

If a termination petition has been filed along with the adoption petition, then the rules about appointing an attorney or a guardian ad litem for a child must be followed as required by that petition. For more information, see Chapter 12.

If a managing conservator has filed a consent to the adoption, can that consent ever be taken back?

Yes, if the court hasn't already granted the adoption. It's done by signing a paper called a Revocation Statement, and filing it with the court. The managing conservator can then oppose the adoption at the trial. The child can revoke consent through the same process.

Is there a right to a jury trial in adoptions?

No. If a termination petition and an adoption petition were filed at the same time, there is a right to a jury trial on the question of termination. If the jury verdict is for termination, then the judge will hear the adoption case. If termination is denied, the adoption is dismissed.

Can more than one couple ask to adopt the same child at the same time?

Yes. Their requests will be joined, and heard at the same time. A social study and investigation will be conducted on each set of prospective adoptive parents.

Who must attend the adoption hearing?

Both parties seeking to adopt the child. If it would be a hardship for both to be present, the judge can excuse one party if the other party is present.

The child must also attend if she's twelve years old or older. However, the court may excuse the child if that's in her best interest.

At an adoption hearing, what issues does the judge decide?

He decides whether:

- The child is eligible to be adopted;
- That particular court has the power to hear the case;
- The petition contained all the information the law requires;
- All the parties entitled to legal notice received such notice;
- The adoption is in the best interest of the child; and
- To grant other matters requested in the petition, such as change of name, termination of the child's right to inherit from her natural parents, and attorney's fees.

If all of the legal requirements have been met, the adoption will be granted if the judge decides it's in the child's best interest.

When does the adoption become a legal fact?

When the judge signs the Decree of Adoption.

Is there a right of appeal in an adoption case?

Yes. It must be filed within thirty days after the judge signs the decree. After thirty days have passed, if no appeal is filed, the adoption becomes final. If an appeal is filed, the adoption doesn't become final until it's decided.

If no appeal is filed, can an adoption ever be set aside?

Only for a period of six months, in a rare proceeding called a Bill of Review. There are very narrow reasons, and very strict requirements, for a Bill of Review. These are most unusual.

What happens if one of the two parties seeking an adoption dies after the petition is filed but before the adoption is granted?

The surviving party may choose to dismiss the case, or proceed with the adoption.

If there's only one person seeking an adoption, and that person dies, or if both parties seeking the adoption die before it's granted, the case is dismissed.

What happens if the parties seeking the adoption are divorced after they file for adoption but before it's granted?

The Petition for Adoption is dismissed, or changed to ask for adoption by one of the parties. Sometimes, when both parties want to adopt the child, they delay their divorce until the adoption is granted. Then, issues regarding custody, child support, and visitation of the child are decided in the divorce case. An adoption cannot be granted to only one of the parties until their divorce is final.

Once an adoption decree is entered, what is its effect?

The decree creates the same legal parent-child relationship between the child and the adoptive parents as would have existed if the child had been born to them during their marriage. The adoptive parents will receive copies of all information available to any agency involved with the case concerning the child's history. The information will be edited first to remove information about the biological parents' identity.

What are the rights of a child's biological grandparents if the child is adopted?

See Chapter 15.

What rights, if any, do biological parents and biological siblings of adopted children still have regarding one another, once the adoption is granted?

The child retains the right to inherit from and through her biological parents, unless that right is terminated by the court. Some adoptive parents request termination of that right. Whether to grant the request depends upon the child's best interest. For more information on a child's right to inherit, see Chapter 25. Biological parents don't retain the same right to inherit from or through their child after her adoption. Nor do they retain any other right, duty, privilege, or power regarding the child. However, there's no prohibition against such biological parents, biological siblings, or adopted children trying to locate each other by legal means, such as those provided by some adoption agencies. There's no obligation on the part of such biological parents, or biological siblings, or adopted children to respond to any such attempts to contact them.

Is there any voluntary means provided by law through which biological parents, biological siblings, and adopted children may try to locate each other?

Yes. Texas law establishes a voluntary adoption registry through the Texas Department of Protective and Regulatory Services.

Do birth parents, birth siblings, or adopted children have to register with the adoption registry?

No. If they wish to do so, they may. If they don't want to be located by their biological children, their biological siblings, or their birth parents, they have no duty to register. However, there's no guarantee that the identity or location of a biological parent or sibling, or an adult adopted as a child, may not be discovered by such relatives through other means.

Must a child be told she's adopted?

No. Most psychologists and other experts in child development urge adoptive parents to tell the child she's adopted, but they aren't legally required to do so.

5

Liability of Parents for Their Children's Acts

Is it right to hold a person responsible for the acts of another?

Usually not. One adult can't control the behavior of another, and as a rule has no duty to do so.

But what if a person who does have the duty to control someone else's behavior doesn't, and harm results to a third party?

Parents have a duty to use reasonable discipline to control their children. They're supposed to teach them appropriate behavior and see that they follow the rules.

If a child causes harm to someone else, the child usually has no money of his own to pay for the third party's loss. So, what's fair? For the third party to bear the loss? Or for the child's parents to do so?

There isn't a perfect answer, but there's a legal one. You may decide to think more carefully about giving Dick or Jane the keys to the family car.

Can parents be held liable for their children's acts?

Sometimes.

When?

A parent has the duty to control and discipline a child. Therefore, if a child's negligence causes property damage, and his negligence is due to his parents' failure to control or discipline him, the parents can be held liable for the damage. The child's age doesn't matter, as long as he's under eighteen.

Furthermore, if a child of twelve through seventeen willfully and maliciously does something that results in property damage, the parents are liable, period. If the child is under twelve or over seventeen, they aren't liable. Nor are they liable if the child was married when the damage occurred.

Is there any limit to the dollar amount of property damage for which parents can be held liable?

Yes. The most parents can be required to pay for their child's willful and malicious conduct is $25,000, plus court costs and attorney's fees. They can only be held liable for the actual amount of the damages, not for punitive damages, but the $25,000 limit applies to a single incident. If the child does the same thing next week, his parents can be held liable for up to $25,000 in damages all over again.

A law concerning property damage to hotels says one incident doesn't cover incidents in separate rooms or on separate days.

As for damage negligently caused by a child, if it happened because his parents weren't controlling or disciplining him, there is no legal limitation on the amount of property damages the parents may be required to pay.

How is parental liability determined?

A lawsuit is filed by the damaged party. The parents of the child who caused the damage must be given proper notice and the chance to hire an attorney. Unless the attorneys reach an agreement, a judge or jury will decide the issue of whether the parents are liable for damages, and if so, the amount they must pay.

Can a child sue a parent?

Well, it depends. In the past, children couldn't sue their parents for injuries arising from the parents' negligent acts if those acts occurred in the course of the performance of customary parental duties. Those duties are wide-ranging.

But since 1971, a series of cases has allowed a child to sue a parent for damages in certain circumstances where the act which caused the injuries wasn't basically the performance of a normal parental duty.

For example, children have been permitted to sue parents for injuries received in automobile accidents resulting from the parents' negligence.

A child has been permitted to bring a wrongful death action against the estate of his father, for the death of his mother in an airplane crash in which the father was the pilot of the plane.

6

Children and Divorce

With nearly two out of every three marriages now ending in divorce, children who grow up amid the chaos and pain involved in broken homes are commonplace.

Parents who are hurt and angry with one another often yield to the temptation to make their child the pawn and the prize in their battle.

There may never be a time in your child's life when she more urgently needs your expression of unselfish love. And there may never be a more difficult time for you to give it. But if reassuring your child is truly more important than retaliating against your spouse, there are positive steps you can take.

- Tell the child together that you're getting a divorce (unless you truly can't even be in the same room without shredding each other). Agree in advance on what you'll say. Explain that the divorce isn't the child's fault, and that you'll both still be her parents. Tell the child that you both love her, and will be there for her as before.

- Give the child as much information as possible about what will happen to her. For example, let her know that, for now, she'll go right on living in the same house with her mother, and will see her father often. As the situation changes, keep the child advised of those changes.

- Don't withhold child support as a weapon. It costs money to feed and clothe a child, as well as to provide medical care. If you don't keep up with those expenses, your behavior ultimately hurts no one as much as it hurts the child. Besides, it says to her you don't love her enough to provide for her needs.

- Make sure the child knows it's okay to love the other parent, and that she's not being disloyal to you by doing so. Each of you may feel the other is every unspeakable name in the book, and you may be right. But a child has two parents. She needs and has the right to know and love them both, and to have a relationship with both. Perhaps your spouse was a terrible husband or wife. But such people can still be good parents. And in any case, your child has the absolute right to love both of her parents without feeling guilty. It's the greatest gift you can give her.

- Don't say derogatory things about your child's other parent. For all of the reasons already mentioned and then some. Your unkind remarks about a parent she loves put your child in a terrible position. They seem to tell her you think it's wrong for her to care for such a person, and unfair to you when she does. If she tries to defend her other parent, she may hurt you, but if she doesn't, she feels disloyal. Either way, the child loses. Be careful what you say about her other parent in her presence. If that person is really such a loser, the child will figure it out for herself one day. But she'll never thank you if you're the one to tell her. She has the right to make her own decision.

- Keep your promises to the child. With everything around her changing, she's bound to feel some insecurity. Now, more than ever, she needs to know she can count on you. Do what you say you will do. And if for any reason you can't, let her know as soon as possible, tell her why, and make plans right then to make it up to her.

- Don't use the child as a messenger or go-between. If you can't communicate directly without bloodshed, do so through your attorneys. That's one of the things they get paid for. Don't put your child in the middle. It's just not fair.

- Don't deny visitation with the child to the other parent, and don't sabotage visitation with the other parent. One ever-popular means of doing just that is to deliberately plan activities your child is bound to enjoy for the time visitation is scheduled with the other parent. The child must either miss out on the fun, or the parent must give up the time. That's a dirty trick, and in the end it's the child who pays. On the other side of the coin, be flexible. Older children especially have activities of their own. Try to accommodate their needs, too. If you are the noncustodial parent, exercise your right to visit your child every time you can. She needs to spend time with you and be reassured that you will remain an active participant in her life.

- Don't use your child as a spy to find out what your former spouse is up to these days. The child feels disloyal to her other parent if she reports to you and dishonest if she lies or doesn't answer when you ask her a question. Don't cross-examine her about what went on during her visit. (The only exception is when you have honest reason to believe the other parent is placing the child in danger of physical, sexual, or emotional abuse. And folks, sending a child home with dirty clothes and a couple of mosquito bites is not what we're talking about here.)

- If both parents want custody, and your child's preference is sought, don't pressure her. Let her know that she's free to make whatever choice she wishes, and it'll be okay. Also, let her know her choice is only one of many factors the judge will consider in making her final decision, and that the child isn't responsible for that decision.

Hard? You'd better believe it. Worth it? Ask your child when she turns thirty.

What happens to the legal relationship between a child and her parents when they divorce?

Until a judge or jury decides otherwise, a child's parents share exactly the same rights, duties, privileges, and powers regarding the child.

When parents divorce, a judge or jury must decide how those rights, duties, privileges, and powers will be divided. That's necessary because the parents can no longer share them in exactly the same way.

For example, if both parents kept the right to decide where the child will live, how would they resolve the question if each wanted the child to live with him or her?

The framework provided in the law for assigning these rights, duties, privileges, and powers is called managing conservatorship and possessory conservatorship.

7

Managing and Possessory Conservatorship

If a child has been born or adopted during the marriage, then a managing conservator for that child must be appointed when the parents divorce.

What is a managing conservator?

A complicated term, dreamed up by lawyers. It means the person who has primary custody and makes the major decisions regarding the child.

What is a possessory conservator?

The person who usually pays the child support and has the right to visitation with the child.

What are the rights and duties of a managing conservator and a possessory conservator?

A parent appointed as either managing conservator or possessory conservator upon a divorce keeps all the rights, duties, privileges, and powers of a parent, except as they're limited, removed, or changed by the judge, who may:

- Appoint another person to serve as a joint managing conservator with the parent and give that person some of the rights, duties, privileges, and powers regarding the child;
- Appoint a possessory conservator and assign that person some of the parental rights, duties, privileges, and powers, such as visitation and child support; and
- Order specific limitations on who may see or associate with the child.

The court can't limit rights and duties of a parent appointed as managing or possessory conservator without first finding that it's in the child's best interest.

Unless the court says otherwise, a parent appointed as either managing conservator or possessory conservator always has these rights:

- As specified by the court, to receive information from the other parent, as well as other persons, about the child's health, education, and welfare and to confer with the other parent before decisions are made regarding those matters;
- To share access to the child's medical, dental, psychological, and education records;
- To consult with the child's doctor, dentist, or psychologist or with school officials about the child's welfare;
- To be informed of the child's school activities and to attend them;
- To be named as a person to call in case of an emergency involving the child;
- To consent to emergency medical, dental, and surgical procedures where there's an immediate danger to the child's health or safety; and
- To manage that property of the child which comes from that parent or his family.

When the child is with a parent who is either the managing or possessory conservator, that parent has these rights and duties:

- The duty of care, control, protection, and reasonable discipline of the child;
- The duty to support the child and to provide food, clothing, shelter, and medical and dental care which doesn't involve an invasive procedure;
- The right to consent to such medical and dental care as well as to emergency medical care and surgery if there is an immediate danger to the child's health and safety; and
- The right to direct the child's moral and religious training.

Unless a court says otherwise, a parent appointed as a sole managing conservator has rights which the other parent doesn't have, including the right to:

- Decide where the child will reside;
- Consent to medical, dental, and surgical treatment which does involve invasive procedures, as well as psychiatric and psychological treatment;
- Receive child support and use it for the child's benefit;
- Represent the child in legal action and make decisions with legal significance for the child;
- Consent to the child's marriage and enlistment in the armed forces of the United States;
- Make decisions about the child's education;

- Receive the child's services and earnings; and
- Act as the child's agent regarding the child's estate in legal matters.

May parents who are getting a divorce both be appointed as joint managing conservators for their child?

Yes. In fact, that's what the law says the judge must do unless someone proves that in this case it wouldn't be in the child's best interest.

What if parents want to agree that they should both be managing conservators?

They can file a written agreement with the court and ask the judge to make it the court's order. For the judge to approve it, the agreement must:

- Either decide what county the child will live in, or which parent has the sole right to make that choice;
- Specify each parent's rights and duties concerning the child's physical care, support, and education;
- Provide ways to keep disruption of the child's life to a minimum; and
- Assign any other rights and duties of a parent set out in the Family Code to one parent or to both.

The agreement also must show that each parent made the agreement voluntarily and understood what it meant.

Neither party can have changed his or her mind about the agreement at the time the judge decides to approve it.

Most importantly, the judge has to find the agreement is in the child's best interest.

If parents don't want to agree to joint managing conservatorship, but do want to agree about such things as who is to be the managing conservator, periods of possession, and child support, what can they do?

They can file a written agreement covering such matters, and the judge must approve it if it's found to be in the child's best interest.

The agreement doesn't have to follow any guidelines in the Family Code for visitation or child support.

May a judge decide to appoint both parents as managing conservators of the child even if neither wants the other to be a joint managing conservator?

Yes, but first the judge will consider how the parties get along with each other. If the judge appoints both parents as managing conservators, then he must decide how to assign the various rights, duties, privileges, and powers of a parent. The judge may let them continue to share some of the rights, while awarding others to only one parent.

The judge will decide "periods of possession," the time each parent will have with the child. The periods don't have to be of equal length. Usually, the judge will designate one parent's home as the child's primary residence; this tells the child where home is, and may provide him with a degree of stability.

Sometimes the judge will give one of the parents the right to decide where the child will live. At other times, the judge will designate the county in which the child is to live and require a hearing if either parent wants to change that decision.

If the parents don't agree to be joint managing conservators, why would a judge decide to appoint them anyhow?

Again, the child's best interest is the most important consideration. To determine the child's best interest a judge may examine:

- Whether the child will be better off, physically, emotionally, and psychologically, and will develop more fully, if the parents are joint managing conservators;
- The ability of the parents to place the child's welfare first and reach shared decisions;
- Whether each parent can encourage and accept a positive relationship between the child and the other parent;
- Whether both parents helped rear the child before the suit was filed;
- How close the parents live to one another; and
- If the child is twelve or older, whether the child wants joint managing conservators.

The judge can also look at any other relevant facts.

What is alternative dispute resolution, and when does it play a role in conservatorship decisions?

Alternative dispute resolution includes arbitration and mediation. In arbitration, a third party hears both sides and decides the issues. In mediation, a third party acts as moderator between the parties in an attempt to help them reach their own agreement on the issues.

The parties can file a written agreement to take their issues to an arbitrator. It must state whether or not they want the arbitration to be binding. If they ask that it be binding, the judge can't change the arbitrator's decision, unless, in a hearing, one of the parties proves the agreement isn't in the child's best interest.

The parties must give written consent to be referred to arbitration.

The judge can send the parties to mediation whether or not they request it. If, after mediation, the parties reach no agreement, they return to court and go through the regular process of a trial.

If the parties do arrive at an agreement through mediation, the court will approve the agreement and the parties will be bound by it, but only if the agreement:

- Has a separate underlined paragraph saying the agreement can't be revoked;
- Is signed by each party to the agreement and by any attorney who was present when either party signed it.

Mediation is a fairly recent idea, and it's a good one.

It may mean the divorce can be settled sooner. That's especially true in large cities where courts have so many cases to hear that it may take months, if not years, for your case to be reached.

Attorneys are busy, too, and trying to work out a time when everyone can go to court isn't easy.

If parents can agree upon a settlement concerning their child, they're far more likely to feel they've been treated fairly than if a decision is forced upon them by a judge. Bitterness is reduced and everyone is more likely to abide by the decision.

Mediation is a chance to discuss all of the questions more fully than is possible in court, to let it all "hang out" in a less formal and intimidating atmosphere.

Can someone other than a parent be appointed as managing conservator?

Yes. A non-parent, a licensed child placement agency, or an authorized agency may be appointed. Usually, that means a relative or the Texas Department of Protective and Regulatory Services.

How does a judge decide who will be appointed as managing conservator?

There's a strong preference in our law for children to be raised by their parents. Before a judge can even consider naming someone other than a parent as the child's managing conservator, he must determine that a significant impairment of the child's physical health or emotional development would result if either parent were appointed. It's not enough that the child might simply be better off if someone else was his managing conservator.

How does a third party go about asking to be named managing conservator in a divorce action?

By filing a paper asking the judge for the right to become involved as a third party in the divorce case. It's called "intervention."

First, the judge must decide whether the person should be allowed to intervene. Usually, if the would-be intervenor can show any substantial connection to the child, the intervention is permitted.

If the intervention is allowed, the intervenor must prove that appointment of either parent as managing conservator would not only significantly impair the child's physical health or emotional development, but that it would be in the child's best interest if the intervenor were appointed instead.

Unlike a parent managing conservator, a non-parent managing conservator must file a written report with the court each year concerning the child's whereabouts and physical condition.

If the court doesn't appoint either parent, or an intervenor, as managing conservator, who will be the child's managing conservator?

A child whose parents divorce must have at least one managing conservator. If neither a parent nor an intervenor qualifies, the judge will appoint an "authorized agency," usually the Texas Department of Protective and Regulatory Services.

Is there a legal limit to the number of managing conservators a judge can appoint for one child?

No. But, as a practical matter, think of the chaos if he had six!

Are there any limitations on a judge's right to appoint the parents as joint managing conservators?

Yes. The judge can't make the parents joint managing conservators if there's believable evidence of a history or pattern of past or present child neglect, physical abuse, or sexual abuse by one parent against the other parent, a spouse, or any child.

For a definition of what the law considers to be child abuse or child neglect, see Chapter 14.

Sexual abuse of a child doesn't require intercourse. Any behavior of an adult toward a child which contains inappropriate sexual elements may be sexual abuse.

The judge must also consider whether either parent has even once used intentional abusive physical force against the other parent, or any child, during the preceding two years in deciding whether to appoint that person as either a joint or sole managing conservator.

Courts take domestic violence seriously.

What if one party claims the other party committed child abuse, knowing the charge isn't true?

A false report of child abuse is a crime and may be grounds to modify child custody. Most judges would be reluctant to appoint someone who made such charges as a child's managing conservator. And think what damage to the child could result from someone he loved making such an accusation, knowing it wasn't true.

May a judge appoint a parent and a non-parent as joint managing conservators?

Yes. All of the rules previously discussed apply.

Does either parent have a greater right than the other to be appointed managing conservator?

No. Once, mothers were almost automatically chosen over fathers as the child's managing conservator. No more. Now, by law, neither sex has preference. Today, many fathers are chosen as managing conservators, but it's probably still harder for a father to be appointed, especially if both parents have been doing a good job.

Does a child ever have the right to choose who will be his managing conservator?

If he's at least twelve years old, the child may file a written statement stating his preference of sole or joint managing conservatorship, or specifying the one person he wants as his managing conservator. The judge must consider his wishes, but isn't required to follow them if they aren't in the child's best interest.

If the parents are fighting over custody, may the child talk with the judge?

Yes. If the child is ten or older, the judge must interview the child at a parent's request. He may do so if the child is younger. The interview may be done privately, but the child's attorney or the parents' attorneys may also be present. This is a tough situation for a child, and every effort should be made to treat him with sensitivity and not force him to take sides in his parents' conflict.

If the parents are appointed joint managing conservators, how does that affect the court's power to order child support?

It doesn't change it at all. A judge can order one joint managing conservator to pay child support to the other joint managing conservator.

If a parent isn't appointed as managing conservator for the child, what rights to the child does the parent still have?

The fact that the parent isn't appointed managing conservator doesn't change his legal status as parent of the child. It does change those rights, duties, privileges, and powers the parent can exercise regarding the child.

Custody isn't the only issue which must be decided when a child's parents divorce. Visitation, child support, and a division of parental rights and duties must also be resolved. These are the things usually addressed under possessory conservatorship.

If a judge doesn't appoint a parent as a managing conservator, that parent is usually, though not always, named a possessory conservator.

How does a judge decide whether to appoint a parent as possessory conservator when the parent won't be appointed as a managing conservator?

Our law is based on the belief that a child needs to have a positive relationship with both parents.

If a parent wasn't appointed managing conservator, the judge must appoint that parent possessory conservator unless he finds that it wouldn't be in the child's best interest because it would endanger the child's physical or emotional welfare.

May a judge appoint more than one person as possessory conservators?

Yes. Usually the parent who was not appointed managing conservator is appointed possessory conservator. The judge may appoint other or additional possessory conservators when there is an agreement between the parties to do so or the person to be named possessory conservator is an intervenor in the lawsuit. Typically, such intervenors are grandparents or other relatives.

If the judge doesn't appoint a parent as either a managing conservator or possessory conservator, what rights does the parent still have regarding the child?

That person remains the child's legal parent. The child can't be adopted unless another lawsuit is filed, seeking to terminate the parent's rights to the child altogether, and such termination is ordered by the court. The parent must be notified of such action and given the opportunity to oppose it.

The parent may also file another lawsuit at a later date, if certain conditions change, asking a judge to issue new orders naming the parent as managing or possessory conservator.

Can a parent who is neither managing conservator nor possessory conservator be ordered to pay child support?

Yes.

8

Visitation

There are some general rules the judge must follow when deciding the possessory conservator's rights to visitation with a child. They are:

- The judge must consider whether there has been a history of family violence in deciding whether to deny, restrict, or limit a parent's access to a child.
- A parent's access to a child can't be restricted more than is necessary to protect the child's best interest.
- The Family Code contains a Standard Possession Order, which sets forth visitation for parent managing conservators and possessory conservators. The presumption is that this Standard Possession Order represents the possession which should be ordered for a parent possessory conservator or a parent joint managing conservator. A person wanting more or less visitation must prove why that's necessary or best for the child in order for the judge to change it. Visitation varying from the Standard Possession Order may be ordered if the parties agree and the judge approves.
- In deciding whether to follow or change the Standard Possession Order, a judge may consider the age, circumstances, needs, and best interest of the child, and the circumstances of the parents, as well as any other relevant factors. The judge can't consider the sex of either the parent or child in deciding whether to use the Standard Possession Order. The Standard Possession Order applies only to children three and older.

What is the Standard Possession Order for parent possessory conservators of children?

There are two different Standard Possession Orders, one for parents who live less than one hundred miles apart, and one for parents who live more than one hundred miles apart. Some provisions of a Standard Possession Order apply no matter where they live. Obviously, if parents live two or three states apart, it isn't possible to visit the child as often as if they lived just around the corner.

Decrees usually include both orders, because no one knows whether the parents will continue to live in the same place. That prevents the parties from having to come back to court for new orders every time either moves.

Basically, the Standard Possession Order provides in great and unbelievable detail for periods of possession during weekends, Wednesday evenings, spring break, summer vacations, and holidays. The Standard Possession Order is set forth in all its glory in the Texas Family Code.

If the parents agree to do so, can they change the periods of possession set out in the court order?

Absolutely. However, they can't agree to unsupervised visitation when the court orders it to be supervised. Neither can they agree to visitation if the court has specifically prohibited it. Nor can they change conditions imposed by the court for visitations.

Couldn't the judge simply order possession "at all times mutually agreeable" rather than establishing specific times for visitation?

The judge must enter specific orders regarding possession by the possessory conservator unless a party proves that such specific orders wouldn't be in the child's best interest. If the judge were to order visitation "at all times mutually agreeable," without specific times guaranteed to the possessory conservator, that person would have no visitation if the parties failed to agree.

If weekend visitation conflicts with holiday visitation, which takes precedence?

Holidays.

After their divorce is final, if parents continue to argue about issues concerning the child, and clearly aren't acting in the child's best interest, can the judge intervene?

Yes. The judge can order counseling and decide who will pay for it.

What can the judge do if she believes a person might not return a child after visitation?

Require that person to post a bond or security with the court, in an amount set by the court, which will be forfeited if the person fails to return the child as ordered.

What is the law regarding possession of a child under three years of age by parent possessory conservators?

Until a child's third birthday, periods of possession are decided on a case-by-case basis. However, it's presumed that the Standard Possession Order will be included in the judge's final order, to go into effect when the child reaches the age of three.

Most experts believe that shorter, more frequent visits are preferable for such young children, with as few overnight or longer periods of time away from the primary caretaker as possible.

What kind of visitation or possession rights can a parent joint managing conservator expect if she doesn't live with the child?

Generally, at least the same possession rights as those granted by the Standard Possession Order to a possessory conservator.

Does a parent have to exercise her right to visitation each time it's allowed by the order?

No. A judge has no power to order a parent to visit a child. Visitation is a legal right, but not a legal duty.

If a possessory conservator isn't going to exercise visitation, does she have any duty to let the managing conservator know?

Yes. If she repeatedly fails to appear with no notice, that fact can be considered in any future suit to change visitation rights. More importantly, it's devastating to a child who is counting on Mom's visit when Mom simply doesn't show up.

What happens if the managing conservator refuses to let the child leave, or there is no one at home when the possessory conservator arrives for visitation?

If the managing conservator refuses to allow a court-ordered visitation when the possessory conservator arrives to exercise it, the possessory conservator can file a motion with the court, asking that the managing conservator be held in contempt. The same is true if no one is at home when the possessory conservator arrives to pick up the child.

However, the possessory conservator must be physically present and try to exercise her visitation right. Even if the managing conservator has told her in advance she can't see the child, that isn't enough. An actual attempt at visitation must be made and visitation denied. It helps to have a witness along to prove what really happened.

Can a judge ever order that a parent or possessory conservator must pay child support as a condition of visitation?

No.

If the possessory conservator is behind in her child support can the managing conservator refuse to let her exercise her court-ordered visitations?

No. The managing conservator can file a motion with the court, asking the judge to hold the possessory conservator in contempt if the child support isn't paid, but can't deny her her court-ordered visitation.

In other words, one parent disobeying the court's orders doesn't give the other parent the right to do the same. What either can do is file a motion with the court, asking that the other party be charged with contempt.

Contempt is no laughing matter. A person who violates a court order can be put in jail and ordered to pay court costs and attorney's fees.

Does a Standard Possession Order make any provisions regarding travel arrangements for a child's visitation?

The Standard Possession Order requires the judge to decide who makes and carries out travel arrangements. Usually, the judge will decide who pays the costs of travel, who picks up the tickets, and what notice of arrival and departure times each conservator must provide the other.

Any form of transportation may be used, as long as it's legal, unless the judge is convinced it would be in the child's best interest to restrict the choices available.

After a divorce has been filed, but before it's granted, which parent has the legal right to custody or possession of the child?

Each parent has identical rights, duties, privileges, and powers regarding their child until a judge decides otherwise. In order to avoid a tug-of-war over the child while the divorce is pending, either parent may ask for temporary orders in the divorce petition. If the parents don't agree about the child's temporary residence, visitation, and support, the judge will hold a hearing to decide those issues.

Can a judge change the temporary orders regarding custody or possession at the final hearing?

Yes. However, since there has already been either an agreement or hearing on the matter, temporary orders are usually changed only if conditions have changed since the temporary orders were issued or the judge hears evidence which wasn't presented before. If those changes or new facts show the judge that different orders would be in the child's best interest, the temporary orders will be changed.

If some special circumstance, like parents working weekends, would make the Standard Possession Order unworkable or inappropriate, must the judge still use the Standard Possession Order?

No. The judge will follow the Standard Possession Order as closely as possible, but can change or modify it for good reason.

Does the judge ever place conditions on the exercise of possession?

Certainly. For example, the judge can order that the parent not be drinking or on drugs while the child is visiting.

Another order commonly issued forbids the parent to have unrelated overnight guests of the opposite sex while the child is visiting in the parent's home.

Sometimes, a parent will be ordered not to remove the child from the court's jurisdiction during periods of possession.

Does a judge ever specifically order that a conservator be allowed phone calls to the child?

Yes. That isn't part of the Standard Possession Order, but if requested, the judge may order phone calls if it's in the child's best interest.

Do courts ever order parents to return a child's personal possessions along with the child when a period of visitation or possession has ended?

Yes. It's a requirement in the Standard Possession Order.

Must the possessory conservator pick up and deliver the child personally, or can someone else do it for her?

Under the Standard Possession Order, the possessory conservator can pick up and deliver the child herself, or can select another competent adult to do so.

Further, the Standard Possession Order provides that the managing conservator may be with the child when the child is picked up for visitation or can have another competent adult there instead. The judge can change this part of the possession order if there's good reason to do so.

For example, if an ex-husband wants his adult girlfriend to pick up his child, the fact that his ex-wife doesn't like her isn't sufficient reason for the judge to change the Standard Possession Order. On the other hand, if the ex-husband sends his eighty-seven-year-old grandmother, who is legally blind and has no driver's license and no taillights, *that's* a good reason to ask the judge to order Dad to pick up the child himself.

Does one conservator have to notify the other conservator of a move to a new address?

Yes.

Is there ever a time when the judge doesn't require a conservator to give such notice?

Yes, if such notice would expose the child or managing conservator to abuse or injury.

9

Child Support

When parents divorce, who is ordered to support the child?

The parent who is appointed managing conservator still has the duty of a parent to support the child, including providing the child with food, clothing, shelter, medical and dental care, and education.

The parent who is appointed possessory conservator must also provide the child with basic necessities when he has possession of the child.

In addition, a court may order child support payments, to be made by:

- A parent appointed joint managing conservator, without primary possession of the child;
- A parent appointed possessory conservator; or
- A parent not appointed as either.

If the child is placed in the temporary managing conservatorship of the Texas Department of Protective and Regulatory Services, either or both parents may be ordered to pay child support. If the child is placed in that agency's permanent managing conservatorship, parents whose parental rights haven't been terminated must be ordered to pay child support if financially able to do so.

Can a judge consider the gender of the conservators or the child in deciding the amount of child support?

No.

Can a judge consider either parent's remarriage in setting child support?

No.

Can a court order that a possessory conservator must pay child support only if the managing conservator allows visitation?

No.

Is court-ordered support paid in installments, or in a lump sum?

Either or both, depending on what the judge orders. Also, a judge can order a parent to set aside property for the child's benefit. If a parent is the beneficiary of a trust, the trustees can sometimes be ordered to make the parent's child support payments from the trust fund.

How long is a parent obligated to pay child support?

Until the child reaches eighteen or graduates from high school, whichever is later. The obligation is also ended if the child dies, marries, or has his disabilities of minority removed. See Chapter 19.

The death of a parent ends his support obligation, unless it's requested and ordered in advance that his estate be obligated to continue child support payments after he dies.

Does a child's disability affect a parent's duty to pay child support?

Yes. Parents of a disabled child, whether the child is a minor or an adult, can be ordered to pay support for an indefinite period of time. The disability must have existed at the time the child turned eighteen.

Can the parents agree to extend the child support obligation beyond the child's eighteenth birthday?

Yes, and the judge can make such an agreement the court's order. This agreement most often involves payment of college expenses.

Can a judge order retroactive child support?

Yes. Child support can be ordered back to the time of the child's birth. This usually happens only in paternity suits. The judge will consider whether the father was aware of his child and whether he made other contributions to the child.

Can the judge order child support payments to be withheld from a parent's wages by his employer?

It's not a matter of choice; it's required. There are only two exceptions: if both parents agree that withholding is not necessary, or if one of them shows good reason why withholding shouldn't be ordered. Even then, the final decree must contain a wage withholding order, which will go into effect if the parent fails to make child support payments.

If this requirement is omitted in the final divorce decree, either by mistake or because the divorce was granted before 1987, when the law went into effect, the decree is construed to contain a wage withholding provision regardless, and it will take effect if the support payments are delinquent.

Can any payment, other than current child support, be ordered withheld from a parent's wages?

Yes. Child support that is found by a judge to be past due can be withheld whether or not current child support is due.

How much can be withheld for past-due support?

In addition to current support, 20 percent of disposable income, or enough to pay off the arrearage in two years, whichever will pay it off sooner.

If no current support is due, the entire amount of past-due support must be paid within two years. At least theoretically.

Can a judge extend the period of time for repayment of past-due child support?

Yes, if repayment within two years would cause unreasonable hardship.

How does wage withholding work?

It is ordered in the decree, and a separate order dealing only with child support wage withholding is sent to the parent's employer. The employer is ordered to withhold the amount of the support payments from the parent's paycheck, and to forward them to an agency or person designated by the court to receive them.

If a person is paid monthly, the entire monthly child support payment is withheld. If the parent is paid twice a month, half is withheld from each paycheck, and so on.

How soon must the employer begin withholding support payments?

No later than the first pay period after the employer received the withholding order.

Sometimes a payment or two will be due before the wage withholding begins. It's the parent's responsibility to make all payments when due until the withholding process starts.

Is there a maximum amount that can be withheld from a parent's disposable earnings?

Yes. One-half.

Can an employer fire an employee because the employer has been ordered by the court to withhold child support payments from the parent's wages?

No. An employee who is fired or disciplined in any way by his employer because of the withholding order can file suit against his employer and recover his current wages and benefits as well as attorney's fees. Further, he will get his job back when the case is over.

An employer can't refuse to hire a person because of such an order.

What if the employer refuses or fails to send the child support payments as ordered?

An employer who receives the order but doesn't withhold the payments is liable to the person to whom the payments are due for any payment not made under the court order. An employer who withholds the payments but doesn't send them is liable to the employee for the full amount he failed to send.

The employer is also liable for reasonable attorney's fees necessary to straighten out the matter.

If the withholding order requires that health insurance be provided for a child, what is the employer's responsibility?

The responsibility and the liability of the employer is the same as for child support payments.

What happens if the parent under a wage withholding court order quits his job, or is fired?

Both the employee and his former employer must give notice within seven days, to the court and to the person receiving the child support payments, that employment has been terminated. The notice must provide the most recent address of the former employee, as well as the name and address of his new employer, if he has one. The parent obligated to pay the child support is also required to inform any new employer of the withholding order.

How does a judge determine how much child support to order?

The Texas Family Code sets guidelines. The presumption is that the guidelines set an amount which is reasonable and in a child's best interest. The judge must follow them unless the facts presented in court convince him otherwise.

Most people have bills to pay, so the fact a parent has other expenses and obligations usually isn't very persuasive. Judges hear at least once a week the excuse that the other parent "doesn't spend the support money on the child." That complaint doesn't even get a response.

And the sad lament that "she [or he] makes more money than I do and doesn't need child support" will get you nowhere.

The fact that the other parent has behaved badly is just not relevant to the child's need for support, if the child is to be living primarily with that other parent.

The probability is always strong that the judge will follow the guidelines. Judges can and do vary from them, but only after being shown good reason why they should.

What does the judge consider when deciding whether to set child support higher or lower than the guidelines?

All relevant factors, including:

- The ability of the parent to contribute to the child's support;
- The child's age and needs;
- Any financial resources available for support of the child;
- Child care expenses of either party necessary to maintain employment;
- The amount of time of possession of a child;
- Whether either party has managing conservatorship or physical custody of another child;
- The amount of net resources of the party paying child support;
- The amount of alimony being paid or received by either party;
- Educational expenses after high school which either party is paying for a child;
- Benefits such as automobiles or housing received by either party from an employer or any other source;
- The amount of other deductions from either party's wages;
- Provision for health care insurance and payment of uninsured medical expenses;
- Unusual health care, educational, or other expenses of the parties or the child;
- Travel expenses incurred to exercise visitation;
- Positive or negative cash flow from the parties' real property, investments, or businesses;
- Debt assumed by either party; and

- Other reasons consistent with the child's best interest, keeping in mind the circumstances of the parties.

What are the child support guidelines based upon?

If the parent paying support has net resources of $6,000 or less per month, the guidelines are as follows:

- For one child, 20 percent of the net resources;
- For two children, 25 percent of the net resources;
- For three children, 30 percent of the net resources;
- For four children, 35 percent of the net resources; and
- For five or more children, not less than 40 percent of the net resources.

What if the parent paying child support has net resources of over $6,000 per month?

Then the guidelines apply to the first $6,000. Without further consideration of percentages, the judge may order additional amounts depending solely on income of the parties and the proven needs of the child.

Here's how that's calculated: The amount the parent would be ordered to pay with net resources of $6,000 or less is subtracted from the amount proven necessary for the needs of the child. The difference is then divided between the parties according to their circumstances. This amount is added to the child support due on the first $6,000.

What does "net resources" mean?

In relationship to child support, the term has a different definition than it has for ordinary purposes. To determine the "net resources" of the parent who is to pay child support, you must do this:

First, add 100 percent of the following:

Gross salary or wages, commissions, overtime pay, tips, bonuses, interest income, dividends, royalty income, rental income (after deducting operating expenses and mortgage payments), and any other income actually received, such as severance pay, retirement benefits, pensions, trust incomes, annuities, capital gains, Social Security benefits, unemployment benefits, disability and worker's compensation benefits, gifts, prizes, spousal maintenance, and alimony.

Don't include payments for Temporary Aid to Needy Families (TANF), other child support payments received, return on principal or capital, or accounts receivable.

Then, after totaling the above income, deduct the following:

One hundred percent of all Social Security taxes, federal income tax withholding claiming one personal exemption and a standard deduction, union dues, and expenses for health insurance coverage for the child. If a state income tax goes into effect one day in Texas, you'll deduct that, too.

The figure remaining is the "net resources" of the parent.

Deductions from the parent's paycheck for such things as credit union payments, retirement, and health or life insurance for the parent are *not* deductible in figuring "net resources," even if they are not voluntary deductions.

Is overtime pay included in calculating net resources?

Yes. Usually, the judge will examine the past year's wages, not just a month or two, to determine how dependable overtime wages are.

In following the guidelines, how is child support figured?

Determine the gross income of the parent who is to pay child support. This is usually done by examining federal income tax returns for the past two years, financial statements, and current payroll records. This information should be furnished to the attorney, and brought to court for the judge to examine. Then, divide the annual gross income by twelve to determine the monthly gross income.

Subtract the deductions as outlined above from the monthly gross income to determine the monthly net income, or "net resources." There are tables in the Family Code which are revised annually and are helpful in arriving at this figure.

Then, apply the appropriate percentage, based on the number of children involved. The result is what the monthly support payment should be under the guidelines.

What happens if a parent is already paying child support for another child?

Here's how to figure child support when a person pays child support for children living in more than one household:

- Figure how much child support would be due under the guidelines if the children all lived under the same roof.
- Divide that amount by the total number of children the parent is obligated to support.
- Multiply that number by the number of children who are not subjects of the present suit.

- Subtract the amount due for those children from the parent's net resources.
- Using the new figure for net resources, apply the guidelines to the number of children who are subjects of the present suit.

Do the rules differ if the parent paying child support is self-employed?

Yes. Self-employment income includes benefits the person receives from the business, less the ordinary and necessary expenses required to produce that income. Such items as depreciation, tax credits, and other business expenses which would be allowed under federal income tax law may not be deductible in determining net income for the purposes of child support if the evidence shows such deductions would be inappropriate.

The state attorney general's office provides annual tax charts for self-employed persons and for persons who work for others. They differ somewhat. These tables are also found in the Texas Family Code. Once net monthly income, or "resources," is determined, the rest of the rules remain the same.

May parents agree on child support which varies from the guidelines, and ask the judge to approve that agreement?

Yes. If the judge approves their agreement, it becomes the court's order. If not, the judge can issue a different order, or ask the parents to make changes in the agreement and resubmit it.

Is it possible to determine child support if the judge can't tell the amount of the parent's income?

Yes. If it's impossible to determine a parent's income, there's a presumption that the parent earns the current federal minimum wage and works a forty-hour week. That isn't very much money, but it at least allows the court to order *some* child support.

What happens if the parent most likely to have to pay support quits his job during the divorce proceedings and takes another job at a much lower salary?

If a parent can prove that the other parent is intentionally underemployed or unemployed, the judge can order child support payments based on the parent's earning potential, rather than actual current earnings.

If child support is ordered for more than one child in the divorce decree, what happens to the support payments for the remaining children when support for the oldest child ends?

The order must spell out how the support payments for any remaining children will be affected as child support ends for each child.

What if a judge varies from the guidelines and a parent disagrees with the amount of child support ordered?

The parent can appeal the support order. The judge must explain in writing any variation from the guidelines. He must find that it would be unjust or inappropriate to apply the guidelines, and give specific reasons why. If the judge doesn't make these written findings after being asked to do so, it's "reversible error," which means the case will be sent back for a new trial.

Are there any requirements concerning health insurance for the child when parents are divorced?

Yes. The court must order that health insurance be provided for the child. The guidelines presume that the person ordered to pay support will also be ordered to maintain health insurance for the child. Failure to pay those premiums will be treated just like failure to pay child support payments and is enforceable by contempt.

Does the question of whose employer makes health insurance available affect what the judge orders regarding the child's health insurance?

Yes. The judge must consider the cost and quality of health insurance coverage available to both parents and give priority to health insurance provided by one of the parent's employers unless there's good reason to do otherwise. If health insurance for the child is available through the employer of the parent ordered to provide it, the judge will order the parent to cover the child with that insurance.

If such insurance isn't available to the parent who is ordered to carry it, but is available through the other parent's employer, the judge will order that other parent to carry it and be reimbursed by the parent responsible for providing health coverage.

If health insurance isn't available at work to either parent, the court may order the parent paying child support to provide such coverage from another source if it's available and if the parent can afford it.

If a parent obligated to pay for a child's health insurance can't do so otherwise, he must apply for coverage from the Texas Healthy Kids

Corporation, which establishes group coverage plans for children. Parents may be required to pay for such coverage according to their ability. If insurance isn't available through the Texas Healthy Kids Corporation, the parent obligated for such coverage must pay a reasonable amount to the managing conservator for such costs. The amount will be withheld from his wages.

The law presumes that $38.00 per month is reasonable.

What if a portion of the child's medical expenses is not covered by insurance?

The court may order one or both of the parents to pay for that portion.

10

Modification of Custody, Visitation, Support, and the Rights of Parents

Once a divorce is granted, can custody, visitation, child support, and rights and duties of parents ever be changed?

Yes.

How?

By filing a Motion to Modify asking the judge to change the original orders.

Who can file such a motion?

Anybody who was directly affected by the judge's orders, and anyone with the right to file an Original Suit to Affect the Parent-Child Relationship regarding the child.

What must you prove to convince the judge to change sole managing conservatorship from one person to another?

A judge may modify an order to change from one sole managing conservator to another, regardless of the child's age, if:

- Circumstances of the child, the sole managing conservator, or the possessory conservator have materially and substantially changed since the orders were issued; and

- Appointment of the new sole managing conservator would be a positive improvement for the child.

If the child is twelve or older, a court can change the sole managing conservator if the child files a written request naming the person she chooses as managing conservator, and if it's in the child's best interest.

If a motion to change the sole managing conservator is filed within one year of the date of the order to be modified, there are tougher standards to meet. The person filing the Motion to Modify must attach a sworn statement to the motion, stating either that:

- The child's present environment may endanger her physical health or significantly impair her emotional development; or
- The sole managing conservator is the one seeking the change, or consents to it, and the change would be in the child's best interest.

If the child's sole managing conservator has voluntarily given up actual care, control, and possession of the child for at least six months and the modification is in the child's best interest, a court can change the sole managing conservator whenever the request is filed.

If the original decree named one parent sole managing conservator, what must the other parent prove in a Motion to Modify to be named as a joint managing conservator?

She must prove that:

- Circumstances of the child or the conservator have materially changed since the order was issued;
- Retention of the sole managing conservator would be detrimental to the child's welfare; and
- The appointment of the parent as joint managing conservator would be a positive improvement and in the child's best interest.

Until 1987, the judge couldn't order a joint managing conservatorship unless both parties agreed. Since then, it doesn't matter whether they agree or not. The fact that the court now has that power is itself a material and substantial change in circumstances, sufficient to justify a change from sole managing conservatorship to joint managing conservatorship if the decree ordering sole managing conservatorship was issued on or after September 1, 1987. It is not, however, if the decree was issued before September 1, 1987. Also, the change must be shown to be in the best interest of the child.

If the judge decides to appoint a parent who has been a possessory conservator as a joint managing conservator, that change alone will not change the amount of child support the parent must pay.

What must a parent prove to replace joint managing conservatorship with sole managing conservatorship?

The parent must prove:

- The child's present living environment may endanger the child's physical health or significantly impair the child's emotional development;

- There has been a substantial and unexcused violation of the present conservatorship order; or

- The circumstances of the child, or one or both of the conservators, have so materially and substantially changed since the order was issued that it's now unworkable or inappropriate.

The parent must also show that appointment of a new sole managing conservator would be a positive improvement and in the child's best interest.

What must a parent prove in a Motion to Modify in order to change child support?

Any party affected by the order can file a motion to either increase or decrease, or otherwise change, the court's child support order. She must show that the circumstances of the child, or another person directly affected by the order, have materially and substantially changed since the order was entered, or that it's been three years since the last order for child support and that order differs by either 20 percent or $100.00 from the amount which would be ordered under the Texas Family Code guidelines.

Any support order may only be modified as to support payments due after the citation of the other party or the other party's appearance in court on the motion, whichever comes first.

No change in support ordered will be retroactive.

If a child moves from the home of a parent who was appointed sole managing conservator and starts living with the possessory conservator, how does that affect child support?

The support payments continue to be due and payable as ordered until the court changes the order. The best idea is for both parties to enter an Agreed Motion to Modify. The fact that the child has been living with the possessory conservator, and has been supported entirely by the possessory conservator, would probably be a good defense against a contempt charge for failure to pay child support as ordered, but don't bet the farm on it. Even though a person may be given credit for time the child was in that party's possession, the length of time and other facts may be debatable. Just get the order changed.

If the parent who's been paying child support payments remarries, is the new spouse's income included with the parent's income to figure the amount of support to be ordered in a Motion to Modify?

No.

If the parent paying child support remarries, may the costs incurred because of the new spouse, or the new spouse's children, be deducted from the parent's net income in a motion to reduce child support?

No.

If a parent wants to change the terms and conditions for possession of a child, or to change the rights and duties assigned to each parent, what must the parent prove?

She must show that:

- The circumstances surrounding the child or other person affected by the order have materially and substantially changed since the court order was issued; or
- The order the parent wants modified or changed has become unworkable or inappropriate; or
- Notice of a change of conservator's address was not given as ordered; or
- A conservator has repeatedly failed to give notice that visitation would not be exercised.

What effect is there on orders concerning managing or possessory conservators if a conservator is convicted or receives deferred adjudication for child abuse?

That is a material and substantial change of circumstances, sufficient to justify modification of orders concerning the child. It seems to me that's just common sense, but to remove any doubt the lawmakers put it in black and white.

If a parent who is sole managing conservator dies, does the other parent automatically become managing conservator?

No. If that happens, the child has no managing conservator. However, the surviving parent retains the status of parent, which gives her the primary right to possess the child unless a court orders otherwise.

The judge must appoint the surviving parent managing conservator unless she finds that:

- Appointing the surviving parent wouldn't be in the child's best interest because it would significantly impair the child's physical health or emotional development; or
- Someone other than a parent has filed a motion asking to be named managing conservator, and the parent has voluntarily relinquished pos-

session and control of the child to someone else for one year or more, a portion of which was within ninety days of the time the motion was filed.

If either of these conditions is met, then the judge can appoint some-one other than a parent as managing conservator, provided it's in the child's best interest to do so.

Do these rules for modification apply only when someone is trying to change a divorce decree?

No. The same rules apply for any attempt to change any order concerning conservatorship, possession, child support, or parental rights or duties. A divorce decree isn't the only place such orders can be issued. They are also contained in orders establishing paternity, and a prior order for modification may itself be modified.

11

Interference with the Possession of Children

Few rights are more precious than the right to possession of one's children, and the law reflects that. When judges issue orders concerning child custody or possession, they are dead serious. You break those orders at your peril.

All sorts of civil, and even criminal, consequences can result.

Children need stability. Parents need to be secure in the fact that no one will arbitrarily take their children away from them.

Lawyers who've been around for a while will tell you that few things are sadder than seeing a child snatched in violation of a court order and hidden away, only to be snatched back and hidden away again, until the object of the tug-of-war isn't much more than a tiny basket case. The adults always claim they do what they do "for the child's sake." They seldom realize what their efforts do to the objects of their benevolence.

What can a person with court-ordered possession of a child do when another person interferes with that possession?

There may be one or more of these possibilities:

- Filing a Motion for Contempt;
- Discussing with the district attorney the possibility of filing criminal charges;
- Filing a civil suit for actual and/or punitive damages; or
- Filing a Writ of Habeas Corpus.

Does the "possession" ordered by the court have to be "custody" for legal help to be available, or can it be "visitation"?

It can be either.

Does the same law apply for possession granted in temporary orders?

Yes.

When is it appropriate to file a Motion for Contempt to enforce possession orders?

If a person was awarded possession of a child in a temporary or final order, and the person who has possession of the child when the visitation is scheduled refuses that visitation.

It's also appropriate if a person who was awarded possession failed to return the child when the period of possession was supposed to end, but returned him later.

Is there ever any acceptable reason to disobey possession orders?

Of course. Common sense would dictate that if a parent arrives falling down drunk and wants to drive away with the child, you say no. But be ready to prove your contention. Witnesses help.

If a child is ill, and the physician says the child must remain home in bed, follow his instruction. But have a written statement to back you up.

In short, if there would be a genuine threat to the child's welfare by permitting the visitation, the child's welfare comes first. But don't play games with the court. If there's a reason to deny visitation each time it rolls around, go back to court and ask the judge to change the order. Otherwise, follow it.

How do you go about having someone held in contempt for violating a court order regarding visitation?

You file a motion with the court, setting out the exact portion of the judge's order which was violated, and each date, time, and place it was disobeyed. There will be a hearing for the judge to decide whether the person is in contempt and what the punishment will be.

What can a judge do if he finds you in contempt for violating possession orders?

He may fine you, send you to jail, and require you to pay costs of court and the other person's attorney's fees. He also may place you on probation, with rules of probation you must follow.

Does a person who's charged with contempt have the right to an appointed attorney if he can't afford to hire one?

If the motion asks to have him sent to jail, yes. He should appear at the proper time in court and ask the judge to appoint an attorney to represent him. He must be prepared to prove he can't afford to hire a lawyer.

If the judge finds he's able to hire a lawyer, the judge will usually give him a reasonable amount of time to do so.

Can a person be held in contempt for violating a possession order if the other person voluntarily gave up that period of possession?

No. If Mom doesn't show up for her court-ordered visits with her child, she can't file a motion claiming Dad denied them to her.

If Dad agrees to let Mom keep Johnny an extra week in the summer, he can't file a contempt motion because she didn't return the child when the court order said she must.

Is there any other protection a court can provide to ensure that violation of a possession order doesn't occur repeatedly?

Yes. If a person denies court-ordered possession to someone twice or more, the court can order the person to execute a bond, or deposit security with the court, to ensure that its orders will be followed in the future. There must be notice and a hearing before a court can issue that order.

After the court has ordered a bond or security, what happens if the person continues violating the order?

The person whose right of possession is being violated can ask the court to forfeit the bond or security. If the judge finds there has been another violation, he can forfeit the bond or security and pay those funds to the person whose visitation rights were violated.

Does such a forfeiture mean a person can't be held in contempt again for violating the possession orders?

No. In fact, a contempt motion and a motion to forfeit a bond can be filed together.

What can be done if a child is wrongfully removed from the United States?

The United States was a party to the Convention on the Civil Aspects of International Child Abduction at the Hague in 1980. That convention established procedures for the return of children wrongfully removed from or retained outside their country, and for securing the exercise of visitation rights. Congress then established laws and procedures in this country for a person to seek that international help.

What kinds of criminal charges can be filed against persons who violate a court's possession orders?

The act may be:

- Interference with child custody;
- Kidnapping;
- Agreement to abduct from custody;
- Enticing a child; or
- Harboring a runaway child.

Contact the district attorney to determine whether it's appropriate to file charges in your case.

If a person takes or keeps a child in violation of a court order, may he be liable for damages to the person whose possessory rights he violated?

A person who takes or keeps a child in violation of a court order may be held liable for damages to the person whose visitation rights were violated.

This is true even if the person only concealed the child's whereabouts and didn't actually take or have possession of the child.

What if the person who violated the court order wasn't a party to the suit where the orders were issued?

Imagine that Peter and Pamela are divorced, and Pamela's parents don't think Peter should see little Paul every other weekend, and certainly not for any time in the summer. So, they take Paul off to the Grand Canyon and points west from June through September. Peter had a court order allowing him to take his son for six weeks each summer, and he showed up at the proper time, only to be told that Paul was somewhere in Arizona with his grandparents. Are the grandparents liable to Peter for money damages? Yes, if:

- The grandparents had actual notice of the existence and contents of the order; or
- They had reasonable cause to believe that Peter had the right to visitation with Paul under a court order and their action would probably violate a court order.

What damages may a person recover if someone interferes with his court-ordered possession of a child?

Damages may be awarded for the actual costs incurred in locating and recovering the child and in filing suit to enforce the court order. This includes attorney's fees.

The value of mental suffering and anguish the person suffered from his loss of possession can also be awarded.

These damages could amount to a great deal of money.

Can a person be liable for damages if all he did was help the person who actually took or retained the child?

Yes. He has equal liability with the person who actually took the child. Such persons have no right to notice of the violation before the lawsuit for damages is filed. Such notice and chance to comply must only be given to the person who actually took or kept the child.

Obviously, if Grandma and Grandpa help their daughter take little Becky and hide her from her father, who has the right to possession, they are in a very dangerous position. Their daughter must be given notice, and a chance to comply, before a lawsuit can be filed against her. There's no such requirement regarding them.

When are such lawsuits for civil damages usually filed?

This is a rarely used remedy. It can be used for any violation of possession, but usually is more appropriate for serious, ongoing violations. An example would be if Mom has the right of possession and Dad disappears, taking the children with no intention of returning them. It's especially useful if friends or relatives have assisted in the violation.

If you file for damages, can you also file contempt or criminal charges, or seek a Writ of Habeas Corpus?

Yes. You can use every means available to enforce an order of the court, or to punish its violation.

What is a Writ of Habeas Corpus?

"Habeas corpus" is Latin for "you have the body." A Writ of Habeas Corpus is a court order telling one person who is detaining another person to bring that person to court, to "produce the body" at the date and time set by the court.

In cases where possession of a child is disputed, the judge requires the person who has the child to bring the child to court, so the question of who has the right to possession can be decided.

When is a Writ of Habeas Corpus the proper way to seek the return of a child?

When the person seeking the writ has the right to possession of the child under a court order and another person is refusing to turn over the child.

How does a person obtain a Writ of Habeas Corpus?

By filing a motion with the court asking for the writ. A hearing will be set and notice given to all parties.

What does the judge decide at a hearing for a Writ of Habeas Corpus?

Usually, the only issue is who has the legal right to possession of the child. If an existing court order spells that out, that's almost always enough for the judge to require that the order be obeyed.

If there's a court order giving possession of a child to someone, is there any way to convince the judge not to return the child to that person?

Yes. Even if there's a valid court order giving possession to someone, the judge won't order the child returned to that person if:

- The order was issued by a court that didn't give both sides reasonable notice of the hearing and a chance to be heard; or
- The person with the right to possession gave up possession, or agreed to another's possession, for at least six months just before the suit was filed. This is true even if the person with possession took the child back for brief periods of time during that six months; or
- There's a serious, immediate question concerning the child's welfare if he were returned.

If the judge doesn't order the child returned, what happens?

The judge will issue temporary orders for the safety and welfare of the child. These orders may include temporary custody, temporary visitation, and temporary child support.

Is habeas corpus ever used when there's no valid court order awarding possession of the child?

Yes. In such cases, a parent may still ask for a Writ of Habeas Corpus on the grounds he has a superior legal right to possession over a non-parent who presently has the child.

If the child is being held by a non-parent and no Suit to Affect the Parent-Child Relationship has been filed, the judge will order the child returned to the parent. Until a judge orders otherwise, a parent's legal right to possession of his child is superior to anyone else's. That's true even if the parent has never seen the child and the other person has had possession of the child since birth.

This kind of case typically involves a grandparent or other relative who has raised a child, when suddenly a long-absent parent appears and demands possession of the child. The child will be turned over to the parent unless the person with possession can show that such a change would create a serious, immediate question concerning the child's welfare.

The only other course of action available to the person with possession is to file his own suit seeking managing conservatorship of the child. This must be done as quickly as possible.

If the person with possession does seek managing conservatorship, what effect will it have on the judge's decision about whether to return the child to his parent?

If a suit has been filed by the person with possession of the child, and if it also asks for a hearing to establish temporary orders, and if that hearing is set at the same time as the habeas corpus hearing, and if the parent gets notice of the hearing, the judge doesn't have to return the child to the parent at the hearing. He may do so, but he also may issue temporary orders continuing possession with the non-parent.

As you can see, a lot of "ifs" are involved, and it's important that the non-parent move quickly if he wants to fight for possession of the child.

Suppose there are no court orders giving either parent possession of a child. Can one parent seek a Writ of Habeas Corpus to gain possession from the other?

No. In that instance, the proper thing to file would be a divorce or a Suit to Affect the Parent-Child Relationship.

If there are no parents involved, and no valid court orders, can one non-parent seek to gain possession of a child from another non-parent by using a Writ of Habeas Corpus?

No.

Does it matter if a child consents to the violation of a possession order?

No. If Daddy takes Johnny on a fishing trip to Colorado and keeps him an extra two weeks in violation of the court order, it doesn't matter that Johnny caught a lot of fish and he heartily agreed with staying longer.

If Mary's mother lets Mary spend the weekend with a friend rather than with her father during his court-ordered time of possession, Mom's in violation, even if Mary begged her for permission.

Is there any defense a court will accept for having interfered with possession of a child?

Yes. There are two.

First, that the person violated the order with the express consent of the person with the right to possession.

Second, that after receiving written notice that he had violated the order, the person immediately and completely complied with it.

If a child doesn't want to go on a visitation, must a parent force him to do so?

Many parents say it's unfair to require them to make a child spend time with the other parent when the child doesn't want to. Perhaps, but the law says the child cannot make that decision. So, it's up to the parent with custody to see that the child follows the court's order. There are particular problems with older children who have their own activities. Good parents will work out some flexibility.

12

Termination of the Parent-Child Relationship

Ending the relationship between parent and child is a new concept. Until recent times, children were considered the property of their parents. A person's property belongs to her, and what she does with it is no one's business. Only when children were finally recognized as individuals with rights of their own were standards established for their treatment by their parents. And only then did the idea arise of termination of the parent-child relationship when parents' conduct failed to meet those standards.

We no longer believe that a father has a right to beat a child senseless because the child is his son. Or that a woman has a right to offer a child's services for prostitution because the child is her daughter. Or that parents can abandon, neglect, and otherwise abuse their children while society stands silent and does nothing.

In the entire area of the law dealing with children, lawyers and judges will tell you that no issue is more painful to try, or more difficult to decide, than termination of the parent-child relationship.

It's a last resort in an effort to protect a child from her parents when all else has failed. Although it may be necessary, and although it may be the turning point toward a better future for the child, it is always profoundly sad.

Sad for parents, because their children are no longer their own. In the eyes of the law, it's as if the relationship between the parents and children never existed. They have no right to play any further part in their children's lives, or even to see them, ever again.

Sad for children, because whatever their parents may have been, and whatever they may have done, they were still the children's parents. There's no longer the hope that their parents will change, that they can be happy and safe with those they know and to whom they are bonded, no hope that their parents will at last become what they remember seeing in brief, promising flashes. The loss is enormous.

As you would expect, the law in Texas is very specific about grounds for termination, and those grounds must be precisely proven. Termination must be in the child's best interest. Even when that's true, no one involved ever walks away without a heavy heart.

What is termination of the parent-child relationship?

The legal ending, termination, or cutting off of any rights, privileges, duties, and powers a parent and child have regarding one another.

What is the legal effect of such termination?

Following termination, the former parent has no different relationship to her former child than if the child had never been hers. There's one exception. The child keeps the right to inherit through and from the former parent, unless the judge specifically rules otherwise.

How may the parent-child relationship be terminated?

By the death of the parent, or by a court granting a termination of the relationship.

May a child ever be adopted before her relationship with her parents has been ended by death or court order?

No. Unless she is being adopted by a stepparent. In that instance, the rights of the parent married to the stepparent are not terminated, though the other parent's rights must be.

Who may file a petition to terminate the relationship between a parent and his or her child?

- A parent;
- A child, acting through an authorized representative;
- A custodian or person having the right to visitation resulting from the order of a court in another state or country;
- A guardian of the child's person or estate;
- A governmental entity such as PRS;
- An authorized adoption agency;
- A licensed child placement agency;
- A man who claims to be the biological father of a child who has no presumed father;
- A person who has had actual possession and control of the child for at least six months immediately prior to filing the petition;
- A person named as a managing conservator in an Affidavit of Relinquishment, or to whom written consent for adoption has been given;
- A person with whom the child and her parent, guardian, or managing conservator have been living at least six months just before the petition was filed; or

- A foster parent in whose home the child has been placed by PRS for at least eighteen months preceding the filing of the petition.

If the petition for termination is joined with a Petition for Adoption, it may also be filed by:

- A stepparent;
- An adult with whom a child has been placed in anticipation of adoption, and who has had actual possession of the child at any time during the thirty days just before the petition was filed;
- An adult who has had actual possession of the child for at least two months during the three months just before the petition was filed; or
- Any other adult the judge decides has had enough contact with the child in the past to give her the right to file a petition for termination.

Can a parent ask that her own parent-child relationship with her child be terminated?

Yes. If the court decides it's in the child's best interest, the court can grant such a request. Needless to say, it's very hard to convince a judge to do it unless it is done for the purpose of freeing the child for adoption and in anticipation that an adoption will occur.

Can the parent-child relationship be restored once it has been terminated?

No. Once the decree of termination is final and the time for appeal has passed, it's irreversible.

What has to be proven for the judge to terminate the parent-child relationship?

A judge must determine, by clear and convincing evidence, that two things are true:

First, that a parent has committed an act which is grounds for termination, and

Second, that termination of the parent-child relationship is clearly in the child's best interest.

One or the other isn't enough.

What are the grounds for termination?

There are six so-called abandonment grounds. They are that the parent has:

- Voluntarily left the child alone or in the possession of someone other than a parent, and has expressed an intention not to return;
- Voluntarily left the child alone or in the possession of someone other than a parent, without expressing any intention of returning, without providing for adequate support of the child, and remained away for a period of at least three months;
- Voluntarily left the child alone or in the possession of someone other than a parent, without providing adequate support for the child, and remained away for a period of at least six months;
- Abandoned the child without identifying the child or furnishing any means of identification, and the child's identity cannot be discovered by the exercise of reasonable efforts; or
- Voluntarily, and with knowledge of the pregnancy, abandoned the child's mother, beginning while she was pregnant with the child and continuing through the birth, failed to provide adequate support or medical care for the mother during that time of abandonment before the birth of the child, and remained apart from and failed to support the child since her birth; or that
- The child has been in PRS custody for at least a year, that agency has made reasonable efforts to return the child to the parent, but the parent hasn't visited or maintained contact with the child and has shown inability to provide the child with a safe environment.

There are two grounds for termination involving abuse or neglect of the child. They exist if the parent has:

- Knowingly placed the child, or knowingly allowed her to remain, in conditions or surroundings which endanger the physical or emotional well-being of the child; or
- Engaged in conduct, or knowingly placed the child with persons who engaged in conduct, which endangers the physical or emotional well-being of the child.

Nonsupport of the child is an element of some of the abandonment grounds. It can also be grounds for termination in and of itself when a parent failed to support the child in accordance with her ability during a period of one year, ending within six months of the day the petition to terminate was filed.

If a parent is willing to consent voluntarily to the termination of her parental rights, a petition need not set forth any grounds. All that's necessary is for the parent to execute an Affidavit of Relinquishment of parental rights before or after the filing of the petition.

There are two grounds for termination which deal with the conduct of the parent toward other children:

- The parent has been found by a judge to be criminally responsible for the death or serious injury of any child; or
- The parent has had her parent-child relationship with another child terminated because of abuse or neglect.

Further grounds for termination are:

- If a child was removed from the home because of abuse or neglect and has been in PRS temporary or permanent custody at least nine months, and the parent failed to do what the judge said she must do in order to have the child returned;
- If a parent's use of a controlled substance endangered a child, and the parent failed to complete a court-ordered drug treatment program, or if, after completing the program, the parent continued to use drugs repeatedly in a way that endangered the child;
- If a parent knowingly committed a crime resulting in at least two years' imprisonment and inability to care for the child; or
- If the parent is the cause of a child being born addicted to alcohol or a controlled substance which wasn't obtained by prescription.

There are three other grounds I've never seen used, but they do appear in the Texas Family Code. They are, if a parent:

- Contumaciously refused to submit to a court order under Chapter 264 of the Texas Family Code (How do you like that "contumaciously"? Why didn't they just say "stubbornly"?);
- Was the major cause of failure of a child to be enrolled in school; or
- Was the major cause of a child's running away from home without parental consent and not intending to return.

These grounds are all very strictly interpreted, and must be proven exactly as stated in the Family Code. Termination of the parent-child relationship is such a drastic measure that it can only be granted under very narrow circumstances.

Once again, even after one or more of the various grounds for termination are proven, the judge must still be convinced that termination is in the child's best interest.

Can a Petition to Terminate the Parent-Child Relationship be filed before a child is born?

Yes.

What is necessary to terminate the rights of an alleged or probable father?

The parental rights of an alleged or probable father of a child who has no presumed father may be terminated on the same grounds as any parent's.

In addition, his rights may be terminated without proving any of the grounds listed above if, after being given proper notice, he doesn't take legal steps to establish his paternity.

Is it ever possible to terminate the rights of a parent for no reason other than she simply cannot take care of the child?

Yes, but only under these very narrow terms:

- The petition must be filed by the Texas Department of Protective and Regulatory Services (PRS);
- The judge must find that the parent has a mental or emotional illness or a mental deficiency that makes the parent unable to provide for the child's physical, mental, and emotional needs, which inability will probably continue to exist until the child's eighteenth birthday;
- PRS must have been the child's permanent managing conservator for the preceding six months; and
- The judge must determine that termination will be in the child's best interest.

Is it possible to terminate a parent's rights in a similar situation, where the disability is a physical one, rather than an emotional or mental one?

No.

Is any protection afforded a mentally or emotionally impaired parent when the Department of Protective and Regulatory Services seeks to terminate her parental rights?

Yes. An attorney must be appointed to protect her rights. A hearing can't be held earlier than 180 days after the petition is filed. The proof must be by clear and convincing evidence.

May a parent's rights be terminated solely because she is financially unable to take care of the child?

No.

How does a parent voluntarily give up her parental rights?

By filing a document called an Affidavit of Relinquishment with the court. If the court finds termination is in the child's best interest it will be granted.

May a parent who is under eighteen years old sign an Affidavit of Relinquishment?

Yes.

When does a child have a right to a court-appointed attorney in a termination case?

Always, when a state agency is seeking termination. When anyone else is doing so, the judge may appoint an attorney for the child if the judge feels it's necessary.

Who pays the attorney?

The parents, unless they're indigent. In that case, the county pays if the state filed the petition. In private cases, the person who filed the petition may have to pay.

When does a parent have the right to a court-appointed attorney in a termination case?

If the parent is:

- A minor, and hasn't signed an Affidavit of Relinquishment;
- Incompetent; or
- Indigent, and opposes the termination.

Who pays for the parent's attorney?

The county, if the state is the petitioner. In private cases, the person who filed the petition may be ordered to pay.

Can parental rights be terminated solely because the parent is a minor?

No.

If a person signs an Affidavit of Relinquishment, can he or she take it back?

Sometimes. The affidavit itself must contain a statement that it either can or can't be taken back, is revocable or irrevocable, or can't be revoked for a specific period of time not to exceed sixty days.

An Affidavit of Relinquishment can also name the child's managing conservator.

If the Texas Department of Protective and Regulatory Services or an authorized adoption agency is designated as managing conservator, the affidavit can't be taken back once it's signed.

An affidavit in which anyone else is designated as managing conservator may be revoked at any time if it states it's revocable. If it states that it's irrevocable for a specific time, it may be revoked only after the expiration of that time, providing termination hasn't already been granted. Even if an affidavit is revocable, it remains in effect unless or until it's revoked.

Is there any way an alleged or probable father can give up his parental rights without admitting paternity?

Yes. Instead of signing an Affidavit of Relinquishment, he can sign an Affidavit of Waiver of Interest. In essence, that says, "I'm not the father, but just in case, I give up whatever parental rights I have."

Is there a right to a jury trial in a termination case?

Yes.

If termination is granted, what happens to the child?

A managing conservator is appointed for the child, and she's free to be adopted.

What happens if termination isn't granted?

The judge can dismiss the petition or enter any order the judge decides is in the child's best interest. This gives the court very broad power. Even if the termination petition isn't granted, the court can appoint a managing conservator, set child support, or provide for visitation.

Is there any restriction on when a judge can appoint the Texas Department of Protective and Regulatory Services as a child's managing conservator following termination of a parent's rights?

Yes. If only one parent's rights are terminated, the court can't appoint PRS as the child's managing conservator unless the judge finds that PRS has made a diligent effort to find the other parent or her relatives. If the parent or relatives can be found, they must be provided a reasonable opportunity to seek managing conservatorship.

13

Removal of a Child from the Home

Laws giving the State the right to take children from their parents, either temporarily or permanently, are new in our century, and they are still developing.

The *Case of Mary Ellen*, in 1874, was the first child abuse case in the United States. But only in 1972, after the abuse of children was brought to public attention by publication of *Helping the Battered Child and His Family* by C. Henry Kempe, did the nation begin to awaken to the problem, and our legislatures begin to respond.

Until recently, children were considered the property of their parents. Just as a man's mules belonged to him, so did his sons and daughters. If he chose to beat them, many might disapprove, but few would intervene.

With our dawning awareness of children as individuals, with their own rights, has come the realization that the State has an obligation to protect the well-being of its smallest citizens, not only because they embody its future, but because it's the decent thing to do. Yet, the family is so basic to our whole system of values that removing a child from his home is a drastic last resort in an effort to ensure the child's health and safety.

Removing a child from his parents, even when it's necessary for his protection, isn't without its own problems. A child may feel he's the one being punished, rather than those who hurt or failed him.

A child may want desperately to stay with even the worst of parents because whatever meager attention and affection he has received has come from them and, in spite of everything, he loves them.

A child may feel guilty if he was the person who blew the whistle on his abuser when he realizes the effect such revelations have had on his family.

All of us tend to fear the unknown. A child who has already suffered abuse, neglect, and abandonment has little reason to look forward to what may lie ahead for him. When strangers remove him from all that is familiar to him to face an uncertain future without even the comfort of anyone or anything he knows to cling to, he's afraid.

The fear, guilt, and sorrow these children experience, and the hopelessness that comes from their realization that they are in the hands of others to do with as they will, often generate a rage in them, astounding in its intensity. These new feelings, together with what they have already been through, create emotional problems that may require long-term counseling to resolve. Sometimes there's never a resolution.

In addition to the question of what emotional trauma a child will suffer if removed from his parents is the related question of how the separation will affect the future relationship of the child and his parents. The bonding between parents and children is an ongoing process; its interruption can have serious, sometimes permanent, consequences, not only for the child as an individual, but for his relationship with his parents as well. Of special concern is the removal of infants and very young children. If bonding, that ability to form emotional attachments and relate to others, is disrupted at a critical time, especially during the first two years of a child's life, he may never learn to trust or form lasting relationships with others.

There's also the very practical consideration of what alternatives are available for placement if a child is removed from his home. Sometimes, there are appropriate relatives who are willing to care for the child. If so, they are certainly the best choice. Sometimes, a child will require hospitalization or residential treatment for emotional problems, which the State can provide. But often, foster care is the only option. And foster care is not without its own problems. Children are often moved from one foster home to another. Despite their desperate need for stability, just as they begin to feel comfortable in one family, they may have to move to another.

Despite all the problems, however, our society has set minimum standards which reflect the view of our people concerning how parents must treat their children. When parents don't meet those minimum standards, the State has the right to remove their children from their care. The judge must weigh the damage to the child's welfare if he remains in the home against the damage he may suffer from removal.

We've made progress. Society no longer simply abandons children to whatever abuse or neglect their parents may choose to visit upon them. But what a tragic situation remains! Perhaps one day soon we'll pour our energy and resources into addressing the underlying problems which bring about the need to remove children from their homes. I believe that's the only long-term answer.

Who, as a representative of the State, may remove children from the possession of their parents?

Law enforcement officers, juvenile probation officers, or caseworkers representing the Texas Department of Protective and Regulatory Services (PRS). Children's Protective Services is a division of PRS.

When can such representatives of the State take possession of a child?

At any time with a court order, but without a court order only under the following conditions:

- Upon discovering a child in a situation which is dangerous to his physical health or safety, if the sole purpose is to return him as quickly as possible to his parents or other person with the right to his possession.

  For example, if a policeman finds a two-year-old wandering alone in a shopping mall, he can take possession of the child long enough to return him to his mother.

- If the parent or person entitled to possession voluntarily delivers the child. A suit must be filed within sixty days if delivery was to a law enforcement officer or a juvenile probation officer.

  For example, a father may take his child to a police officer because he's ill, the mother is deceased, and he's simply unable to provide for him.

- Upon personal knowledge of facts that would lead the ordinary person to believe there's an immediate danger to the physical health or safety of the child, if there's no time to obtain a court order.

  For example, a police officer may find a five-year-old child in a crack house where shots have just been exchanged.

- Upon information from someone else, which is corroborated by personal knowledge of the facts, all of which would lead the ordinary person to believe there's an immediate danger to the physical health or safety of the child, and there's no time to get a court order.

  For example, a teacher reports to PRS that a child came to school with bruises which he claimed resulted from a beating by his father. The caseworker investigates, and confirms that the child is bruised. The child says he's beaten frequently, and is afraid to return home.

- Upon personal knowledge of facts that would lead an ordinary person to believe that a child has been sexually abused, and there's no time to get a court order.

  For example, a juvenile probation officer investigates a report that a child is a runaway. It's obvious that the child is going to have a baby, and she says she's pregnant by her own father.

- Upon information from someone else, which is corroborated by personal knowledge of the facts, all of which would lead the ordinary person to believe that the child has been sexually abused, if there's no time to get a court order.

  For example, an eight-year-old child tells a school counselor that his mother's boyfriend has been forcing him to perform oral sex and has threatened to kill him if he tells. The counselor reports to PRS, whose worker talks with the child and his six-year-old brother. They both indicate they are being forced to have sexual contact with their mother's boyfriend, and they're afraid of him.

- By PRS, when a child is born alive after an abortion. Or
- During a criminal investigation relating to the child's custody, by a law enforcement officer who learns that a child is missing and thinks someone may run away with or hide the child.

For example, Dad has custody but Mom has filed to change managing conservatorship to herself, claiming Dad uses drugs around their six-year-old girl. The officer uncovers evidence which seems to indicate Mom may be right.

Dad behaves in a strange way and mumbles about no one taking his child away. He closes his bank account and quits his job. At that point, the officer takes possession of the little girl and turns her over to PRS.

How does a person, on his own, get a court order to remove a child from the child's home?

By asking a judge for a temporary restraining order, or a Writ of Attachment. When that's filed, it's necessary to convince the judge that a person of ordinary prudence would believe there's an immediate danger to the physical health or safety of the child, or that the child has been sexually abused and would be in danger if the judge waited for a full-blown hearing with everyone present before ordering the child removed from his home.

Does a person who is aware of abuse, neglect, or abandonment of a child have a legal duty to report it to the authorities?

Yes. It's a criminal offense not to do so.

Does PRS investigate anonymous reports?

Yes, but they must find evidence to support the report to proceed any further.

Will the identity of the person making such a report be revealed?

It remains confidential unless a judge orders otherwise. To do so, a judge must find disclosure is necessary for the administration of justice and wouldn't endanger the child, the person who made the report, or anyone involved in the investigation.

If a person makes such a report to the Department of Protective and Regulatory Services, must PRS investigate?

PRS investigates when the report concerns abuse by someone who is a caretaker of the child, while a law enforcement agency investigates reports of abuse by noncaretakers.

Especially in counties with very large populations, PRS can and does set priorities and investigates those situations first which appear to be most urgent.

Does PRS have the right to talk to the child and to conduct medical and psychological examinations as part of its investigation?

Yes, and parental consent isn't necessary. If the child is the alleged victim of abuse, the interview must be audio- or videotaped unless PRS decides there's good reason not to do so. The caseworker must inform the child's parents within twenty-four hours that the interview took place.

During an investigation, does the caseworker have the right to examine medical and mental health records of the child, parent, or person taking care of the child?

Yes.

If the caseworker has reason to believe someone may try to take the child out of state before the investigation is completed, what can he do to prevent it?

If there's sufficient evidence, it may be possible to remove the child immediately, even without a court order. If there isn't, a caseworker can ask a judge for an immediate order forbidding travel with the child. However, such an order probably won't stop someone who decides to grab the child and run.

If the investigating caseworker finds no evidence of abuse, what happens next?

The file will indicate that the report couldn't be substantiated, and it will be closed.

If the investigating caseworker does find problems in the home, is the child always removed?

No. Sometimes the child can remain in the home while the caseworker offers services such as counseling, parenting classes, or assistance in finding a job, housing, or relatives to help care for the child. The law allows removal of a child only when an ordinary person would prudently believe there's a threat to his physical health or safety if he's allowed to remain.

If a caseworker finds after a time that the problems at home have been resolved, the file will be closed, and that will end it.

If efforts to improve the situation are unsuccessful and the problem intensifies to the point it meets the criteria for removal, the child will be taken from his home and a lawsuit filed. Often, the first contact a caseworker has with the family presents facts which require immediate removal, but this certainly isn't always so.

Can the person who abused a child ever be removed from the home instead of the child?

Yes. PRS can file a suit asking for that person to be removed from the home. For a judge to grant the request, PRS must show that:

- There is an immediate danger to the child's health or safety, or the child has been sexually abused; and
- There isn't time to wait for a full-blown hearing if the child is to be protected; and
- The child isn't in danger of abuse from anyone else who will continue to live in the same home; and
- Removal of the person is in the child's best interest.

I really like this law. Sometimes it isn't feasible, because the person left in the home won't protect the child, but when it can be used it's great. Children who've suffered abuse don't need the additional trauma of being removed from their homes to live with strangers. Whenever possible, it's the abuser who should be required to move.

What steps must PRS take after removing a child from his home?

The state must do four things:

- Give legal notice of the removal to the child's parent or guardian;
- File a lawsuit asking for managing or possessory conservatorship, or for termination of parental rights;
- Ask the court to appoint a lawyer for the child; and
- Have the required court hearing.

What if the parent or guardian can't be located for notice of removal?

The judge can waive the requirement that he be notified.

How does PRS decide whether to file a lawsuit for termination of parental rights, or just managing conservatorship?

Two questions must be answered:

First, are there legal grounds for termination of the parent's rights, or are there only grounds to ask for permanent managing conservatorship? PRS must prove the same grounds as anyone else who goes into court seeking termination.

If there are grounds for termination, the next question is whether termination is in the child's best interest. If not, or if there aren't grounds for termination, permanent managing conservatorship will be requested.

It is PRS's goal, whenever possible, to avoid termination and eventually reunite children with their parents.

Does PRS ever file for managing conservatorship, then reconsider and file to terminate the child-parent relationship instead?

Yes. And sometimes the opposite is true. A petition originally filed asking for termination may be changed to ask only for managing conservatorship.

The reason these changes sometimes occur is simple: the original petition must be filed very quickly after the child is removed. The original assessment of the case may be flawed, or altered as new information comes to light. Also, as the case progresses, everyone else involved is also taking steps and making moves; and all of those actions can change whether the case moves toward termination, managing conservatorship, or return of the child to his home.

How soon must a hearing be held after a child has been removed from his home?

The first hearing, requesting temporary managing conservatorship for a period of fourteen days, must be held before a judge by the next working day after the child has been removed.

If a judge isn't available for this first, or "emergency," hearing, it can be held up to the third working day after removal. If there's no hearing within that time period, the child must be returned.

What does PRS have to prove at the emergency hearing to be allowed to keep possession of the child?

PRS must either prove that there's a continuing danger to the physical health or safety of the child if he's returned to his parent or legal guardian, or that evidence shows the child has been sexually abused and is at risk for further sexual abuse. If neither of these things is proven, the child goes home.

In addition, PRS has to show that the nature of the emergency and the continuing danger to the child make return of the child impossible or unreasonable.

Must the child actually have been physically injured for the judge to find there's a danger to the child's physical health or safety at home?

No.

In making his decision, may the judge also consider whether there's a person in the household to which the child would be returned who has caused serious bodily injury or death to another child by abuse or neglect, or has sexually abused another child?

Yes.

Must a parent be present for the emergency court hearing to be held?

No. The parent or legal guardian has the right to be there, and to bring an attorney, but the hearing will take place whether or not that person is present or even knows of it.

What if PRS proves at the emergency hearing all of the necessary facts required to keep possession of the child?

The judge will give PRS temporary managing conservatorship of the child until the next hearing, and PRS may decide to place the child with relatives, in foster care, or in a treatment facility.

When is the next hearing?

Any order issued at the emergency hearing is only good for fourteen days, so the next hearing must be held within that time if the child hasn't been returned home. This second hearing is designed to give parents a full opportunity to be heard.

Do the child's parents or legal guardian have to be given notice of this second hearing?

Yes. At least one parent or guardian must be served with a copy of the petition and notice of the second hearing, which is called a "show cause" hearing, or a "fourteen day" hearing.

What if notice to them isn't possible because they can't be found?

Every fourteen days, PRS can ask the court to extend the original order, showing the same danger to the child still exists.

If PRS still can't find a parent or legal guardian after doing everything possible, then service of citation must be done by publication. At that point, an attorney will be appointed to represent the missing parents or guardian, and the case will proceed.

What happens at the show cause hearing?

PRS, the parents, and the child's attorney are all permitted to present evidence. When the evidence is complete, the judge will either appoint PRS as the child's temporary managing conservator or send the child home.

The judge may also issue a wide variety of other temporary orders involving visitation, child support, counseling, psychological or psychiatric evaluations, and placement.

Placement and managing conservatorship are two different things. Managing conservatorship carries a whole laundry list of rights, duties, privileges, and powers concerning the child as discussed earlier. Placement merely means where the child will actually live. Unless the court orders a specific placement, the decision is left up to the managing conservator.

What must PRS prove at the show cause hearing to continue as temporary managing conservator of the child?

PRS must show that:

- There was a danger to the physical health or safety of the child which was caused by the act, or failure to act, of the person entitled to the child's possession;
- The urgent need for protection required the immediate removal of the child and makes efforts to prevent the child's removal impossible or unreasonable; and
- Despite reasonable efforts to eliminate the need for the child's removal and to enable him to remain at home, there's a substantial risk of continuing danger if he's returned home.

    In deciding whether there's a continuing danger to the child the court can consider whether someone is living in the home who has caused serious injury or death to, or has sexually abused, another child.

How long do the orders issued at a show cause hearing remain in effect?

Until the case is dismissed or the judge issues other temporary orders or final orders. Any party always has the right to file motions asking for further temporary orders or for a final hearing.

Does the child have the right to representation at the show cause hearing?

Yes. The court must appoint both an attorney ad litem and a guardian ad litem for the child. They may be the same person. See Chapter 1.

Do the parents or legal guardian have the right to an attorney?

Yes. If they can't hire an attorney, they have the right to a free court-appointed attorney, but only if a termination petition is filed, they oppose the termination, and they can prove they are indigent. If both parents' interests are the same, they may be represented by one attorney. If there's a conflict, each parent will be appointed an attorney.

Also, in termination cases, an attorney must be appointed to represent a party served with citation by publication.

An attorney may also be appointed for any party to a suit if the court believes such an appointment is necessary to protect the child's interest. The parties for whom the attorneys are appointed may be required to pay the fees.

A guardian ad litem, usually an attorney, is also appointed for a parent who is a minor or a party who is incompetent.

What can a parent do to regain possession of his or her child once the child has been removed by PRS?

I can't emphasize enough the importance of having your own attorney. If you can't hire one and don't qualify for a court-appointed lawyer, talk with your local bar association about what low-cost or free services may be available.

Many people whose children have been removed by PRS view PRS as the enemy. That's only human. But the truth is, these people are there to help children and their families. Whether or not the specific allegations are true, the very fact that a situation leading to removal of a child arose almost surely means there are problems in the home. PRS may be able to offer some solutions, with its wide variety of programs and forms of assistance. If you approach the PRS caseworker as a parent who knows he has problems at home and is willing to accept help to solve them, that's the first step toward the return of your child.

It's vital to find out what the caseworker wants you to do in order to have your child returned. If possible, have the caseworker set out in writing what he expects of you. Typically, you may be asked to participate in: psychological evaluations, counseling, parenting classes, Alcoholics Anonymous meetings, and drug screenings. You may also be required to have a steady job, an adequate place to live, and frequent contact with the caseworker.

Depending on the facts in your case, you may be asked to comply with some or all of the above conditions. By all means, do so. Those requirements aren't made to punish you. Their purpose is to determine what the problems are which led to the child being removed, and to help eliminate the problems so the child may be returned. Many times, parents find that the services offered help them to be better parents and result in greater happiness and harmony for the entire family.

Try to establish a good relationship with your caseworker. That person's opinion carries a lot of weight.

If you aren't promptly referred to the agency providing counseling, parenting classes, or other services your caseworker has asked you to attend, ask him to follow through so that you can begin participating as soon as possible. Be persistent. Don't fall between the cracks. Your worker is busy, and without your reminder may forget to pursue the services you need.

Keep your appointments. With your caseworker. With your counselor. And with anyone else you've been referred to for services. Each appointment you miss just delays the return of your child. And it leaves the impression, whether true or not, that you aren't very reliable and your children really aren't your top priority. If you must miss an appointment, call and let the other person know. Explain why you can't be there, and ask for another appointment.

If your work schedule or a lack of transportation makes it difficult to attend counseling, parenting classes, or other scheduled services, explain the problem to your caseworker and ask what alternative arrangements might be made.

Ask your caseworker what visitation you may have with your child. Request as much visitation as possible. And be there every chance you get. Your child loves and misses you and needs to be reassured that you still love him. Whatever you do, don't say you're coming and then fail to appear. That's devastating for a child. If you must miss a visit, let your caseworker know as far ahead of time as possible. Explain why you can't come, and set up another visit.

Make your visits with the child pleasant occasions. Crying the entire time and repeating how much you miss him is no favor to the child. Don't discuss the case or the facts that caused the child to be removed from home. Talk to your child about school, friends, and activities. Play a game. Read a book. Enjoy your time together.

Ask your caseworker about bringing gifts, especially for the child's birthday and holidays. If it's allowed, write and make phone calls. Use every chance for contact with your child.

Never encourage your child to break the rules of his placement, to run away, to disobey those in charge, or to phone you when it isn't permitted.

Never, ever, try to persuade your child to change the statements he has already made about the problems which prompted his removal from your home. It's a bad mistake to do that for a number of reasons, not the least of which is the damage it can do to your child.

If his statements were false, the decision to "come clean" should be based on his own desire to tell the truth, not on pressure from you to do so. That decision can be the beginning of his emotional healing, but it needs to be his own.

If his statements were true, your efforts to get him to change them are truly destructive. They say to him either that you do not believe him, or that he is not as important to you as hiding the truth so that you may be protected.

Keep a written record of all of your telephone contacts with your child, your caseworker, and your counselor, and all of your appointments with them. Write down the details of what happened so you can show a judge the specific efforts you've been making.

Be present and on time for all court hearings. Make sure your attorney has information concerning all that has been happening.

Talk with your child's attorney and guardian ad litem, whose support is very valuable.

At the start, provide the caseworker with names and addresses of any relatives who might be willing to have your child placed with them until he can be returned to you, and ask that home studies be done on them. If it's possible for your child to be placed in a relative's home rather than foster care, seize the opportunity. He'll probably be far happier with people he knows, and will have greater stability, since he won't be moved from one place to another as sometimes happens to children in foster care. He'll still be within the family, and your visitation may be more frequent and flexible.

Be aware that if you haven't done the things the judge told you to do to get your child back, once the child has been with PRS for nine months your rights may be terminated.

What happens after the second hearing?

Everyone will return to court for the judge to see how things are going and for the court to hear any motions asking for such things as new temporary orders, orders for psychological or psychiatric evaluations, or a final hearing date. Meanwhile, the caseworker will be offering services to the child and the family and assessing whether progress is being made toward reunification of the family or whether the case is moving in another direction.

Unless PRS and the parents agree on a resolution, there will be a trial. The parents have the right to a jury trial if they wish, as well as the right to appeal the decision if they don't agree with it.

What happens to the child from his removal until he's returned to his parents?

Each case is different. Sometimes the agency will return the child to his home under supervision to see if the situation will work out. After a few months, if everything is okay, the suit will be dismissed.

If a child has special needs, they'll be addressed. If he needs medical or psychiatric care or counseling, he'll receive it in or out of a hospital or residential treatment facility.

The first choice, if home isn't an option, is to place him with suitable relatives.

If he has no such relatives, he'll go to a group home, a licensed foster home, or some other approved facility. The length of time a child can now remain in foster care is limited to twelve months, with one six-month extension at the judge's discretion.

For a number of reasons, children must sometimes be moved from one foster care placement to another. Foster parents move, become ill, or simply decide they no longer wish to be foster parents. A child's behavior may improve or deteriorate, causing his transfer to a less restrictive or more restrictive environment.

School-age children attend school while they are in care. Older children, sixteen or seventeen, may be placed in programs to prepare them for independent living, since they'll no longer be in anyone's legal custody when they turn eighteen.

If a child is returned to his parents, the case usually isn't dismissed immediately. PRS may keep the case open for a few months to monitor the family. When the case is dismissed, managing conservatorship will revert to the parents.

If the case ends with parental rights being terminated, PRS, or occasionally a relative or foster parent, will be given managing conservatorship, and the child will be free for adoption.

If PRS asked for termination but it was denied, the judge can give permanent managing conservatorship to PRS or a third party intervenor, or return the child to his parents.

If PRS is appointed managing conservator, the child may be placed in whatever placement PRS believes appropriate.

As long as the child's under the permanent managing conservatorship of PRS, his placement will be reviewed by a judge every six months until he's eighteen.

Are there any specific rules about becoming a foster parent?

Yes. You must be a licensed foster parent to have a child placed in your home if you're not related to the child. Contact PRS to learn more about becoming a foster parent.

Your home will be inspected to make certain it meets state health and safety standards and is appropriate for children. You'll be investigated and trained before receiving your license.

Special training is given persons who want their homes to be licensed as habilitative foster homes. These foster parents learn to care for children with special health needs or severe emotional or behavioral problems.

Foster parents are paid to care for children in state custody. But most of the foster parents I've known are involved simply because they love children. By and large, they perform a needed service with dedication and generosity.

Children Who Are Victims of Abuse, Neglect, and Crime

By their very nature, children are the most vulnerable of human beings. Their size, their dependence, and their relative lack of credibility make them easy victims of abuse, neglect, and crime.

A child is a victim of abuse when someone does something to harm her, a victim of neglect when someone who is supposed to provide for her basic needs fails to do so, and a victim of crime when someone commits an illegal act against her.

Even today, when evidence abounds that child abuse is all too common, most people have difficulty believing it occurs as frequently as it does, and that its effects are as devastating as they are.

Is child abuse a new phenomenon? I don't think so. In earlier times, attitudes were different. Parents could treat their children as they pleased. It was a personal matter, to be decided and dealt with in the privacy of the family. Outsiders either were unaware of maltreatment or looked the other way. Is child abuse more widespread today? It's difficult to tell. We may just be more aware of what has always been there. But the increase of drug use, the breakup of the family, the less frequent availability of the extended family, poverty, the increase in teen pregnancy, urbanization, and the increase in single-parent families all contribute to the stress on families and the likelihood of abuse. On the other hand, help that was never offered before is available to parents and children alike in the form of counseling, education, and other services designed to prevent abuse.

Victims of abuse and neglect are robbed of a normal childhood. Children learn through play, but abused children often lack the capacity for play.

Abused children are more likely to have learning disorders. Abused children are more likely to run away. Abused children don't develop properly, emotionally.

The vast majority of abuse isn't committed by a stranger lurking in a dark alley, but by the child's own parent, family member, or close family friend. And that makes the abuse infinitely worse.

If a child is hurt by one of the very people she trusted to love and care for her, she may never recover the ability to trust. She may always see herself as worthless or bad.

And she may never learn to develop healthy relationships with others.

The helpless anger, fear, and hurt which she is unable to fully express may prevent her development of compassion and concern for others.

Counseling for an abused child in an attempt to rehabilitate her so that she can become a healthy adult costs remarkably little in comparison to the cost to society if she grows up unhealed. Set aside the cost in human misery alone, and consider the implications in dollars and cents as you contemplate this fact: Findings show that 97 percent of the inmates imprisoned in Texas for crimes of violence were abused as children.

Numerous studies indicate there is a far higher risk that people who were abused as children will grow up to abuse their own children. In many such instances, the State then assumes custody of the children. And the cycle continues:

Victims of childhood abuse are more likely to have mental health problems.

Victims of childhood abuse are more likely to have substance abuse problems.

Victims of childhood abuse are more likely to be on public welfare.

Physical abuse is usually easier to detect than emotional or sexual abuse. It's more often observed by others while it's happening. And physical scars are easier to see than emotional ones.

Here are some facts about sexual abuse:

- Children as young as two months old have been raped; the average age of a child sexual abuse victim is seven.
- Approximately 83 percent of adolescents who are raped make no report to the police.
- In surveys of adults who said they were raped as children, the majority said they had never told anyone.
- Both boys and girls are sexually abused.
- Women, as well as men, commit sexual abuse.
- The majority of children who are sexually abused have normal physical examinations.
- As in other types of abuse, the abuser is usually a parent, family member, or close family friend.

When do the experts say sexual abuse should be suspected? These are some of the symptoms. While each of these may be indicative of sexual abuse, especially if several are present together, there are also other possible explanations. However, their occurrence should at least alert you to the possibility the child may have been sexually abused, and they do require further investigation. They are:

- Changes in eating or sleeping habits;
- Sudden behavior changes;
- Poor peer relations;
- Running away;
- Unusually frequent urination;
- Pain in the genitals;
- Chronic abdominal pain;
- Torn undergarments;
- Blood on undergarments;
- Bruises;
- Anal or genital discharges; or
- Explicit sexual behavior beyond the child's development level.

Because children are vulnerable and because of how they are taught to behave, it's easy for sexual abuse to occur.

They learn it's okay to say no to strangers who offer rides or candy, but children are taught to be affectionate toward family members and close friends, and to obey the adults who are a part of their lives.

When abuse first occurs, children usually don't resist. They don't know how to say no to a trusted adult. They don't know how to resist threats, or where to turn for help if those they trust betray them.

Typically, the abuse takes place more than once, and the child usually doesn't tell immediately. The more times the abuse occurs before the child reveals it, the less likely it is that the child will be believed. Adults don't understand why a child didn't tell at once, because they believe that's what they would have done. They fail to see the difference between their position and experience, and the fear, guilt, and vulnerability of a child.

The longer the abuse continues without the child telling, the worse her position becomes. It's too threatening to blame the trusted adult who is the abuser, so the child can only believe that she herself is to blame. The child tries to do exactly as the abuser says, because then, maybe, everything will be okay.

When the abuse is finally revealed, the child has still further strikes against her. It's often the word of a child, who is confused, frightened, and inarticulate, against that of a trusted adult. The consequences, emotional and financial, when other adults accept as fact that the child was abused can be enormous. Small wonder children's stories of abuse are often dismissed.

Yet, the fact is that the overwhelming majority of children who claim to have been sexually abused are telling the truth.

Sadly, many of them retract their stories at some point. Why?

For one thing, the abuser is often someone the child loves. It's not at all uncommon for children to protect the abuser.

For another, there may be pressure from other family members. They may tell the child it's her fault if the abuser goes to jail and there's no money coming in and the family is torn apart.

Then, too, children are usually shy about sexual matters, and it's embarrassing for them to discuss with total strangers the abuse they suffered at the hands of someone they trusted.

And finally, the child sees all of the terrible consequences of telling. The abuser may lose his or her job or go to jail. The other family members may not believe the child and blame the child for all that has gone wrong. And the child may even be removed from her home.

The wonder to me is not that children often retract their claims of sexual abuse, but that some of them stick to their stories, no matter what.

In addition to being assured that she is loved and being protected from further abuse, what the child needs most is to be believed. And experts say that a child may be as damaged by someone who rejects her plea for help as by the person who actually abuses her. An abused child needs to have the reality of the abuse acknowledged and to be reassured that she is not the one to blame. If that doesn't happen, the child internalizes her feelings of guilt, rage, and pain, and a time bomb has been created that's just waiting to explode.

Another wrenching example of parental behavior harmful to children is neglect.

Unlike abuse, which involves the commission of a harmful act, neglect is characterized by omission, by not acting, when there's a duty to do so for the child's well-being.

Neglect involves patterns of failure to provide basic necessities to a child, such as food, clothing, shelter, medical care, supervision, and a safe environment. It's a form of abandonment.

Its chilling hallmark is indifference. Apathy has as many causes as anger. But often it is the result of ignorance, drug or alcohol abuse, or feelings of hopelessness and futility.

Some experts believe that even the negative attention of an abuser is easier for a child to deal with than the indifference of a parent who just doesn't care, one way or the other.

The most extreme example of neglect is actual physical abandonment. The figurative tossing away of a child, as if the child were irrelevant, is the ultimate rejection. It says to her that she simply wasn't worth having.

A common form of neglect is failing to provide basic necessities. One major and obvious cause of neglect is poverty. If a parent is living in poverty, there may not be adequate food, clothing, or shelter; if she's doing the best she can, that isn't neglect. But when a parent could provide those things and her priorities lead her to other choices, such as spending the money on drugs, neglect occurs.

Lack of supervision, another form of neglect, may result from a lack of parenting skills and understanding of the child's needs, or it may be the result of a parent's emotional withdrawal.

But, sad as it is to think of a child's physical hunger, perhaps the most poignant form of neglect is emotional neglect. That leads to hunger of the heart.

Children must receive emotional support from their parents. It's as necessary as food, and to withhold it is neglect. Babies must be touched and held and made to feel loved and safe. The extreme example of what can happen if a child is deprived of such nurturing is nonorganic failure to thrive. This is medical terminology for a condition brought about by emotional neglect. A child so diagnosed will show actual damage in her physical development. The condition is especially dangerous for children under one year old. They can die.

Older failure-to-thrive children have retarded bone growth. Quite simply, they don't grow because they're not loved. When they're removed to emotionally healthy environments, such children typically grow quickly, and their IQs often improve dramatically.

Today, in tragic numbers, children are the victims of abuse, neglect, and crime. We must find a way to raise public awareness, arouse public outrage, and stir public action to stop the assault on the bodies and souls of society's most vulnerable victims.

What, exactly, is child abuse?

Child abuse can be physical, mental, emotional, or sexual. The Texas Family Code lists a number of acts or omissions in its definition of child abuse. Abuse includes these acts or omissions by a person:

- "Mental or emotional injury to a child that results in an observable and material impairment in the child's growth, development, or psychological functioning." This is one of the most difficult forms of abuse to uncover and prove. Yet it can be one of the most damaging. Emotional wounds may affect a child long after physical injuries have healed.

Isolation, humiliation, and ridicule can destroy a child's self-esteem and so thwart her emotional development that she stumbles through a lifetime of failure.

- "Causing or permitting a child to be in a situation in which the child sustains a mental or emotional injury that results in an observable and material impairment in the child's growth, development, or psychological functioning."

In the first point above, the person commits abuse by herself inflicting the emotional injury. In the second, the person commits abuse either by putting the child into a situation where she receives the mental or emotional injury or by allowing the child to remain in the situation.

Of course, the person must be aware of the abuse which is happening, or likely to happen, before placing the child or allowing her to remain in the situation that is abusive. Typically, this kind of abuse occurs when a spouse is emotionally abusive to a child and the other spouse is aware of the problem but does nothing and allows the child to remain in the abusive situation.

- "Physical injury that results in substantial harm to the child, or the genuine threat of substantial harm from physical injury to the child, including an injury that is at variance with the history or explanation given and excluding an accident or reasonable discipline by a parent, guardian, or managing or possessory conservator that does not expose the child to a substantial risk of harm."

Physical injury doesn't have to be life threatening or require hospitalization to be abusive. Neither must physical injury occur more than once. A single incident is enough.

- "Failure to make a reasonable effort to prevent an action by another person that results in physical injury that results in substantial harm to the child."

A person can't just stand by and watch someone physically harm a child without her own failure to act being abusive.

- The Family Code also lists a whole range of sexual conduct prohibited by the Texas Penal Code. Under these provisions, sexual abuse can range from a single incident where a child's breast is deliberately touched to a pattern of incestuous rape. And it can vary from a sexual assault on the child to intentional sexual behavior in a child's presence. Any sexual conduct of an adult which involves a child is abusive.

- Compelling or encouraging the child to engage in sexual conduct, including everything from arranging child prostitution to placing young girls as topless dancers.

- Failure to make a reasonable effort to prevent the above sexual abuse. Again, there must be knowledge that the sexual abuse was occurring, or likely to occur.

- "Causing, permitting, encouraging, engaging in, or allowing the photographing, filming, or depicting of the child if the person knew or should have known that the resulting photograph, film, or depiction of the child is obscene as defined by Section 43.21, Penal Code, or pornographic."

  This is fairly self-explanatory.

- Current use of a controlled substance in a way that causes mental, physical, or emotional injury to a child. And

- Causing, permitting, or encouraging a child to use a controlled substance.

If a child's physical injuries don't fit the explanation or history provided by the parent, what then?

The law specifically defines such instances as abusive. These are very difficult cases. Typically, a child appears at the hospital with a fractured skull, or a spiral fracture of a leg, or some such injury, and the doctor who treats the child says it is impossible or very unlikely from a medical standpoint that the injury could have occurred in the way the parents claim. Then there's an impasse. The inconsistency is enough under the law to permit a judge to treat the incident as abuse. However, that isn't a perfect answer.

No one wants to remove a child from her parents. Such removal in itself can do great damage to a child emotionally, to say nothing of the trauma inflicted on the child's parents and her family. Yet, the child's safety must be protected.

Often judges will order such things as psychological evaluations, counseling, or parenting classes in order to arrive at the truth with the help of experts. Even then, it may not be possible to know with certainty how the injury occurred. So, there may come a time when the judge realizes that all the information that's likely to be obtained is available and there still is no clear answer. Then the judge must weigh the need of the child and her family to be reunited, and to have finality to the case, against the degree of risk to the child in placing her back in the home. It's a very tough decision.

What right does a parent have to discipline a child?

The law gives parents the right to exercise reasonable discipline of children and imposes the duty on parents to control their children.

What is "reasonable discipline" as opposed to abuse?

It's discipline that doesn't expose a child to a substantial risk of physical, mental, or emotional harm. This is a subjective matter to a degree. And while everyone would agree that deliberately burning a child is abuse, there are degrees of severity of abuse. Not all judges may agree upon when the line is crossed from reasonable discipline to abuse. Parents might wish to consider these suggestions:

Appropriate forms of discipline include grounding, time out, loss of privileges, and extra chores. Even these may become abusive if carried to an extreme. Sending a child to her room is one thing; locking her in the room for a week is another.

Inappropriate forms of discipline include sleep deprivation; locking the child out of the house; threatening or frightening the child; abandoning or threatening to abandon the child; prolonged isolation of the child; depriving the child of food, water, clothing, or medical care; keeping the child out of school; forcing the child to perform humiliating or degrading acts; embarrassing the child in front of others; forcing any substance down the child's throat; and exposing the child to extreme heat or cold.

Is physical discipline always considered abusive?

That's a hard question to answer because opinions differ widely.

Almost any judge would agree that physical discipline is abusive if it results in substantial injury to the child, even if the parent inflicting the punishment didn't intend it to result in actual harm. But then you run into conflicting ideas of what's permissible.

Some judges believe that any form of physical punishment is abusive.

Others believe it's acceptable so long as it's only administered with the hand and leaves no marks.

Others believe a belt or switch is okay, but not a board or extension cord.

Still others believe that as long as no marks are left, physical discipline isn't objectionable.

Other considerations are: the age of the child, on what part of the body the child was struck, how many blows were struck, and how frequently the child was struck.

As you can see, a parent who administers discipline by physically striking the child is running the risk that her actions may be considered child abuse.

For parents who prefer not to use physical discipline but don't know alternative means of effective discipline, there are parenting classes available through many churches and community agencies.

Some experts believe that physical punishment sends a message to a child that violence is an acceptable way to get someone to do what you want, especially if you're bigger and stronger.

If a child suffers harm as a result of an accident, is there child abuse?

No. But it's possible, although not always true, that child neglect is involved.

What can happen if a parent is guilty of child abuse?

All of the following are possibilities:

- The parent may face criminal charges;
- The child may be removed from the parent's custody and placed in the managing conservatorship of some other person or agency; and
- The parent-child relationship may be terminated, and the child freed for adoption. See Chapter 12.

What if one parent is guilty of child abuse and the other isn't?

The result will depend on the attitude and actions of the nonabusive parent, and whether that parent is willing and able to protect the child from the abusive parent, and whether the nonabusive parent could have protected the child from the abuse initially and failed to do so.

If a child consents to sexual behavior with an adult, is it still abuse?

Yes. Children under eighteen don't have the legal capacity to consent to sexual acts. Adults involved in such acts with a child are legally responsible, even if the child agrees to the act, and even if the child initiated the behavior.

Must physical harm have resulted to a child in order for sexual abuse to have occurred?

No.

What is child neglect?

The Texas Family Code, Section 261.001(4), defines neglect as including: "The leaving of a child in a situation where the child would be exposed to a substantial risk of physical or mental harm, without arranging for necessary care for the child, and the demonstration of an intent not to return by the parent, guardian, managing conservator or possessory conservator of the child."

This deals with abandonment of the child in a situation where the child could be in danger. The abandonment must be by a parent or other person legally responsible for the child's welfare. The parent must have made no provisions for necessary care of the child and must show an intent not to return.

It's also neglect if the person responsible for a child's care, custody, or welfare permits the child to return to the child's home after she's been absent for any reason, including having run away or been in residential treatment, without arranging for the necessary care of the child. For example, a hospital can't simply release a ten-year-old who's been receiving treatment without some authorized adult to assume responsibility for her. A staff member can't even take her to her home and leave her there without making such arrangements.

Can a child be neglected by someone who isn't a parent or other person legally responsible for a child's welfare?

Yes. The legal definition of neglect continues with the following acts or omissions by anyone:

- "Placing a child in or failing to remove a child from a situation that a reasonable person would realize requires judgment or actions beyond the child's level of maturity, physical condition, or mental abilities and that results in bodily injury or a substantial risk of immediate harm to the child."

  This section deals with a lack of supervision or protection. For example, watching a two-year-old wander onto a busy highway and making no attempt to remove the child from danger, or leaving a five-year-old in a shopping center with no supervision.

- "Failing to seek, obtain, or follow through with medical care for a child, with the failure resulting in or presenting a substantial risk of death, disfigurement, or bodily injury or with the failure resulting in an observable and material impairment to the growth, development, or functioning of the child."

  An interesting aspect of this section, and the next, is that it requires no intent to harm, or even any knowledge that harm would result to the child from the act.

- "The failure to provide a child with food, clothing, or shelter necessary to sustain the life or health of the child, excluding failure caused primarily by financial inability unless relief services had been offered and refused."

Children who beg for food in the neighborhood because their parents spend their money on drugs are an example.

Another such case would be where a child's home is so dirty and the physical conditions so deplorable that they present a health hazard to the child living there.

- "Placing a child in, or failing to remove the child from a situation in which the child would be exposed to a substantial risk of sexual conduct harmful to the child."

How extensive must the failure to provide food, clothing, shelter, or medical care be to constitute neglect?

It's a judgment call. Behavior can range from failure to provide which is so severe no one has any doubt it is neglect, to occasional, less severe lapses. Here, common sense must prevail.

Some general examples of children who most judges would probably agree have been neglected are:

- A child who has been prescribed medication for a serious illness, but whose parents forget to give her the medication, leading to a relapse;
- A child suffering a high fever, whose parent does not seek medical treatment;
- A child suffering seizures for which the parents seek no medical evaluation;
- A child who repeatedly threatens suicide, then finally attempts suicide after the parents have made no effort to obtain professional help for the child;
- A child suffering malnutrition because her parents are spending their money on drugs and making no effort to provide adequate food for the child;
- A child whose parents have left her home alone, without adequate food or money to buy food, while they visit relatives for a couple of days; or
- A child who lives in a car with her parents even though they could go to a family shelter.

Examples of behavior I don't believe most judges would find neglectful are:

- Buying a child inexpensive jeans instead of designer brands and fewer clothes than she would like;
- Allowing the child to miss an occasional meal, so long as a healthy diet is usually provided;
- Not taking a ten-year-old to the doctor for a common cold; or

- Having the beds unmade, newspapers on the floor, and dirty dishes in the sink on occasion.

As you see, there is quite a range of behavior, from what is definitely neglectful to what isn't. A judge must consider the total circumstances, the frequency of the behavior, and the degree of risk of harm involved to decide if the behavior was neglectful.

Is it neglect for a person who isn't legally responsible for a child to refuse to risk her own life or safety to remove a child from a dangerous situation?

No. For example, she isn't required to dash in front of a car to push a child out of harm's way.

Is there a legal age under which a child may not be left alone?

No. Obviously, it's neglect to leave a two-year-old alone. Is it neglect to leave a ten-year-old alone? You must look at the facts. What was the time of day? How long was the child alone? Did the child have access to help if needed? Why was the child alone?

Do parents have the right to refuse medical treatment for their child because of their religious beliefs?

No. Parents have a legal duty to provide the child with medical care. It may fall within the definition of neglect if a parent doesn't seek, obtain, or follow through with medical care for a child, regardless of the reason.

May a parent refuse certain types of medical treatment for a child which violate the parent's religious beliefs, while agreeing to alternative medical treatments which do not?

This is a much more complicated question. Often, judges rely upon the testimony of medical experts concerning the child's needs and the relative value of the treatments proposed.

Obviously, off-beat, bizarre treatment, with no support in the medical community, will be rejected. But alternative methods of treatment which do have the support of some, if not the majority of, medical authorities become a much closer call.

The child's own religious beliefs may be considered, especially with an older child.

Does a person who believes a child has been or will be abused have any duty to report it?

Yes. The law requires any person who has reason to think child abuse or neglect has occurred, or will occur, to report it.

To whom must the reports be made?

Any local or state law enforcement agency; the Texas Department of Protective and Regulatory Services, if the suspected abuse involves a person responsible for the child's care; the state agency which operates, licenses, certifies, or registers any facility in which the abuse occurred; or the agency designated by the court to be responsible for the protection of children.

The number for the Abuse Hotline of the Texas Department of Protective and Regulatory Services is 1-800-252-5400.

How soon must the report be made?

A report is to be made immediately upon learning of abuse or neglect.

Do attorneys, doctors, nurses, clergymen, daycare employees, teachers, social workers, psychologists, and other professionals have the same duty to report abuse or neglect as other individuals?

Yes. The only difference is that the professional's report may be made within forty-eight hours of the time abuse or neglect is first suspected, instead of immediately. A professional can't delegate the duty to anyone else, but must make the report personally. Generally, information given by a person to his or her attorney, doctor, or minister is considered confidential, and they can't be compelled to disclose it. This is called "privileged communication," but it doesn't apply here.

Is anyone exempt from the duty to report abuse or neglect?

No.

Is a person who reports abuse or neglect or helps investigate such a report immune from civil or criminal liability which might otherwise be incurred or imposed?

Yes. Except that a person who reports her own conduct, or who otherwise reports or helps investigate in bad faith or with malice, isn't protected by such immunity.

Is there any penalty for making a false report?

Yes. If a person knowingly makes a false report, it's a Class A misdemeanor.

In a suit between the parents, if one accuses the other of child abuse, knowing that's not true, it's not only a misdemeanor, but it may be considered by the judge in deciding conservatorship of the child.

What if a person knows of child abuse or neglect or potential abuse or neglect and fails to report it?

If a person has cause to believe a child's physical or mental health or welfare has been or may be further adversely affected by abuse or neglect, and doesn't make a report, it's a Class B misdemeanor.

Are there criminal offenses specifically based on the need to protect children?

Yes. The Texas Penal Code, which defines most crimes in our state, lists a number of offenses in which children are always the victim and others in which the victim can be either a child or an adult. The law makes the punishment for some such offenses more severe if a child is the victim.

What should a person do if she believes a crime has been committed against a child?

Take the necessary steps to insure the child's safety for the moment, if you can legally do so. Call the police at once.

What are some of the reasons a district attorney might decide not to try a case?

Every criminal offense consists of specific elements. There must be believable evidence to support each one of those elements, or it cannot be proven that the defendant committed the crime. Sometimes, the district attorney doesn't believe she has evidence to support each necessary element of the case.

There are also a number of defenses to the commission of crime. Some of them are general ones, which apply to the commission of any crime. Others are defenses related only to a particular crime. The DA may believe that the facts show the defendant has a valid defense.

Also, the district attorney may believe that further facts will come to light later which will strengthen her case against the defendant. She may prefer to wait, rather than go to trial now and risk losing the case because the evidence is weak.

May a child be a witness in a criminal case?

Yes. However, the judge may refuse to allow the child's testimony if she decides the child doesn't seem to possess sufficient intelligence or maturity to relate events about which she is questioned.

May the out-of-court statement of a child abuse victim be admitted in a criminal trial?

Yes. Usually, hearsay can't be admitted into evidence at a trial. Hearsay is an out-of-court statement offered to prove the truth of its content. Hearsay isn't considered reliable evidence because the person being quoted was not under oath when the statement was made and isn't available for cross-examination at the trial.

The law permits the hearsay statement of a child abuse victim to be admitted into evidence in a criminal trial under certain circumstances.

Are there legal ways to make it easier for young victims of child abuse to testify in a suit for conservatorship or termination?

Yes. Legislators were aware that children who had already experienced the physical and emotional pain of abuse often had to undergo still more trauma when they appeared in court to tell what had happened to them. They usually had to sit in a courtroom where the very person who abused them was staring at them, with total strangers coming and going throughout their testimony. It's very difficult for anyone, much less a child, to talk about such personal things publicly. Additionally, children are afraid of being punished for what they say, losing their parent's love, or hurting someone close to them. They often feel tremendous guilt because they believe the abuse, with all of its consequences, is their fault for having spoken out. In an effort to make the experience easier for such children, and still protect the rights of all sides to a fair trial, these laws were passed:

In any suit affecting the parent-child relationship, where a child twelve or younger is alleged to have been abused, the child's oral statement, made and recorded prior to the hearing, is admissible as evidence if:

1 no attorney for a party was present when the statement was made;
2 the recording is both visual and aural and is recorded on film or videotape or by other electronic means;
3 the recording equipment was capable of making an accurate recording, the operator was competent, and the recording is accurate and hasn't been altered;

4 the statement was not made in response to questioning calculated to lead the child to make a particular statement;

5 each voice on the recording is identified;

6 the person conducting the interview of the child in the recording is present at the proceeding and available to testify or be cross-examined by either party; and

7 each party is afforded an opportunity to view the recording before it is offered into evidence.

A child twelve or younger who is alleged to have been abused may be called to personally testify in court in a suit affecting the child-parent relationship, rather than simply introducing her recorded statement.

If so, any party may ask the judge to order that the child's testimony be prerecorded and videotaped or taken in another room and televised by closed-circuit television into the courtroom for viewing by the judge, the jury, and the parties. If this is ordered:

- Only an attorney for each party, an attorney for the child, or other person whose presence would be of help to the child, and the operator of the equipment may be present in the room with the child during her testimony.

- Only attorneys for the parties may question the child.

- The person operating the television equipment must be in an adjacent room, or behind a screen or mirror, so that she can see and hear the child but the child cannot see or hear her.

- The recording must be both visual and aural and recorded on film or videotape or by other electronic means.

- The recording equipment must be capable of making an accurate recording, the operator must be competent, and the recording must be accurate and not altered.

- Each voice on the videotape or film must be identified.

- Each party to the proceeding must be given the chance to see the film or videotape before it is presented in court. If a child's testimony is taken in any of these ways, she may not be required to testify in open court.

These rules also apply to the oral statement or testimony of a child of any age who is an alleged victim of child abuse and is incapable of testifying in court because of a medical condition. These rules don't apply to trials in the adult criminal courts, where such protection doesn't exist.

15

Rights of Grandparents and Other Non-Parents

If a child is lucky, his parents aren't the only ones who love him. Grandparents, stepparents, aunts, uncles, brothers, and sisters are also there, to nurture and protect him and help him grow.

A supportive extended family is a valuable asset to any child. No matter how dedicated and capable his parents may be, they can't meet his every need, every day. Other members of the family make their own unique contributions as role models, teachers, and providers of love and attention. Such people make a real investment of themselves in the child over the years, and that makes them extraordinarily vulnerable. As for the child, such relationships become a vital part of his life.

What happens to those relationships when the parents die, divorce, or change custody, or there is a termination of parental rights?

Some of the most wrenching moments I've ever witnessed in a courtroom have been those when such relationships have been torn apart. Saddest of all is that such pain is often the result of situations which those affected did not create, and over which they had no control.

In the past several years, the law has been moving toward greater rights for such people, and I believe that's a good thing. Too often, they, and the children they love, have been the innocent victims of the actions of others.

But even today, in spite of the progress that has been made, painful questions remain. How do you assure fairness to natural and adoptive families, to children, and to the third parties who have a relationship with them when death, divorce, or termination turns their lives upside down?

So far, there are no perfect answers. I doubt that the law alone can ever ensure that what's best for everyone involved will always be the outcome. That time can come only when we understand and accept that loving one person doesn't limit our ability to love another. That hope may be realized only when parents who love a child understand that one of the greatest gifts they can give him is the freedom to love whomever he wishes, with no strings attached.

Can a non-parent ever establish legal rights concerning a child?

Yes.

How?

By filing an Original Suit to Affect the Parent-Child Relationship, or by intervening as a third party in a Suit to Affect the Parent-Child Relationship which has already been filed by someone else.

What is a Suit to Affect the Parent-Child Relationship?

It's a suit regarding a managing conservatorship, a possessory conservatorship, access to or support of a child, adoption, establishment of paternity, or termination of the parent-child relationship. Every divorce in which the parties have children includes such a suit.

Are requirements for becoming a party in a suit already filed by someone else different from requirements for filing your own Original Suit to Affect the Parent-Child Relationship?

Yes. It's far easier to meet the requirements for entering as a third party in a lawsuit already filed by someone else. You file a Petition in Intervention, asking the judge to let you participate as another party to the lawsuit. It's up to the judge whether you'll be allowed to do so. Usually, if you've had significant contact with the child in the past, the judge will permit you to intervene.

To file an Original Suit to Affect the Parent-Child Relationship, a non-parent must have the legal authority to file such a suit. The legal right to file a lawsuit is called "standing" to sue.

Not everyone has standing to file an Original Suit to Affect the Parent-Child Relationship, and that makes sense. Imagine the possibility for chaos if it were otherwise. I could come out of nowhere to file for custody of your little boy because I thought he was just the sort of child I'd like to raise as my own. Or five hundred people who saw a child selling cookies on television might decide they would like to have the right to spend time with her, and they'd each file a lawsuit seeking visitation.

Obviously, that's ridiculous, but it illustrates why it's necessary to have limitations on who can even ask a court for legal rights concerning a child.

The first thing a non-parent must do is determine whether he fits into one of the legal categories of persons who do have standing to file a Suit to Affect the Parent-Child Relationship. The law establishes who has standing. If you have it, well and good. If you don't, you're out of luck; there's no way you'll be permitted to present your case to a judge.

Who has standing to file an Original Suit to Affect the Parent-Child Relationship?

- A parent of the child;
- The child (but the suit must be filed on behalf of the child by a person authorized to do so by the court);
- A custodian, or a person having visitation rights with the child, who was appointed by order of a court of another state or country, or of the State of Texas before January 1, 1974;
- A legally appointed guardian of the person or estate of the child;
- A government agency;
- Any authorized agency;
- A licensed child placement agency;
- A man claiming to be the biological father of a child who has no presumed father (however, the only original suit he can file is one to establish his paternity);
- A person who has had actual physical possession and control of the child for at least six months immediately before filing the suit;
- A person designated as managing conservator in an Affidavit of Relinquishment by a parent, or to whom written legal consent to adopt has been given;
- A person with whom the child and the child's parent, guardian, or managing conservator have resided for at least six months before filing the suit if the child's parent, guardian, or managing conservator is deceased;
- The Office of the Attorney General, which may file for child support or to establish paternity;
- Under carefully limited circumstances, a former stepparent, who may ask for adoption (see Chapter 4); or
- A foster parent who has had the child placed in his home by PRS for at least six months before he filed the suit.

As you can see, the most likely grounds for standing which a non-parent may have are actual physical possession of the child for the preceding six months, or the designation of the non-parent as managing conservator in a parent's Affidavit of Relinquishment.

By the way, that six-month possession, which can serve as a basis for standing, must have been aboveboard. You can't take the child against the will of the person who has the legal right to custody, hide him for six months, then reappear and claim to have standing.

There's one other very important provision for granting standing to seek managing conservatorship, and it's this: A grandparent, or any other person the court decides has had enough past contact with the child to justify it, may be granted standing to file for managing conservatorship or custody by proving either of the following:

- The child's present environment presents a serious question concerning the child's physical health or welfare; or
- Both parents, the surviving parent, the managing conservator, or custodian either joined in filing the suit or consented to it.

Before you get too excited, however, consider whether you truly have a "serious, immediate question concerning the child's welfare." The fact that you once saw Daddy drink three beers in an evening, or that Mom's housekeeping standards don't match your own, won't get you more than a polite shake of the head from the court. If you're lucky.

A judge may grant anyone the right to intervene in a suit concerning a child if he decides that person has had past contact with the child sufficient to justify intervention.

Concerning suits for adoption, or adoptions combined with suits to terminate the parent-child relationship, see Chapter 4 for the categories of people who have standing.

When can grandparents file a suit asking for possessory conservatorship of a child?

A grandparent can seek possessory conservatorship only by intervening in a lawsuit already filed by someone else with standing to file a Suit to Affect the Parent-Child Relationship, as outlined above.

If a judge grants a grandparent the right to intervene in the suit, the grandparent must then prove that it's in the child's best interest for the grandparent to be appointed a possessory conservator.

Does it make any difference whether the child is their biological or adopted grandchild?

No.

When can grandparents file a suit asking for access to a child?

Access and possessory conservatorship are different. A possessory conservator acquires rights and duties which a person who merely has the right to access doesn't have.

Grandparents have standing to ask for access if:

- The grandparent is a parent of a parent of the child, and that parent has been in jail for three months immediately preceding the filing of the suit, or the parent is dead, or the parent has been found incompetent by a judge;

- The child's parents are divorced, their divorce has been filed but has not been heard, or the parents have been separated for the three months immediately preceding the filing of the suit;

- The child has been abused or neglected by a parent;

- A judge has found the child delinquent or in need of supervision;

- The child has lived with the grandparent for at least six months within the twenty-four-month period immediately preceding the filing of the suit; or

- The grandparent is the parent of a person whose parent-child relationship with the child has been terminated (but see the next question concerning what happens if adoption follows the termination).

How does a grandparent go about gaining access to a child if the grandparent is the parent of a person whose parent-child relationship with the child has been terminated?

By filing an Original Suit to Affect the Parent-Child Relationship, or a motion to modify an order already issued, or a petition for further action. Your lawyer will have to guide you in determining which is appropriate. The grandparent must then show that he fits one of the fact situations described in the answer to the immediately preceding question, and that his access to the child will be in the child's best interest.

When a child is adopted, what rights, if any, do his biological grandparents still have regarding him?

They have no standing to ask for any rights regarding the child, unless the child has been adopted by the new spouse of the former spouse of the former parent, whose rights were terminated, or who died.

For example: Johnny's biological parents are Mary and Joe. Mary dies. Joe remarries, and his new wife, Ann, adopts Johnny. Mary's parents still have standing to ask the court for reasonable visitation with Johnny.

The situation would be the same if Mary had not died, but if, instead, her parental rights had been terminated by a court. It's important to note that Mary's parents do not automatically have the right to visitation with Johnny. They only have standing to sue, asking a judge to grant them such visitation.

Consider a different situation: Assume that Jane's biological parents are Betty and Tom, and Betty and Tom are killed in a plane crash. Bill and Jenny adopt Jane. The parents of Betty and Tom, Jane's grandparents until the tragedy, have no standing to ask a court to grant them even reasonable access to Jane. The result would be the same if, instead of being killed in a plane crash, Betty and Tom had both had their parental rights terminated by a court before the adoption.

When a child is adopted, what rights do his biological brothers and sisters, or aunts and uncles, still have regarding the child?

None. Their only possible avenue for pursuing further contact is registration with the voluntary central adoption registry. By registering, they may be able to reestablish contact once the adopted child becomes an adult. See Chapter 4.

When a child is adopted, what rights does he have in relation to his birth family?

None, except that he retains the right to inherit from his biological parents if the court didn't terminate that right at the time of the adoption. When he's an adult, he has the right to register with the central adoption registry and, in that manner, may be able to reestablish contact with his birth family. See Chapter 4.

What happens to a child when his parents die?

Usually, if one parent dies, the other parent will have the right to possession and control of the child, whether or not he was a managing conservator of the child when the other parent died.

This isn't always true, however. Sometimes it's possible for another person to gain custody by filing a Suit to Affect the Parent-Child Relationship. That person must have standing to file the suit as outlined earlier.

If he does have standing and files suit, he must prove to the judge that it would significantly impair the child's physical health or emotional development to name the surviving parent as managing conservator, and further, that it would be in the child's best interest to name the person filing the suit as managing conservator instead.

After one parent dies, a child is in a difficult spot if the surviving parent doesn't want him to continue a relationship with grandparents, uncles, aunts, or cousins from the deceased parent's side of the family.

As a practical matter, there's nothing the child can do. If those relatives want to maintain a relationship with the child, they must be the ones to take the initiative by filing suit to gain the legal right to see him.

If one or both parents die, it's significant to note that a child twelve or older may not be adopted without his consent. Further, he has the right to select his managing conservator, subject to the court's approval.

However, the fact is that whatever his age, a child must wait for adults to file a lawsuit to determine who has what rights concerning him. Until or unless they do, he's powerless concerning his relationship with non-parents. Our Texas Family Code does give a child the right, through a representative authorized by the court, to file a Suit to Affect the Parent-Child Relationship. However, as a practical matter, the child can't act alone and must rely on the actions taken by others.

What legal rights does a stepparent have regarding a child?

Very few.

Following a divorce from a parent, a stepparent has no right to any further contact with the child based simply on having once been a stepparent.

However, stepparents are specifically granted standing to file suit to adopt a stepchild, or a former stepchild under certain circumstances, as explained earlier. If a child's parent or parents die, the stepparent has no automatic legal rights regarding the child. But a stepparent who can qualify under one of the categories for standing to file a Suit to Affect the Parent-Child Relationship may be able to take legal steps to establish rights regarding the child. Let me give you a couple of examples; they're extreme, but they illustrate the law.

Mother and stepfather, who have been married seven years, are in the middle of a divorce. The child's natural father is deceased. Mother is a drug addict, physically abuses the eight-year-old child, and sometimes disappears for days at a time. Stepfather loves the child, has been the child's primary caretaker during the marriage, and is the only father the child has known. I believe the stepfather could qualify for standing to file a Suit to Affect the Parent-Child Relationship, joined with the divorce, and ask the court for custody of the child.

Let's consider another case. Assume the father dies after a ten-year marriage to stepmother. Suddenly, the birth mother, who hasn't seen the twelve-year-old child since he was six months old, reappears. She's heard about the life insurance proceeds and Social Security benefits her son is about to receive. I think there's no doubt the stepmother has standing to file for custody.

Once again, if both parents are deceased, or there has been termination of the parent-child relationship, stepparents have no automatic legal rights concerning the child. But the facts may well bring them within one of the categories for standing to sue, giving them the opportunity to ask a court for rights regarding the child.

What rights do aunts, uncles, brothers, and sisters have regarding a child?

None. However, they may be able to acquire standing to sue to ask a court to grant them rights to a child. Their most likely basis for standing is six months' possession of the child prior to filing their suit, or their designation as managing conservator in an Affidavit of Relinquishment signed by the parents.

What must any non-parent who has standing to file for managing conservatorship prove in order for a judge to grant his request?

Once a person has met the requirements for standing, he has only begun to fight.

If either of the child's parents is asking for appointment as managing conservator, a non-parent must show that the appointment of either such parent would significantly impair the child's physical health or emotional development, and that appointment of the non-parent would be in the child's best interest.

It isn't enough to show the child would be "better off" with the non-parent. Unless you can show the "significant impairment" mentioned above, you won't even get to the question of the child's best interest.

It's not easy for a non-parent to gain managing conservatorship of a child when a parent is asking for custody. There's a deeply rooted belief in our society, reflected in our laws, that ultimately, children fare best with their own parents, even if the situation isn't an ideal one. Non-parents do convince a court on occasion. It doesn't happen often.

16

Children Who Run Away from Home

Why do children run away? Those who do often run away more than once if the reason they left the first time isn't discovered and addressed.

Some children leave because of problems within the home, such as a divorce, or a stepparent they don't like.

Others run away because they are being physically or sexually abused, and they don't know how else to escape.

A child may leave because she wants to do something that wouldn't be permitted at home, like using drugs. Peer pressure is a powerful influence among adolescents. A child may feel the rules at home are too strict. She may carry rebellion beyond that which is normal for children who are growing up and breaking away from their parents.

Almost always, one factor involved is the emotional isolation of the child from her family. Children who are loved and valued and know it, children who communicate with their parents, children whose parents spend time with them, don't usually run away from home.

Today, the concern for children who run from their homes is greater than ever. A runaway's education is interrupted, her emotional, and often her physical, health are affected. The streets are more dangerous than ever. Drugs, AIDS, and violence are very real threats to children on their own.

The legislature recognized the potential for harm to children who are runaways and enacted laws concerning the problem.

How old must a child be to leave home without a parent's permission?

In most cases, eighteen. If she has ever been legally married, she may live wherever she wants, whatever her age.

She may live wherever she chooses once her disabilities of minority have been removed for general purposes.

What are the legal consequences of a child running away from home?

If she's under seventeen, and doesn't fall into one of the categories listed above, and she leaves home without parental permission, the police can pick her up and turn her over to the juvenile probation department.

If the child is under ten years old, she'll be returned immediately to her parents or managing conservator.

If the child is ten or older and under seventeen, she may have to appear before a judge, accused of being a child in need of supervision. If the judge finds that the child left home without a parent's permission, and stayed away for a substantial period of time, or simply didn't intend to return at all, the judge can find that she's a child in need of supervision.

The judge can then send the child home on a year's probation or place her in whatever placement the judge decides would be in the child's best interest.

The judge can't send the child to the Texas Youth Commission.

If a child's parents refuse to allow her to live at home, what can she do?

Call the Department of Protective and Regulatory Services (PRS), which has offices in each county in Texas.

The agency can provide shelter, food, clothing, and medical care. It can also help to find relatives or foster families willing to provide a home for the child.

In some instances, the agency can also ask a judge to order the parents to pay child support.

There's a National Runaway Switchboard, which is open twenty-four hours a day. It's confidential. The number is 1-800-621-4000. The number for the hearing impaired is 1-800-621-0394.

May a person who isn't a relative provide shelter for a child who has run away from home?

It's a very risky proposition. You may be inviting charges of harboring a runaway or interference with child custody. Obviously, you needn't shut the door in the face of a child who needs shelter or is in danger. But you should call the police and PRS as soon as possible to protect yourself. If you want to offer the child a home, let those agencies know and it may be possible for such arrangements to be made with the law's blessing. Also, be aware of insurance questions and other legal responsibilities you may incur. In short, discuss such plans with an attorney.

Is there any special provision to help minor mothers?

Yes. An emergency shelter facility may provide shelter and care to a minor mother who's providing the sole financial support for her child.

But that care may be provided only if there's an immediate danger to the health or safety of the minor mother or her children.

The shelter may only be used for fifteen days, unless consent is given by the minor mother's parent or guardian, or she's qualified for Temporary Assistance to Needy Families and on a waiting list for housing.

17

Children and Marriage

If there's anything in the world that children don't need, it's to be married.

A happy marriage is one of life's greatest pleasures. But even for adults, it isn't easy to achieve. Maturity is a necessary ingredient. For children, marriage can be disastrous.

They aren't prepared financially or emotionally for the responsibilities it involves.

Often it interrupts or ends their education, resulting in a lifelong limitation on job opportunities.

Just as often, young married couples have children while they're still children themselves, before they are ready in any sense to assume the role of parents.

Even under the best of circumstances, marriage propels children into an adult lifestyle, with adult decisions to make and adult responsibilities to shoulder. It robs them of a part of their childhood which they can never go back and reclaim. It cuts short the fun of school activities, the chance to meet many people and have many kinds of experiences that will prepare them to be happier adults before they actually reach adulthood.

Now that I've gotten that off my chest, yes, sometimes the law permits children to marry. Each case is different. Once in a while marriage for a teenager may be the best choice available.

Years ago, a streetwise sixteen-year-old was my client. She had awful parents, who really cared nothing for her. She'd been out of their home, on the streets, for two years when she stole some things from a store. The one good influence in her life was her boyfriend. He was several years older, and he really loved her. He was trying to get her to go back to school. He had a job, and he wanted to marry her. I made a deal with them. I'd try to get the judge to approve their marriage if she'd go back and finish high school. The same judge who found her delinquent agreed to perform the ceremony. The prosecuting attorney was best man. I was matron of honor and we had the wedding at my home.

It actually worked out. The last I heard she had completed school and they had twin boys. I guess you never know. I still don't think marriage is for children.

How old must a person in Texas be to get married?

He or she must be eighteen years old.

If a child is at least fourteen, but not yet eighteen, that person may marry with the written consent of a parent, court-appointed managing conservator, or legal guardian. A person of any age under eighteen may marry if a judge, after a hearing, consents to the marriage.

What is required to obtain a marriage license if a child is under eighteen but over fourteen and his parents consent to the marriage?

The county clerk provides a consent form which the parent, managing conservator, or guardian of the child must sign before a county clerk of the State of Texas.

What if the parent lives in another state and can't come to Texas to sign such a consent in person before a county clerk?

The parent may sign and swear to the consent form before a person authorized to issue marriage licenses in that state.

If a parent is ill or incapacitated, making appearance before a county clerk impossible, what then?

The parental consent form may be signed before a notary public, accompanied by a sworn affidavit of a doctor, stating the person is unable to appear before a county clerk to sign the consent form.

Is there any time period after which a signed consent form is no longer valid?

Yes. It must be signed on the day of the application for the marriage license, or within the thirty days immediately preceding.

If a child is under eighteen and his parents won't consent to his marriage, is it still possible for him legally to marry?

He can file a petition in district court asking the judge to give him permission to marry. If the judge consents, parental consent isn't necessary. A parent, managing conservator, or guardian must be notified of the suit.

How does a judge decide whether to permit a child to marry?

By determining what's in the best interest of the child.

Is the law any different for boys and girls regarding marriage?

No.

If a child between fourteen and seventeen marries without the required legal consent, what can be done?

The marriage can be annulled.

If a child under fourteen marries without a judge's permission, what can be done about it?

The marriage can be annulled.

How is a marriage annulled?

By filing a petition in district court asking the judge to declare the marriage void and having him grant it.

Who has the right to file such a petition?

A parent, a managing conservator, or a legal guardian can file such a petition. The child can also file it by having an adult act on his behalf.

Is there any time limit for filing a petition to declare the marriage void?

Yes. If a child under the age of fourteen is the person seeking to have his marriage annulled, the petition can't be filed later than ninety days after the child's fourteenth birthday. If it isn't filed by then, it can never be filed by the child.

The rule is different if the petition is filed by a parent, managing conservator, or legal guardian of the child under fourteen. Then, the petition for annulment can be filed anytime before the child's fourteenth birthday, and afterward within ninety days of the time the person filing the petition knew, or should have known, of the marriage. If it isn't filed by that time, it can never be filed by that person.

A petition to annul his own marriage may not be filed by a child fourteen through seventeen years of age who married without the necessary consent. A child lacks the legal capacity to file a lawsuit. Therefore, the suit must be filed on the child's behalf by an adult acting for the child. This person, usually a parent, stands in the place of the child, and is called the child's "next friend." The suit must be filed within ninety days of the marriage, or within ninety days of the time the child realized he was married. If the petition isn't filed within this time period, the child loses the right to ask for an annulment based on his age.

A child's parent, managing conservator, or legal guardian may file a petition to annul the marriage of a child who married between the ages of fourteen and seventeen without consent, but must do so within ninety days of the time that person knew, or should have known, of the marriage.

If one parent knew of the marriage but did nothing to have it annulled, can the other parent, who learned of the marriage later, file to have it annulled?

Yes. So long as it's within ninety days of the date the other parent learned of the marriage.

Can a child's parent, managing conservator, or legal guardian ever file to annul the marriage of a child who was underage at the time of the marriage but has since turned eighteen?

No.

Is there a right to a jury trial in a suit to annul the marriage of a child who was underage and married without consent?

No.

If no one files a suit to annul the underage marriage of a child who married without legal consent, is the marriage a legal one?

Yes. It's a valid marriage until or unless a judge rules otherwise.

Can a child seek to have his marriage annulled for any reason other than age?

Yes. He may use the same grounds for annulment that are available to adults.

Can anyone other than the child seek an annulment on grounds other than age?

Only the actual parties to the marriage, the children who are husband and wife, can file suit to annul their marriage on any grounds other than age, with one exception:

The legal guardian or the next friend of the child may, with the judge's permission, file a petition to annul the child's marriage on the grounds the child is incompetent.

If a child's parent has been paying child support and the underage child gets married, must the parent continue paying child support?

No. Once a child marries, any legal rights, duties, and privileges between the child and his parent, managing conservator, or legal guardian end.

Does being married change the age at which a child may vote?

No.

Does being married change the age at which a child may legally operate an automobile?

No.

Does being married change a child's capacity to enter into a legal contract?

Yes. Children who have never married don't have the legal capacity to sign a contract until they are eighteen years old. A child of any age who marries acquires more than a spouse; he also acquires the legal capacity to enter a contract, and he can't use his age as a basis for voiding that contract.

Do a married child's property rights with respect to the marriage differ in any way from the property rights of a married adult?

No.

If an underage child is married, and then the marriage is annulled, is the law regarding him the same as though he had never been married?

Yes. An annulment has the effect of saying a valid marriage never existed; legally, it simply never happened.

If an underage child marries, and then gets a divorce before he's eighteen years old, is the law regarding him the same as though he had never married?

No. It's the same as it would have been if he'd never been divorced.

Once a child of whatever age marries with legal consent, if the child's marriage ends, through death or divorce, does the child require the same legal consent to remarry?

No. If the child was ever legally married, the child may remarry without anyone's consent.

If a child under seventeen who is legally married commits a crime, is he tried in juvenile or adult court?

He'll be tried in juvenile court just as any other child.

Changing a Child's Name

Shakespeare asked, "What's in a name?" Often, the answer is "quite a lot."

It has to do with who we are and where we came from. And it says where we belong.

People feel deeply about having their children bear their name. That makes it seem as if a part of them lives on, even after they're gone. Continuation of their family matters.

Children whose last name is different from that of their parents and brothers and sisters often feel like outsiders, not quite a part of the circle that is the family.

So changing a child's name can become an important matter indeed. And does the law provide a way to do so? Of course.

How is a child's legal name established?

A child's legal name is the name that appears on her birth certificate.

What if the name is misspelled on the birth certificate?

It's her legal name until it's corrected and an amended birth certificate issued.

Who has the right to change a child's name?

Only a judge.

How can you get a child's name changed?

By filing a petition in the district court, asking for the name change.

Who has a right to file such a petition?

A parent, managing conservator, or legal guardian of the child.

What information must the petition contain?

It must contain:

- The present name and address of the child;
- A request that the child's name be changed;
- The full name to be given to the child;
- The reason for requesting the name change; and
- Information concerning whether any court has already heard any case regarding the child, other than an adoption. If so, that court has the right to hear any other matters regarding the child.

A person who files the petition must attach a sworn statement that the information contained in the petition is true.

Is the child's consent to the name change required?

If she's under twelve, no. If she's twelve or older, yes. Her written consent to the name change must be attached to the petition.

Must anyone be given notice that a name change petition was filed?

Yes. Legal notice and a copy of the petition must be given to each parent whose rights haven't been terminated, any managing conservator of the child, and any legal guardian of the child. Each has the right to appear at the court hearing to oppose or support the name change.

What has to be proven in order for the child's name to be changed?

That the name change is in the child's best interest.

May a name change request be included in another petition being filed regarding the child?

Yes. In fact, the request to change a child's name is most often made in an adoption suit or in a suit to establish paternity.

Is it necessary to change a child's name when she's adopted?

No. The child's last name is generally changed, and sometimes her first or middle names as well. There are cases, however, where the child's name isn't changed. She may be older and prefer to keep the name she has had all her life. Also, if the child's father has died and the child is being adopted by a stepfather, the child may wish to continue the biological father's name.

May persons seeking managing conservatorship of a child, without adoption, ask that a child's name be changed in their petition for conservatorship?

Yes. The judge may find that the necessary legal requirements have been met and grant the change. However, it's less likely than in an adoption, because parental rights may not have been terminated if a person is seeking only managing conservatorship. Also, conservatorship is a relationship more subject to change than adoption.

What is the legal effect of changing a child's name?

A new birth certificate may be issued.

The name the judge orders will become the child's new legal name.

The child has the same rights and liabilities she had under her previous name.

What can a parent do if the parents are divorced, or were never married, and the other parent keeps referring to the child by a last name other than her legal name?

A father has a legal right to have his child continue to bear his surname after a divorce, or after a paternity suit where a child has been given his surname. The mother can't change the child's name without a court order. If she tries to do so, the father can file a request with the judge that she be ordered to refer to the child by her legal name.

By the same token, if a judge doesn't change a child's surname to the father's in a paternity decree, but the mother refers to the child by the father's last name, the father can file a suit asking the judge to stop her from doing so.

19

Removing Disabilities of Minority

Childhood. A time for learning and growing and becoming the person you will be.

A gentle time, free of the responsibilities which will be a part of each day for the rest of your life.

A time for dreaming, and playing, and being sheltered from life's pain.

That's what we'd like childhood to be for all children. But it isn't always so. And sometimes there are reasons to cut childhood short and allow a child to grow up and assume the responsibilities of adulthood before the calendar says it's time. When these situations arise, the law provides a way, through removal of the disabilities of minority.

What do the terms "minority" and "majority" mean?

Minority exists until you turn eighteen. Majority begins at that point and continues for the rest of your life.

What are "disabilities of minority"?

The inability to enjoy all of the legal rights granted to an adult, simply because you are a minor.

For example, adults have a right to live where they choose, and a right to their earnings. Children do not have these rights, because they are children. Parents have the right to decide where their children live, and the right to their children's wages. These are some of the disabilities children experience because of their minority.

What does it mean for a child to have his "disabilities of minority" removed?

It means he is no longer subject to restrictions on certain of his legal rights, which are imposed because he is a minor.

What specifically does the removal of disabilities of minority permit a child to do that he couldn't do before?

It depends on whether his disabilities of minority are removed for limited purposes or general purposes.

If the removal is for a limited purpose, the only right the child can then exercise that he couldn't before is the right or rights given him in the decree signed by a judge. If the removal is for general purposes, it means the child can then exercise all of the rights of an adult, which he could not enjoy before because he was a minor.

This can be misleading, because a number of laws with specific age requirements still apply. For example, a child whose disabilities of minority have been removed for general purposes still can't vote until he is eighteen. And the same age requirements still apply regarding driving, drinking, and attending school whether his disabilities have been removed or not.

Removal of disabilities of minority for general purposes does give a child the capacity to enter into a valid contract.

How does a child go about having his disabilities of minority removed?

By filing a petition which makes that request with the district court.

Can any child file such a petition?

No. The child must be a resident of Texas and either sixteen or seventeen years old.

If he's seventeen, he may file even if he's living with his parents, managing conservator, or legal guardian and isn't self-supporting. A seventeen-year-old may also file for removal of his disabilities of minority if he isn't a resident of Texas and is an adult under the laws of the state in which he lives. A sixteen-year-old who files must be living separate and apart from his parents, managing conservator, or legal guardian, be self-supporting, and be managing his own financial affairs.

May a child who is eligible to file a petition for removal of his disabilities of minority file the petition himself, or does he have to have an adult file it for him as his "next friend"?

Usually a child has no legal capacity to file a lawsuit because he is a minor, and an adult acting for him must file the suit as the child's "next friend." The suit for removal of disabilities of minority is an exception. He can file it himself. But it must be sworn to by his parent, managing conservator, or legal guardian. If the whereabouts of such persons are unknown, or if no such person is available, the guardian ad litem of the child must swear to it after the judge appoints him to represent the child.

What information must be contained in a petition for removal of disabilities of minority?

It must contain:

- The child's name, age, and address;
- The name and address of each parent, managing conservator, and legal guardian;
- The reason why removal of disabilities would be in the child's best interest; and
- A statement whether the request is for removal for general purposes or for limited purposes, and if for limited purposes, what limited purposes.

There's a special requirement if the child is a seventeen-year-old resident of another state. A certified copy of his birth certificate, or some other acceptable proof of age, must be attached to the petition. He must also attach a copy of the law of that state showing that a person his age is considered an adult in that state.

Who must be served with citation on the petition?

The child's parents, managing conservator, and legal guardian.

Who must be present at the hearing on the petition to remove a child's disabilities of minority?

The child, unless he isn't a Texas resident. In that case, he doesn't have to appear in person if his attorney or guardian ad litem is present to represent him and he's only asking for removal of his disabilities for limited purposes.

The guardian ad litem of the child must be present.

The child's parents, managing conservator, and legal guardian have a right to be present and to speak for or against the removal of disabilities. They don't have to be present so long as they received legal notice of the hearing.

How will the judge decide whether or not to remove the child's disabilities?

The request will be granted if the judge believes it's in the child's best interest.

Does the removal of disabilities of minority change the law regarding the age at which a child may legally drop out of school?

No.

If a child who had his disabilities of minority removed for general purposes in another state moves to Texas, are his disabilities removed in Texas, too, or is he still a minor in Texas?

He can file a certified copy of the decree removing his disabilities in the deed records of any county in Texas. When that's done, he has the same status in Texas he would have if his disabilities had been removed in Texas. The only limitations which may apply are those imposed by the decree itself and any applicable statutory and constitutional provisions.

Children and Health

Today's children face many more health problems than measles and chicken pox.

At the same time that medicine has found the answers to such former childhood killers as polio, diphtheria, and scarlet fever, new dangers have arisen from our society, which threaten the health, and often the lives, of our children.

Drug usage, AIDS, teenage suicide, teenage pregnancy, and violence are all at near-epidemic proportions. And they are killing or injuring young people.

Many children are affected even before they are born, because of drug use by mothers during pregnancy. A mother's parental rights may be terminated if her baby is born addicted to alcohol or drugs.

The involvement of children with drugs isn't news to anyone living in today's society. Children not yet in school are involved in the sale of drugs. Children in elementary schools are approached by drug dealers. And almost any high school student can tell you who sells drugs in the neighborhood.

Even those children who don't sell or use drugs themselves are affected by the drug use of others around them. Drugs are a major factor in child abuse, accidents, homicide, and other violence of which children are so often the innocent victims. Drugs are often the reason children break the law.

Among the most chilling threats to our children's lives is AIDS. Here are some facts from the U.S. Department of Health and Human Services Centers for Disease Control:

Since 1981, when AIDS was first reported in the United States, the virus that causes the disease has created an epidemic that is unprecedented in U.S. history.

A high percentage of teenagers engage in activities that place them at significant risk of contracting the HIV virus.

Sexual contact with an infected person and sharing needles with an infected person are the two primary methods of getting AIDS. Such knowledge should provide real protection, but it hasn't, and there seem to be two main obstacles in the way.

First, children simply can't accept their own mortality. Studies show that even when children engage in behavior they know will put them at risk of contracting the HIV virus, they just don't believe it will happen to them. The reality of the danger to them personally seems to elude them. One study showed that 70 percent of teenagers between sixteen and nineteen admitted they were sexually active, but only 15 percent said they had changed any part of their sexual behavior because of concern about AIDS.

Second, parents think of AIDS as a disease someone else's children might contract, but find it difficult to believe that their own children would do the things that put them at risk, so they take the comfortable path and ignore the subject.

That they're wrong is illustrated by the fact that, according to figures quoted by the Centers for Disease Control, the average age of first intercourse for females is just over sixteen. The percentage of never-married girls who said they had intercourse was 24 percent of the fourteen-year-olds, 35 percent of the fifteen-year-olds, 45 percent of the sixteen-year-olds, 56 percent of the seventeen-year-olds, and 66 percent of the eighteen-year-olds.

As for male homosexual intercourse, another important risk factor for the HIV virus, one study showed 5 percent of boys aged thirteen to fifteen and 17 percent of boys aged sixteen to nineteen reported having at least one homosexual experience.

There's no second chance, once the virus is contracted. As of today, there's no cure. Perhaps your child wouldn't be involved in such risky behavior, but it's too dangerous to take the chance, however slight, that you might be wrong.

Please, talk with your children about AIDS, and do it soon.

Here's some information which you can use as you feel appropriate.

- AIDS is caused by the HIV virus.
- Most infected people are adults, but children get it, too.
- Scientists everywhere are working hard to find a cure, but as of now, there is none.
- People of all races get AIDS.
- Females, as well as males, get AIDS.
- It sometimes takes several years after being infected with the HIV virus before the symptoms appear. An infected person may not know for a long time that he or she is HIV positive.
- HIV may be transmitted by:

+ *Sexual contact, in any of the following ways: penis/vagina, penis/ rectum, mouth/vagina, mouth/penis, mouth/rectum;*
+ *Using needles or other injection equipment that an infected person has used;*
+ *An infected mother to her infant before or during birth;*
+ *Direct exposure to infected blood; some doctors and other health workers have been infected in this way; and*
+ *Transfusions using infected blood. (Since 1985, this country's blood supply has been tested for HIV, and the risk today is considered almost nonexistent.)*

- The risk of becoming infected with HIV today can be virtually eliminated by not engaging in sexual activities and by not using illegal intravenous drugs.
- AIDS can't be contracted by touching someone who is infected, by being in the same room with her, or by donating blood.
- Teenagers should know that even if their sexual partner is totally honest (and not everyone is), their partner may be infected and not know it. When two people have sex, they not only have each other as partners, but everyone else the partner has ever had sex with, too. Any one of them could have been infected with the HIV virus.
- There's no safe sex except a monogamous relationship with an uninfected partner.
- People who insist on engaging in sexual activities with persons whose HIV status is unknown should use a latex condom, not natural membrane. It must be applied properly and used from start to finish for every sexual act. It doesn't provide complete protection because it may break, leak, or slip off, but it's better than no protection at all. Some additional protection may be provided by using spermacides in conjunction with a condom; they appear to be active to a degree against HIV and other sexually transmitted organisms.

For more information about the HIV virus and AIDS, phone the Centers for Disease Control National HIV and AIDS Hotline at 1-800-342-2437 or the CDC National AIDS Hotline—Spanish, for Spanish-speaking callers, at 1-800-344-7432. For information about HIV and AIDS, as well as other sexually transmitted diseases, call the Sexually Transmitted Disease National Hotline, 1-800-227-8922, your local health department, or your own physician.

Teenage suicide, another real threat to today's child, has tripled in the United States since 1950, according to the National School Safety Center News Service. It is the third-leading cause of death among teenagers, after accidents and homicide.

No parents want to believe their child could ever consider, let alone follow through with, committing suicide. But children do. This is a problem that is especially common among gay teenagers fearing parental rejection.

So, how do parents minimize the risk?

By keeping open the lines of communication between themselves and their children, establishing trust and awareness between them.

By listening, and hearing what their children's actions, as well as their words, are saying.

Here are some of the things you should know:

- Children who are severely depressed are at risk for suicide, but not all depressed children are suicidal. And not all children who are suicidal are obviously depressed.

- Most suicidal people don't really want to die. But they are so overwhelmed by their problems, they feel unable to cope and see no alternative to their pain.

- Children don't yet have the maturity and experience to be able to look beyond the present. What may seem trivial or easily resolved to you may appear hopeless to them.

- There's a common belief that people who threaten suicide never actually do it. That isn't true. People who've committed suicide have often made direct or indirect threats of suicide, such as "I wish I were dead" or "you'd be better off if I were dead." Such statements are clear danger signals and a cry for help. To ignore them, or to react with anger or disbelief, is to invite tragedy. It's true that many people who threaten suicide don't go through with it, but many others do.

- As well as direct and indirect suicide threats, other warning signals are:

  + *Depression. If the depression is persistent, and accompanied by loss of appetite, hopelessness, crying bouts, or sleeplessness, it's cause for concern.*

  + *Behavior change. Abrupt changes may signal trouble. If an outgoing child becomes withdrawn suddenly, a quiet child starts getting into trouble, or a curious, involved child loses interest, you should be alert to the fact problems exist.*

  + *Preoccupation with death.*

  + *Giving away treasured personal possessions.*

- Those who've tried suicide, and failed, are at increased risk. Eighty percent of those who commit suicide have made at least one prior attempt.

Sometimes suicide occurs just when the family believes the child is back to normal. The first three to six months are most critical, but there's an increased risk for up to two years after a failed suicide attempt.

- Drugs and alcohol are associated with an increased risk of suicide. Statistics from the Center to Prevent Handgun Violence indicate guns are the most effective means of committing suicide; 97 percent of such attempts are successful. Teenagers who've been drinking are more likely to use guns than any other method. The odds that suicidal teenagers will actually kill themselves go up seventy-five times when there's a gun in the house. The conclusion is obvious: if you have a gun in your home, keep it out of reach of children, especially one who is exhibiting any of the above signs. If you believe your child is potentially suicidal, trust your gut feeling. Get professional help at once. Your doctor, your child's school, or a mental health professional can refer you to the appropriate individual or agency.

Some agencies which provide information concerning suicide are:

- National Mental Health Association, 1-800-969-6642;
- Youth Suicide National Center, 1-650-342-5755;
- The Resource Center on Substance Abuse, 1-202-628-8080; and
- National Clearinghouse on Family Support and Children's Mental Health, 1-800-628-1696.

Another serious health problem is teenage pregnancy. The U.S. Department of Health and Human Services says over one million teens get pregnant each year. We know that young girls have more problems during pregnancy. Their health is at real risk. Babies of young mothers are likely to be born with serious health problems. All of which doesn't even acknowledge or begin to address the emotional problems facing a young mother who is herself still a child, or the effect those emotional problems will have on her baby.

The law can't solve all problems. How does one legislate hope in the heart of a child in pain, or wisdom for the choices their parents must make?

There are some health questions involving children to which the law does speak. This chapter will discuss them.

Who has the power to consent to medical, dental, surgical, and psychological treatment for a child?

A parent. However, a court may remove that power and place it in a managing or possessory conservator.

If a person with the power to consent to medical, dental, surgical, or psychological treatment of a child can't be located, does anyone else have the power to consent?

Yes, if the person with the power to consent hasn't given actual notice otherwise, the following people can consent:

- A grandparent;
- An adult brother or sister;
- An adult aunt or uncle;
- A school where the child is enrolled, if the school has written authorization from the person with the power to consent;
- Any adult who has care, control, and possession of the child, and has written authorization from the person with the power;
- Any judge having jurisdiction over the child;
- Any adult responsible for the child's care under a juvenile court's jurisdiction or order, if she has reasonable grounds to believe a child needs immediate medical treatment; or
- A peace officer who has lawfully taken possession of a child and reasonably believes the child needs immediate medical treatment.

Oddly enough, stepparents are not included in this list.

The Texas Youth Commission may consent when a parent of a child in TYC care has been contacted and hasn't refused the treatment.

Is the above information the same regarding consent for immunization of a child?

No. It's slightly different. Any of those listed above may consent to immunization. So may a stepparent, an adult who is the child's primary caretaker, or an adult having care of the child under a juvenile court order.

However, these people can't consent if:

- They know firsthand that the person with the power to consent to immunization has refused to consent;
- They have been denied the power to consent by the person with the power to consent; or
- Permission to consent has been withdrawn by the person with the power to consent.

May a person under eighteen consent to her own medical treatment?

Sometimes, yes. Sometimes, no. Yes, if the child is:

- On active duty with the armed forces of the United States;
- Sixteen or older, living apart from her parents, and managing her own financial affairs;
- Consenting to diagnosis and treatment of either any infectious, contagious, or communicable disease that must be reported to the local health authorities or any sexually transmitted disease;
- Unmarried and pregnant and consenting to treatment related to her pregnancy; or
- Consenting to examination and treatment for drug or alcohol addiction or dependency.

Except for the above, a child under eighteen may not consent to his or her own medical treatment or diagnosis.

A child who is unmarried and has custody of her own child may consent to treatment for that child.

May a child consent to an abortion?

The law says no, but the law may be unconstitutional as written. Attempts in the last (1997) legislative session to restrict a minor's right to consent to an abortion without parental notification, which might be constitutional, failed. In spite of what the law says, minors consent to abortions in Texas all the time and doctors perform them.

Does a doctor need the child's consent to inform her parents of a diagnosis and treatment given to or needed by the child?

No. The decision is up to the doctor. The parents may be informed without the child's consent. However, the law doesn't require the doctor to do so.

May a child consent to counseling for sexual abuse, physical abuse, suicide prevention, or chemical dependency?

Yes. The person authorized to provide such counseling may do so with or without the parent's consent if the child consents. However, the parent isn't required to pay the fee for services to which she didn't consent.

The counselor may inform a parent of the treatment needed by or given to the child, with or without the child's consent. But the counselor isn't required to give a parent such information.

Is anyone's consent required for a doctor or dentist to examine a child believed to be abused or neglected?

No, unless consent is specifically refused by a court order. However, if a child sixteen or older refuses to consent to being examined, no examination may be conducted.

May a parent deny a child medical treatment based upon the parent's religious beliefs?

No. The law imposes a duty upon parents to provide necessary medical care for their children. Failure to do so may result in the state removing the child from the parent's home, based on parental neglect. However, there is a narrower question, concerning whether parents may choose more unorthodox, as opposed to more conventional, courses of medical treatment.

If serious injury to or the death of a child results because of the parent's failure to provide necessary medical treatment, criminal charges may be filed against the parents.

If a woman, knowing she has AIDS or is HIV positive, becomes pregnant and transmits the virus to her baby, has she committed a crime in Texas?

No. It's a third-degree felony for that woman, or anyone else, to intentionally engage in conduct which is likely to transmit the virus. But Texas law specifically says that doesn't apply when a mother transmits the disease to her baby before birth.

What this means is that if a man or woman is HIV positive and deliberately exposes a sex partner to the virus, intending to transmit it, that's a felony. As it should be. But if an HIV positive woman deliberately gets pregnant and gives it to her unborn child—a significant risk—that's not even a misdemeanor. Incredible!

What immunizations are required for a child to be admitted to any public or private school in Texas?

Diphtheria, rubeola, rubella, tetanus, and poliomyelitis. The Texas Department of Health has the authority to add to or delete from this list.

Are there any exceptions to these requirements?

Yes. If the immunization would be injurious to the health or well-being of the child, her family, or other household members, the rule is waived. A doctor's affidavit is necessary.

If the child's parents submit an affidavit stating immunization is against the religious beliefs of a recognized religious denomination of which the child is a member, immunization isn't required.

Finally, such immunizations are waived if the person is a member of the armed forces of the United States on active duty.

If a child has begun a series of inoculations, must she wait until they're completed before she can enter school?

No. She can be admitted to school, conditioned upon her finishing the series of inoculations as quickly as medically appropriate.

Children with Disabilities

A child is a child. The fact that he may have a disability doesn't alter his basic nature. He has the same needs, and the same rights, as any other child. The difference is simply that he, and to a lesser degree, his parents, are challenged in ways that other children and their parents are not. It's sometimes more difficult for such children to have their basic needs met.

Fortunately, the law has taken steps to try to help.

Two federal statutes which address these problems, the Education for All Handicapped Children Act of 1975 and Section 504 of the Rehabilitation Act of 1973, deal with one of childhood's most important tasks, getting an education. They prohibit discrimination against a child in any federally assisted program or activity for which the child would qualify if he were not handicapped.

Perhaps the least malicious, but one of the most damaging, forms of discrimination against the child with a disability is for others to see only the disability and fail to see the child for the individual he is.

Much has been accomplished by parents who fought for a greater understanding and acceptance of their children with disabilities, but much remains to be done. Largely, it's a question of educating others. And parents who insist upon their children's rights are the most effective weapon against ignorance.

May a child or parent be denied benefits or services in programs or activities which receive funding from the U.S. Department of Health and Human Services because of the child's or parent's disability?

No. If an agency receives federal funding, it's usually very responsive to charges of discrimination against a child or parent because of disability. If for no other reason, it's concerned because such discrimination may jeopardize its funding.

Affected facilities and programs typically include adoption agencies, foster homes, day care centers, family health clinics, hospitals, state agencies which administer health care, Medicaid, community health centers, alcohol and drug treatment facilities, and children's protective services.

What should a parent do if he believes he or his child is a victim of discrimination by such programs because of the parent's or child's disability?

File a complaint with the regional office of the Office for Civil Rights for Texas:

Office for Civil Rights
1301 Young St., Room 1169
Dallas, Texas 75202
phone: 1-214-767-4056 and 1-800-368-1019

You may request a complaint form or include the following information in your written complaint:

- Your name, address, and telephone number, and the name of the child and your relationship to him;
- The name and address of the agency or institution you believe discriminated against the child;
- How, why, and when you believe the discrimination occurred; and
- Any other information you believe is relevant.

What educational rights does the law give to children with disabilities?

Federal law requires states to provide a free, appropriate public education to every child with a disability between the ages of three and twenty-one. Children with visual or hearing impairment may also be entitled to services from state and federal agencies.

Who is responsible for seeing that children with disabilities receive the education to which they're entitled?

The Texas Education Agency (TEA). It establishes policies and procedures for local independent school districts.

When the law requires a free, appropriate public education, what is meant by "free"?

Appropriate educational services must be provided to children with disabilities at no cost. However, if fees for a particular educational service are charged to nondisabled children, disabled children may have to pay them as well.

What is meant by an "appropriate" education?

That's determined by the needs and abilities of the individual child. It will include:

- Nondiscriminatory evaluation and placement procedures;
- Periodic reevaluation;
- Educational services designed to meet the individual's educational needs as adequately as those of nondisabled students are met;
- To the extent possible, the education of disabled children with non-disabled children; and
- Establishment of means for parents to review their child's records, and to challenge decisions concerning his evaluation and placement.

What if the school district in which a disabled child resides is unable to provide a free, appropriate education to the child?

It may place the child in, or refer him to, a program other than the one it offers, but must ensure that the education provided is appropriate. Further, the school district must pay any costs of such placement, including tuition, room and board, psychological and medical services for diagnosis and evaluation of the child, and transportation.

What if a school district makes a free, appropriate education available, but the parents prefer to place the child in a private school?

They may do so, but must pay all of the costs of that placement.

Are there any special requirements concerning accessibility to educational programs?

Yes. Facilities used for educational programs must be readily physically accessible to children with disabilities.

What about nonacademic, extracurricular activities sponsored or provided by the school?

The school must give disabled children an equal opportunity to participate in all such activities.

Specifically, what does the law require the public education system to do for children with disabilities?

- Identify them;
- Evaluate or assess them;

- Develop an individual educational plan for each disabled child before the child receives special education services;
- Provide educational and related services in the least restrictive environment possible;
- Provide residential care to students when necessary to give them appropriate educational services;
- Maintain educational records for all children in special education;
- Provide transportation to and from school if necessary; and
- Provide a way for complaints and grievances to be heard and appealed.

What actual disabilities will qualify a child for special education services?

Virtually any physical, emotional, or mental condition which limits or alters a child's ability to participate in regular educational programs or activities may qualify that child for special educational services.

When a child is referred for consideration for special education services, what process takes place?

First, the child's parent must be given notice of the school's plan to assess the child for special education, and must consent to the testing. Parental consent is necessary only for the first placement, but not for subsequent changes in the child's educational plan. If the parent refuses to consent to the initial placement, the school can request a hearing to show that the child should be tested or placed even without parental consent.

Next, testing is done to see if the child needs special education. If the testing shows that he does, it will be used as a basis to design the child's educational program. Eligibility and need for special education services must be reviewed every three years as long as the child is in the program.

Parents have the right to:

- Receive written notice before the school assesses or refuses to assess the child;
- Receive information about the abilities, skills, and knowledge to be assessed;
- Give consent before the school assesses the child for the first time;
- Receive a description and explanation of the tests, reports, or records to be used;
- Inspect and review assessment records before an admission, review, and dismissal (ARD) committee meeting;

- Have the results of the assessment considered at an ARD committee meeting;
- Be assured that the tests will be conducted in the child's native language or other primary form of communication;
- Be assured that no single test will be the sole basis for determining the child's educational program;
- Present a written complaint to the TEA if the parent believes the law and proper procedures aren't being followed;
- Ask the Secretary of Education of the U.S. Department of Education to review the final decision of the TEA regarding the complaint; and
- Request mediation or a due process hearing if there's no agreement on assessment.

Children who are being tested for special education have the right to be:

- Assessed in all areas related to the suspected disability, including, where appropriate, health, vision, hearing, sociological and emotional status, general intelligence, academic performance, communication skills, and motor abilities;
- Tested with instruments designed for the specific purpose for which they are being used;
- Tested in a way that isn't racially or culturally discriminatory;
- Tested by qualified personnel; and
- Evaluated by a group including at least one who is a specialist in the area of the suspected disability.

The assessment must be completed and the report written within sixty days of the referral to the school district, and within thirty school days of its receipt by the district's special education staff.

A parent who disagrees with the assessment may ask the school district to pay for additional testing, provided by a qualified examiner not employed by the school district. The district must comply with the parent's request or ask for a hearing to show that the original assessment and evaluation were appropriate and it shouldn't have to provide another one. If the hearing results in the district having to pay, ask at the district's administrative office for procedures you must follow before obtaining an independent evaluation. A parent always has the right to obtain a further evaluation at the parent's expense.

An admission, review, and dismissal (ARD) committee meeting is held once the child's testing and assessment are complete. This meeting, known as an ARD meeting, is very important. The child's parents are members of this committee, as are school personnel and, when appropriate, the child himself.

The ARD committee determines the child's eligibility to receive special education services after reviewing the results of the child's testing. If the child is eligible for special education, the ARD committee plans the child's educational program based upon his needs.

ARD committee meetings are scheduled at least once a year to review the child's progress. However, a parent may request an ARD meeting at any time. It's a good idea to meet informally with the school's special education people before asking for a formal ARD meeting. Any change in the child's education plan, such as placement, must be made by the ARD committee.

In the ARD process, a parent has the right to:

- Receive written notice of ARD meetings at least five school days in advance of the meeting;
- Receive written notice of what the school proposes for the child as a result of the meeting;
- Have the ARD meeting at a time and place convenient to the parent and the school. If neither parent can attend, their input may be provided through letters or phone calls, but the meeting can be held with or without them;
- Have an interpreter present if the parent is hearing impaired, or English is not his primary language;
- Bring one or more persons to the meeting to assist or represent him;
- Be actively involved at the ARD meeting where the child's educational plan and placement are determined;
- Discuss any service the parent believes will help the child;
- Receive information about the Texas School for the Blind and Visually Impaired if the child has a visual disability or the Texas School for the Deaf if the child is hearing impaired;
- Tape any ARD meeting after informing everyone present that the meeting is being recorded;
- Sign the individual education plan for the child, indicating the parent's presence, and note agreement or disagreement with the ARD committee's decisions and to the child's initial placement; and
- Give consent to the child's initial placement in special education.

The next step is the development by the ARD committee of an individual education plan for the child. It will state what services the child needs, and how, when, where, and by whom they will be provided.

If possible, there must be agreement on the plan between the parents and the other committee members. If not, the parents may request that the meeting be recessed for ten school days to gather more information. Then, if no agreement is reached, the school's plan will be followed. However, the parents retain the right to request mediation or a due process hearing, or file a complaint.

The ARD committee will decide which related services—such as transportation, therapy, counseling, occupational therapy, and parent training—the child needs. The school must pay all costs of such services and see that they are delivered by qualified people.

What guidelines are followed in determining where the child will receive his education?

Whenever possible, the child will be placed in a regular education classroom.

He will remain there so long as it's appropriate and as long as fulfilling his educational needs doesn't prevent other students in the class from learning.

The child has the right to be considered for a variety of educational settings, including those within his local school district, home instruction, special schools, or residential placements.

The child must be placed in a program as close to home as possible.

What if a parent believes his child needs educational services beyond the regular school year?

The regular school year is 175 days. In some cases, students may be eligible for educational services in excess of that. Parents can ask the ARD committee to consider this possibility. The decision should be based upon whether the child is likely to lose a significant amount of the skills acquired during the regular school year if he doesn't receive additional services.

What is the policy concerning discipline of children in special education?

Unless his individual education plan states otherwise, a special education student is subject to the same conduct requirements and discipline as any other student.

However, a special education student's plan may provide for additional or different disciplinary options.

May a special education student be expelled from school for inappropriate behavior?

Yes, but only if the ARD committee finds that the child's misbehavior wasn't due to his disability or inappropriate placement.

If a special education student is expelled from school, do all services extended to him stop?

No. The ARD committee will decide which services he'll continue to receive while expelled.

Does the school provide special education students assistance in preparing for adult living in addition to their individual education plans?

Yes. When the child turns sixteen, the school will develop an individual transition plan, designed to prepare the child for community living and work when he is no longer receiving public school services. The plan is reviewed each year, and parents may participate in its preparation.

What is the educational goal of special education?

To provide skills that will permit the children involved to lead productive lives. Depending upon the individual, the goal may be college, vocational school, or employment.

The goal should be a realistic one, based upon the child's abilities.

What must a special education student do to graduate?

The ARD committee must determine that he has completed an:

- Individual educational plan that contains the same requirements made of regular education students;
- Individual educational plan that leads to full-time employment, and acquired self-help skills that enable him to maintain that full-time employment without further help from the school district;
- Individual education plan that leads to mastery of employable skills, and acquired self-help skills which don't require further help from the school district;
- Individual education plan which leads to college, employment, or acceptance by an adult service agency; or
- Individual education plan and no longer meets age eligibility requirements.

If a child is transferring to a new school district, what should his parents do to make the transfer easier?

Ask his prior school to send his records to the new school as soon as possible. After he enrolls in the new school, an ARD meeting will be held. It may be possible to develop a new educational plan for the child and place him based on tests already available. If not, he may be placed temporarily and a new assessment made for another ARD meeting, which must be held within thirty school days.

If a child is in the custody of PRS, does the caseworker take the place of the child's parent at ARD meetings?

No. Neither state employees nor employees of private child care agencies receiving funds to care for the child may serve as surrogate parents at an ARD meeting. Foster parents, the child's attorney, CASA volunteers, or other persons the school district may find qualified—in addition to parents—are permitted to serve as surrogate parents when a child is in PRS custody.

Where can a parent go for additional information concerning the education of disabled children?

Call the Texas Education Agency's toll-free Parent's Special Education Hotline: 1-800-252-9668.

The Texas Association for Children and Adults with Learning Disabilities is located at 1011 W. 31st Street, Austin, Texas 78705. The telephone number is 1-512-458-8234.

The Texas Department of Mental Health and Mental Retardation also has a toll-free number: 1-800-252-8154.

Advocacy, Inc., can be reached at 1-512-454-4816.

If a parent believes a school district has violated the law concerning the education of a disabled child and wants to file a complaint, what should the parent do?

Talk with school officials and schedule an ARD meeting. If the dispute isn't resolved at that meeting, you may file a complaint with the Texas Education Agency at:

Division of Complaints and Administration
Texas Education Agency
1701 North Congress Avenue
Austin, Texas 78701

The complaint must be in writing, stating that the parent believes the school has violated state or federal law, and must request an investigation. It should include all facts upon which the complaint is based.

Usually, the investigation will be completed within 60 days, and the parent will receive a report. The parent may request that the report be reviewed by the office of the U.S. Secretary of Education.

Another option is to ask for a hearing with an impartial hearing officer, who has no connection with the school. The Commissioner of Education will appoint the hearing officer. The request for a hearing must be in writing, must explain the reason for the request, and must be sent to the school's board of trustees and delivered to the superintendent's office. A copy should be sent to:

Commissioner of Education
Texas Education Agency
1701 North Congress Avenue
Austin, Texas 78701

Be sure to file the request within 15 days of the action which is the basis of the complaint. If it's filed later, the right to a hearing still exists, but the school may already have acted on the ARD committee decision.

The hearing office will notify the parents of the date of the hearing. Both the school and the parents will have the opportunity to present their side of the issue.

It's not necessary for either side to be represented by a lawyer, but both sides may be if they choose. The school will almost certainly have an attorney. It's a formal hearing, and conducted under the rules of legal procedure for administrative hearings. Most parents would be at a disadvantage without their own attorney. Sometimes parents may be able to receive reimbursement for their attorney's fees. They should discuss this question with their attorney.

Each side must provide the other side all evidence they intend to present at least 5 days before the hearing. If they don't, the evidence can't be used at the hearing.

Each side may ask the hearing officer to subpoena witnesses. It's important to provide their names and addresses early.

Parents have the right to have the hearing at a reasonably convenient time and place, to have the child present, and to decide whether the hearing should be closed or open to the public.

Each side will receive a written copy of the hearing officer's decision within 45 days.

Usually, the child will remain in his present education placement until a final decision, including a decision about an appeal, is made.

Each side has a right to obtain a written transcript of the hearing and to appeal the decision to a state or federal district court.

The third choice of a parent who believes a school has discriminated is to file a complaint with the U.S. Department of Education. It must be filed within 180 days of the discriminatory act, although the agency may extend that time for good reason.

Parents don't have to go through the school's procedures for handling complaints, as set forth above, before filing directly with the U.S. Department of Education. However, if they do, the complaint filed with the U.S. Department of Education must be filed within 60 days of the last step in the state process.

For further information, and to obtain a discrimination complaint form, contact:

Office for Civil Rights, Region VI
U.S. Department of Education
1999 Bryan St., Ste. 2600
Dallas, Texas 75202
phone: 1-214-880-2459

The process used when a parent is dissatisfied with decisions concerning the child's education, but isn't claiming the school violated the law regarding discrimination, is called mediation. Specially trained, impartial third parties work with both sides to try to find a satisfactory solution.

Mediation may only be used if both sides agree to participate. If it doesn't result in agreement, the parent still has the right to request a hearing.

To request mediation, write to:

Division of Complaints and Administration
Texas Education Agency
1701 North Congress Avenue
Austin, Texas 78701

Can a parent consent to sterilization of a mentally or physically impaired child?

No. A person under the age of eighteen can't be sterilized in Texas. Neither a court nor the child's parents have the right to consent to such a sterilization unless it's medically necessary. "Medically necessary" doesn't mean necessary as a means of birth control, or for sanitation purposes.

Can a parent consent to an abortion for a pregnant mentally impaired child?

A tough question. Probably not. At least not unless it's medically necessary. A parent may not force a pregnant child to have an abortion without the child's consent. Texas courts, insofar as I know, have not addressed the question of who may consent to an abortion for an incompetent adult, much less a mentally impaired child.

What happens if a child who is mentally impaired or emotionally disturbed is accused of breaking the law?

See Chapter 28.

What financial assistance is available to disabled children?

Supplemental Security Income (SSI). This is a federal program, handled by the Social Security Administration. It provides financial assistance for children who are disabled and meet certain financial eligibility requirements. Those requirements can be very detailed, so it's best to check with Social Security to determine whether eligibility exists in a particular case.

22

Children and Drugs

It's hard for today's child to escape the effects of drugs. Many children are damaged, even before they're born, by their mothers' use of drugs during pregnancy.

Statistics show that parents who are involved with drugs are many times more likely to abuse or neglect their children. And they may not be physically or emotionally available for an infant's bonding, so necessary to her lifelong emotional health. Movie, TV, and sports heroes, as well as role models closer to home, provide children the pattern for their own behavior. When they abuse alcohol and drugs, it's small wonder that many children do likewise.

Alarming numbers of children become drug users, and many help perpetuate the cycle by selling drugs to others. Often, such activities bring them into early involvement with the law. About eight out of every ten children referred to juvenile authorities in Texas come from families which abuse alcohol or use other drugs.

Even if a child's parents are drug free and the child is neither a user nor dealer, she may still be touched by drugs. Many crimes and much of the violence in our society, of which children are often innocent victims, are drug induced or drug related.

And our society itself, for all of its crusades against drugs, may be sending children the message that drugs are actually okay.

Our children are growing up in a culture which teaches that all pain, however minor, must be avoided, whatever it takes. Children are bombarded with TV commercials—one out of every four offering a veritable smorgasbord of pills, liquids, and powders to ease any discomfort. And physicians dole out millions of psychoactive prescription drugs to calm us or elevate us or do whatever is indicated to "fix" whatever ails us. The message seems to be that life's too tough for the ordinary person to get through without a few pills.

How prevalent is drug use by adolescents?

A high school senior survey, conducted by the National Institute on Drug Abuse, provides statistics showing the extent, expressed as a percentage of those surveyed, to which the following drugs are used:

1. Marijuana/hashish	50.9%
2. Inhalants	15.9%
3. Hallucinogens	9.7%
4. Cocaine	16.9%
5. Heroin	1.1%
6. Stimulants (nonprescribed)	23.4%
7. Sedatives (nonprescribed)	10.4%
8. Tranquilizers (nonprescribed)	10.9%
9. Alcohol	91.3%

How many of those children's parents do you suppose would be astonished to learn that their child was among the users? It's only human to believe it's other people's children who use drugs. While it's important for parents to trust their children, they must be aware of the painful truth about drugs.

What is the average age at which children start using drugs?

A survey of children in state-operated institutions, conducted by the U.S. Justice Department, shows the average age at which the children surveyed began using drugs to be twelve.

What specific things can a parent do to prevent drug abuse?

- Be a positive role model; don't use illegal drugs;
- Know where your child is, who she's with, and what their plans are;
- Encourage your child to entertain her friends at home where you can supervise;
- Communicate with your child; everything you do to improve the relationship between you lessens the chances that she will turn to drugs;
- Talk with your child, and make it clear that drugs are not okay with you;
- Watch for indications of drug use;
- Get professional help at once if you suspect your child is using drugs or alcohol; and
- Educate yourself about drugs, and their use and effects. A well-informed parent is more likely to prevent drug use.

What is the drug most commonly used by children?

Experts say that the most dangerous drug for children, the one they use most widely, is alcohol.

Children are starting to use alcohol at a younger age. In the mid-1970's, the use of alcohol characterized a child's transition from adolescence to adulthood. Now, according to Dr. Donald Ian McDonald, Deputy Assistant to the President for Drug Abuse Policy, the average age when children first use alcohol is just over twelve. We're not talking about a taste of wine or a sip of beer. By age thirteen, 30 percent of our boys and 22 percent of our girls drink alcoholic beverages on a regular basis.

The younger a child is when she first starts to drink, the greater the risk of addiction, and the greater her exposure to the other dangers of alcohol consumption. The susceptibility of teens to alcohol is eight to ten times greater than for adults. A teen can become an alcoholic in a month, while it might take several years for an adult.

What is the likelihood that children will become involved with drivers under the influence of alcohol?

Here are two questions, asked of Florida high school seniors: "Have you ever driven while under the influence of alcohol or drugs?" (Forty-eight percent said "yes.") And "Have you ever ridden with a driver who was under the influence?" (Seventy-nine percent said "yes.")

Talk to your children. Help them plan what to do if they are faced with the prospect of riding with a driver who's been drinking. Children sometimes get themselves into frightening situations which they would like to avoid, if only they knew how.

Does the fact that one or more family members abuse alcohol have any relationship to whether a child becomes an alcoholic?

Yes. According to the *Metropolitan Judges Committee Report* to the National Council of Juvenile and Family Court Judges, children of families in which one or more adult members are alcoholics are at four times greater risk of becoming alcoholics themselves than the children of nonalcoholic families. Whether that is due to genetic or environmental factors, or some combination thereof, is still unresolved.

Parents are their children's primary role models. What they do, far more than what they say, sends a message to their children about what substances are safe and acceptable for *their own* use.

In a survey of drug use by young males in the United States, E. Hunter Hurst, in the *Juvenile and Family Court Newsletter*, reported a surprising finding: those young men whose fathers had the most prestigious occupations had the highest prevalence of drug use. I'm not sure what that suggests, but it's food for thought.

What other impact on children is caused by parental use of alcohol?

In a variety of studies, children of alcoholics have been found to have:

- Low self-esteem and low self-confidence;
- Higher anxiety levels;
- More problems in school; and
- A higher incidence of mental illness.

They are also more likely to:

- Be married before the age of sixteen;
- Be placed in a foster home;
- Commit delinquent acts;
- Be suicidal; and
- Be neglected or abused.

Children who do well despite having an alcoholic parent usually have some other positive adult role model to whom they are close. That person is there to say, "It's not your fault. You didn't cause it, and you can't fix it." That person provides consistency, honesty, and reliability, the basic ingredients for building trust.

What are the physical effects of alcohol on adolescents?

Alcohol is a depressant, soluble in water, which flows through all of the body's organs. It takes about one hour for the liver to metabolize one ounce of alcohol.

Alcohol sedates those parts of the brain which control judgment and impulse.

Adolescent bodies haven't yet fully matured, and they are more vulnerable to the toxic effects of alcohol, which may affect the development of the child's central nervous system.

The earlier the individual starts heavy drinking, the more rapid and serious is the damage to the liver and gastrointestinal system.

The three primary causes of death among adolescents—suicide, accidents, and homicide—are, in the great majority of cases, related to the use of alcohol.

In Texas, how old must a person be to legally buy, possess, or drink an alcoholic beverage?

Twenty-one.

Is the age requirement the same for both sexes?

Yes.

Is the requirement the same even if a person is married?

Yes.

If someone under twenty-one buys, has in her possession, or drinks an alcoholic beverage, what can the legal consequences be?

It's a misdemeanor. She may have to appear in court to answer charges. If so, the minor's parent or legal guardian must go to court with her if that person lives in the court's jurisdiction. If the parent or guardian lives outside the court's jurisdiction, legal, written notice must be sent. Only if the parent or guardian can't be found can these steps be waived. If the child is found guilty, the judge can impose a fine.

On the first conviction of a minor for purchase, consumption, or possession of an alcoholic beverage, the court can also order that she attend an approved alcohol awareness course instead of paying a fine. After the first conviction, if the minor is convicted of one of those offenses again, the court must order the child to attend such a course and pay a fine as well. The child must present proof to the court that the course was completed.

What if the child lives in a rural area, where no alcohol awareness program is readily available?

Then the judge may order the minor to perform eight to ten hours of community service instead of attending the program.

What if the child doesn't speak English?

If she requests, the course can be taught in another language.

Is it illegal for a parent to serve an alcoholic beverage to his or her own child under twenty-one?

No. An adult parent, guardian, adult spouse, or person to whom a court has committed a child may serve alcohol to the child. However, that person must be visibly present when the child possesses or drinks it or the possession or consumption is illegal.

Anyone other than one of the persons named above who buys alcohol for a child, or knowingly makes it available to her, commits a misdemeanor.

Are there any other times when it's legal for a person under twenty-one to drink alcohol?

No.

Can a parent legally serve alcohol to her children's under-twenty-one friends at a party in the parent's home?

No.

Is there any other time when it's legal for someone under twenty-one to have an alcoholic beverage in her possession?

Yes. Someone eighteen or older can do so in the course of her lawful employment.

A bar may hire a nineteen-year-old bartender to sell, prepare, and serve alcohol. But she can't serve herself a drink, nor can she take a few bottles to the beach to share with her friends.

Can the holder of a mixed-beverage permit hire a child under eighteen for other work which doesn't require her to sell, possess, or serve alcoholic beverages?

Yes.

What is the law regarding the sale of alcoholic beverages to someone under twenty-one?

It's a misdemeanor, punishable by a fine and/or a year in jail, to sell an alcoholic beverage to a person under twenty-one.

What if the seller didn't know the buyer was under twenty-one?

It's a misdemeanor even if the seller didn't know, provided she didn't know because of her own negligence. For example, she didn't ask for proof of age.

However, no crime is committed by the seller if the minor lied about her age and used an apparently valid ID with a physical description matching the buyer's appearance.

The underage buyer who lied about her age committed a misdemeanor.

Is there any way someone convicted just once of consuming, possessing, or purchasing alcohol before she was twenty-one can clear her criminal record?

Yes. Upon turning twenty-one she can apply to the same court and ask that her record and conviction be expunged.

Is there a legal way to prevent a bar from opening next door to a school?

Yes. When the owner of a business applies for her original alcoholic beverage license, if that business is situated within one thousand feet of a public school, the owner must give written notice of her application to the school before she files it, so that the school may be heard.

Counties and municipalities may enact regulations prohibiting the sale of alcoholic beverages within three hundred feet of a public school.

Is it legal for children to use tobacco?

A child under eighteen who is caught publicly smoking can be fined and can lose her driver's license. It's illegal.

What are the most common drugs, aside from alcohol, used by children, and what are their effects?

The following information is compiled from the Harris County Juvenile Probation Department handbook *Kids and Drugs: A Handbook for Parents.*

Marijuana
The drug is usually smoked in hand-rolled cigarettes. Marijuana is mentally addictive and physically harmful. It's a cancer-causing drug, and one marijuana cigarette can be as harmful as four tobacco cigarettes. Today's marijuana may be as much as twenty times stronger than the marijuana used twenty years ago.

Marijuana interferes with the body's ability to fight infection, and even small amounts can affect memory, vision, and judgment, and greatly impair motor skills.

Regular use of marijuana can cause brain damage and brain changes similar to those found in old age.

Marijuana is especially dangerous because of the widespread notion that it isn't harmful.

Cocaine

A white powder, cocaine can be smoked, snorted, or inhaled. It's a strong stimulant, highly addictive, and it can be deadly.

It increases heart rate, narrows the blood vessels, and raises blood pressure. It can cause seizures, heart attacks, breathing failure, and strokes.

Crack Cocaine

Crack comes in the form of small rocks. It's even more addictive than heroin. It can be smoked. All of the problems associated with cocaine are intensified for users of crack cocaine. It's a deadly drug. It kills.

Inhalants

The primary categories of inhalants are aerosol sprays (hair spray, spray deodorants, cooking oil sprays, and paint), solvents (glue, gasoline, paint, paint thinner, and typewriter correction fluid), and nitrates (liquid incense, room deodorizer, and nitrous oxide).

Inhalants are sniffed through the nose or inhaled through the mouth.

The inhalant may be sprayed into a plastic bag and sniffed, or onto a cloth and placed to the nose. A common method is to spray the substance into a soft drink can and inhale the fumes through the mouth.

Inhalants can cause physical and psychological problems, including permanent brain, liver, and nerve damage. Inhalants can be fatal, even with only one use.

Designer Drugs

The most common designer drug is MDMA, nicknamed XTC or "Ecstasy." It comes in powder or capsules, and can be inhaled, injected, or swallowed.

Ecstasy can cause extreme exhaustion, liver damage, amphetamine psychosis, and even death.

Steroids

Anabolic steroids are a manufactured form of testosterone, the male sex hormone. They may be injected or taken orally.

Young athletes sometimes take these because they stimulate the building of muscle. One survey estimates that 500,000 teenagers have used steroids. Chronic use of the drug can cause cancer, liver damage, heart disease, strokes, mental problems, and severe depression.

They often stunt growth when used by adolescents. They're addictive, and withdrawal symptoms often result from stopping their use.

The use of all these drugs is illegal.

How do you know if a child is using drugs?

A child using drugs may show some of the following signs:

- Personality changes. Is the child more irritable, secretive, hostile, depressed, withdrawn, or indifferent? Does she show sudden mood swings?
- Behavioral changes. Does she fail to complete her chores and homework? Does she forget to let you know she'll be late? Is she tardy for school? Has the child lost interest in her appearance?
- Changes in relationships. Does your child have new friends, and has she lost interest in her old ones? Is her relationship with you and other family members becoming more distant and guarded? Is communication more difficult than it once was?
- Changes in interests. Has your child lost interest in sports, school, hobbies, and other activities she once enjoyed? Does she spend a lot of time alone? Have her grades dropped?
- Physical and mental changes. Is there a weight change, increased or decreased appetite, hyperactivity, sluggishness, or changes in her speech? Does the child's ability to think seem slightly out of focus?

There are other, obvious clues.

- Are you starting to miss items that could easily be sold for cash?
- Have you found things like cigarette papers, burn holes in clothing, empty spray cans or small paint spots on clothing (from inhalants), or empty or watered-down bottles in the liquor cabinet?
- Does the child have large, unexplained amounts of cash? If so, she may be selling drugs.

The common thread is change. Any changes, particularly any negative changes in a child, should be carefully observed.

That's hard to do for several reasons. First of all, you've tried to teach your child about trust. You want her to trust you, and you believe you should show trust in her.

But trusting doesn't mean ignoring or denying what is right under your nose. A parent is responsible for a child's well-being. The very fact that a child is still a child means she still requires supervision and limits from her parents. Just as you check to make sure she takes her medicine when she's ill, and goes for dental checkups when she should, you're responsible for observing and addressing any symptoms that she may be using drugs.

Another reason it's not easy to evaluate whether changes signal drug use is that some changes are the very hallmark of transition from childhood to adolescence to adulthood. Those changes, though they are also sometimes painful, are necessary and normal.

No one ever said being a parent would be easy. Follow your heart, but don't forget to throw in a good measure of common sense.

And if you're in doubt, err on the side of protecting your child. Drugs don't always give you a second chance. They can kill.

What are the high-risk factors for drug abuse by children?

They are:

- Having a dysfunctional family;
- Alcohol or other drug use within the family;
- Tolerance of drug use by family members;
- A child's belief she doesn't fit into her family;
- Problems in school;
- Poor self-image;
- A child's belief she doesn't control her own destiny;
- Family problems;
- Parental indifference toward school;
- Early unacceptable behavior by the child;
- Alienation from others and from societal institutions; or
- Poor ability of the child to communicate with others, defer gratification, and adjust to new situations.

What should you do if you suspect your child is already using drugs?

Get professional help. Don't worry about what it may cost. Treatment is available from a number of sources, sometimes at little or no cost for those who can't afford to pay.

People who can point you in the right direction and provide you with information include:

- Physicians;
- County medical societies;
- County health departments;
- School counselors;
- Churches or synagogues;
- Alcoholics Anonymous (no fees, listed in the phone book);

- Narcotics Anonymous (no fees, listed in the phone book);
- Local chapters of the Council on Alcoholism & Drug Abuse;
- Palmer Drug Abuse Program;
- Association for the Advancement of Mexican-Americans;
- Elks Lodge Drug Awareness Committee;
- Cocaine Hotline, 1-800-COCAINE;
- Al-Anon, 1-800-252-6465;
- Alcohol Hotline, 1-800-252-6465;
- National Institute on Drug Abuse, 1-800-662-HELP; and
- National Parent's Resource Institute for Drug Education, 1-800-853-7867.

There are other individuals and groups who offer help. Don't be afraid to ask, and keep asking until you get the answers you need.

Parents may hesitate to seek help for children on drugs, afraid that revealing the problem may get them into trouble with the law.

Actually, failure to act increases the chance that a child's drug use may lead to other illegal behavior which will get her into even more serious trouble.

Besides, those who provide help to children with drug problems, and even prosecutors who usually might file a case against the child for drug use, are primarily interested in getting the child off drugs. If she hasn't committed any other offense, it's unlikely she'll have to go to court for drug use alone if she's getting help for the problem. At least, it's far less likely than if she were not.

All other considerations aside, it's the child's health, and perhaps her very life, we're talking about.

Is it illegal for a minor to use, possess, or sell marijuana, controlled substances, or dangerous drugs?

Obviously. The same law which applies to adults applies to children.

What is the penalty for giving or selling marijuana or a controlled substance to a person under eighteen?

It's a first-degree felony, punishable by life imprisonment, or a prison term of five to ninety-nine years plus a fine of up to $10,000.

23

Children and School

Where must a child enroll in school?

In the district where he resides with his parent, legal guardian, or spouse, or any other person having control over him by court order. If the child does not live with any such person, where he has established a separate residence. If a child under eighteen establishes a separate residence for the purpose of attending school, he must show that his presence there isn't for the primary purpose of participating in extra-curricular activities.

A child placed in temporary foster care by a state agency attends school in the district where his foster parents live. If he's in grades nine through twelve, a child in temporary foster care is entitled to complete high school at the school where he was enrolled at the time he went into foster care, free of tuition charges.

Is identification of a child required for him to enroll in school?

Yes. He must have a birth certificate or other proof of his identity and a copy of his records from the school he last attended. These documents must be provided within thirty days. If the child's name on the documents provided is different from that under which he's enrolled, the school will notify the Missing Children's Information Clearing House.

If the required documents aren't provided within thirty days, the school will ask the police to investigate whether the child has been reported missing. It's a criminal offense to refuse to provide the documents to a law enforcement agency or to provide false ones.

What shots is a child required to have for admission to a school in Texas?

See Chapter 20.

What is the law regarding truancy?

If a parent, managing conservator, or guardian doesn't make the child attend school, he'll receive written notice that the child must begin to attend school immediately. If the person, after receiving such notice, intentionally, knowingly, recklessly, or negligently fails to follow those instructions, he commits a misdemeanor. The school attendance officer will file a complaint against him, and he'll have to appear in court, where he may be required to pay a fine.

A child who is voluntarily absent from school without parental consent for ten days over a six-month period, or three days over a four-week period, may be required to go to court for conduct indicating a need for supervision. If a judge finds that the child was truant, the judge may enter "an appropriate order" (whatever that may be). If the judge finds that the child's truancy is "recurring" (which is not spelled out either), the judge can send the child to:

- A program leading to a General Equivalency Diploma (GED), which, as its name implies, is the equivalent of a high school diploma;
- An alcohol or drug abuse program; or
- A class for students at risk of dropping out of school. (The parent can be sent, too, and be held in contempt for failure to appear.)

The judge can also require the child to perform community service, to attend school without unexcused absences, or to be tutored.

Of primary importance to children, the judge can also suspend the child's driver's license.

Is a child who is late for school considered a truant?

Yes. Missing any part of a day is counted as an absence.

What if a parent is unable to make a child attend school?

If the parent can prove that's true, the judge won't find him guilty of the misdemeanor described above.

What are the legal excuses for missing school?

Absences are excused if they are due to:

- Illness of the child;
- Illness or death in the child's family;
- Quarantine of the child and his family;
- Weather or road conditions making travel dangerous;
- Some purpose approved by the child's teacher, principal, or school superintendent; or
- Other circumstances found to be reasonable and proper.

Does the state have any legal obligation to provide for the special education needs of children with physical, mental, or emotional problems?

Yes. Extensive legislation, at both the state and federal level, addresses this question. See Chapter 21.

What is the law regarding kindergarten and prekindergarten?

Each school district must provide free kindergarten to children who reside in the district and are at least five years old at the start of the school year.

If a school district has fifteen or more children at least four years old who are otherwise eligible for prekindergarten, it must provide prekindergarten classes. The district may provide such classes if there are fifteen or more eligible children who are at least three years old. To be eligible for prekindergarten, a child must be at least three years of age and:

- Unable to speak or comprehend the English language; or
- From a family whose income, according to State Board of Education standards, is at or below subsistence levels.

What is the minimum number of days a child must attend a given class during the school year in order to obtain credit for the class?

Usually, eighty days. However, under extenuating circumstances, an attendance committee may give class credit to a child who attended fewer than eighty days. The committee develops a policy concerning what constitutes extenuating circumstances, and the school board adopts policies establishing alternative ways for students to make up work or regain credit lost because of absence.

If a child is denied credit for a class by an attendance committee, he may appeal to the school board. The school board's decision can be appealed to a district court, where the matter will be tried by a judge.

May children legally be segregated by race in state-supported public schools?

No.

May a school board require that students who marry withdraw from school, or refuse married students admission to school?

No.

Are any special provisions made under the law for students who are pregnant or are parents?

Yes. A school district may provide a special program which includes both educational and support services for students who are pregnant or are already parents. However, at least 30 percent of the district's students must be of low socioeconomic status, as measured by State Board of Education standards. Such programs must include:

- Individual counseling, peer counseling, and self-help programs;
- Career counseling and job-readiness training;
- Day care for the students' children, on campus or nearby;
- Transportation of the students' children to and from the campus or day-care center;
- Transportation for students, as appropriate, to or from the campus or day-care center; and
- Instruction in child development, parenting, and home and family living.

Is the school required to provide a driver's education and traffic safety course?

Yes. A student who will be fifteen years old before the course ends may enroll in it. The course isn't required, but must be offered.

Is each school district required to provide tutorial services at the school?

Yes. A district may require a student whose grade in a reporting period is below seventy, on a scale of one hundred, to attend tutorials in the subject during the next reporting period. The school doesn't have to provide transportation for tutorials.

What is done to meet the educational needs of children who aren't fluent in English?

The law says that English shall be the basic language of instruction in all Texas schools.

However, the legislature has provided for the establishment of bilingual education and special language programs to satisfy the state policy of ensuring equal educational opportunity to every student.

How does a school district decide whether or not a bilingual or special language program must be offered?

A committee assesses each student at each school in the district during the first four weeks of the school year and determines the number of children at each school with limited English skills. They are then classified according to their primary language. If the committee reports to the school board that there are at least twenty students within the district of limited English ability, in any language classification in the same grade level, the district must offer a program to those students which provides:

- Bilingual education from kindergarten through elementary school; then
- Bilingual education, instruction in English as a second language, or transitional language instruction through the eighth grade; and
- Instruction in English as a second language in grades nine through twelve.

How are children taught in bilingual and English-as-a-second-language courses?

Bilingual education means that the child is taught basic skills in his own, primary language, and is also given carefully planned help with the mastery of English. The program for instruction in English as a second language consists of intensive instruction in English by teachers trained to recognize and deal with language differences. These programs must be designed to consider the student's learning experiences and incorporate cultural aspects of the student's background.

Are all subjects for such students taught as bilingual or English-as-a-second-language classes?

No. These students participate in regular classes in subjects such as art, music, and physical education. Elective courses may be taught in a language other than English, but that's not a requirement.

What about extracurricular activities?

Students in bilingual or English-as-a-second-language programs must be given a meaningful opportunity to fully participate with other students in all extracurricular activities.

How is the decision made whether to enroll a student in a bilingual or English-as-a-second-language program?

The State Board of Education adopts criteria to identify and assess students with limited English fluency who may be eligible for such programs.

If a student is found to be eligible, his parents are notified. They must approve of the child's entry into the program and his placement. Both the school district and the parents may appeal the decision. Parents must also be notified when the child is removed from the program.

Are bilingual and special language programs located in buildings separate from regular schools?

No. They must be conducted in regular public schools.

What about preschool for children with limited English skills?

Each district that is required to offer bilingual education must also offer a voluntary summer program for children with limited English skills who will be eligible for admission to kindergarten or first grade at the beginning of the next school year. Students attend one-half day, for eight weeks.

What about summer school for children with limited English skills?

The school district may provide a full- or part-time summer school, or extended day program of bilingual education, but isn't required to do so.

What is the law regarding the suspension of a student?

A student may be suspended for not more than six school days or may be removed to another school program. Suspension for more than six days during a given semester is considered an expulsion and must comply with the legal requirements for expulsion.

What must be established before a student may be suspended or removed to an alternative school?

It must be determined that:

• The student's presence in class presents a danger of physical harm to himself or others; or

- The student has engaged in serious or persistent misbehavior which violates the district's standard of student conduct, and the student had been advised of that standard of conduct.

If a student meets the above requirements for suspension, what happens?

The school must consider reasonable alternatives, including transfer to an alternative education program. If suspension is most appropriate, the child is suspended.

The child's parent has a right to notice of the suspension or transfer of the child to an alternative education program, and the right to be heard before the school board, whose decision is final and can't be appealed.

What is meant by alternative education program?

Some examples are:

- In-school suspension;
- Transfer to a different school;
- Transfer to a school-community guidance center; or
- Transfer to a community-based alternative school.

If a student is suspended, are the days of suspension considered excused or unexcused absences?

Excused absences, if he satisfactorily completes, within a reasonable timetable, the assignments he missed while suspended.

May a student be suspended for being absent or tardy?

No.

When may a teacher remove a child from class?

A teacher may send a student to the principal's office for appropriate discipline to maintain order in the class.

A teacher may remove a student from class if the teacher has kept a record of the child's repeated interference with the teacher's ability to communicate with the class.

There will then be a hearing with the principal, the parents, the child, and the teacher. After the hearing, the principal will suspend the student, transfer the student to an alternative education program, or return the student to class.

If the student is removed from class a second time in the same semester, only the school superintendent, upon the principal's request, may return him to class.

If removal happens a third time in the same semester, only the district board of trustees, at the superintendent's request, may return the student to class.

Are students' constitutional rights violated by a requirement that for them to enroll and attend class their hair may not be longer than a prescribed length?

No.

How does a student know what behavior constitutes grounds for suspension or expulsion?

The school board must have established rules and regulations regarding student conduct which are sufficiently specific to let students know what conduct is prohibited.

What is the difference between suspension and expulsion?

If a student is removed from classes for more than six days in one semester, and isn't transferred to an alternative education program, he's expelled. If he is removed from classes for six or fewer days during one semester, or is transferred to an alternative education program, he's suspended.

When may a student be expelled?

A student may be expelled if the student, while on school property, or while attending a school-sponsored or school-related activity, on or off school property:

- Assaults someone;
- Sells, gives, delivers, or is under the influence of illegal drugs;
- Sells, gives, or delivers an alcoholic beverage to another person, commits an illegal act while under the influence of alcohol, or possesses, uses, or is under the influence of alcohol on more than one occasion;
- Sniffs glue, aerosol paint, or other volatile chemical;
- Commits arson;
- Commits felony criminal mischief; or
- Possesses a firearm, illegal knife, club, or prohibited weapon.

I'm sure you know what a firearm is. An illegal knife is a:

+ *Knife with a blade over five inches long;*
+ *Hand instrument designed to cut or stab someone by being thrown;*
+ *Dagger;*
+ *Bowie knife;*
+ *Sword; or*
+ *Spear.*

It's a rare student who marches into school with a spear, but sometimes students carry knives with a blade of more than five inches. Many of them don't realize that such a weapon is illegal.

Now, what constitutes a "club"? A club is a:

+ *Blackjack;*
+ *Nightstick;*
+ *Mace (not the kind you spray); or*
+ *Tomahawk.*

As for "prohibited weapons," no surprises here. I doubt if anyone thinks it's okay for Johnny to stow a machine gun in his locker. Prohibited weapons are:

+ *Explosive weapons;*
+ *Machine guns;*
+ *Short-barrel firearms;*
+ *Firearm silencers;*
+ *Switchblade knives;*
+ *Brass or metal knuckles;*
+ *Armor-piercing ammunition;*
+ *Chemical dispensing devices (the kind you spray); and*
+ *Zip guns.*

What happens if a child placed in an alternative education program continues to misbehave?

He can be expelled.

For how long may a student be expelled?

The school board sets the time. It may not extend beyond the end of the current school year unless the conduct involved occurred during the last six weeks of the school year. Then, it may extend beyond the end of the current school year, but not beyond the end of the first semester of the next school year. If a student is expelled for first-time use or possession of alcohol, he can't be expelled beyond the end of the semester unless the offense occurred in the last six weeks of the semester. Then he can be expelled until the end of the next semester.

Does the student have a right to a hearing before he's expelled?

Yes. Before he's expelled, the student must be given a hearing which meets constitutional standards of "due process," or fairness.

What happens if a student who has been expelled enrolls in another school district before his expulsion expires?

The original district provides a copy of the expulsion order, along with a copy of the student's school record, to the new school district. The new district may allow the child to remain in his new classes or require that he complete the term of expulsion before entering the new school.

Does a juvenile court become involved when a child is expelled?

Yes. Every child expelled must be referred to juvenile court for the judge to decide what action, if any, is required.

What if a judge orders an expelled student to attend classes as a condition of probation?

The school district must admit the student, but the student isn't immune from further suspension or expulsion.

Is it legal for a student in public school to possess an electronic pager while on school property, or while attending a school-sponsored or school-related activity, on or off school property?

No. There is an exception, if the student is present in his capacity as an active member of a voluntary fire fighting organization or a voluntary emergency medical service organization. A person who discovers a pager in a student's possession is required to report it. The pager will be forfeited, and the student will be subject to discipline.

Must school districts establish a program especially designed for gifted or talented students?

The district must adopt a process to identify such students. "Gifted and talented" refers to a student who, because of his outstanding mental ability, is capable of high performance. His potential may be in the areas of general intellectual ability, specific subject matter aptitude, ability in creative and productive thinking, or leadership ability. It doesn't include above average physical abilities or potential. An athlete, even one with Olympic potential, is not what they're talking about.

Once the identification process has taken place, the district must establish a program for those students at every grade level. It may do so in cooperation with one or more other districts.

May a student legally be exempted from taking a final exam?

Not if any other student is required to take it.

Under what circumstances are students "skipped" to the next grade?

School districts must develop advance placement exams for each primary grade and for each secondary school academic subject. The exams are supposed to test the student's knowledge of the information presented in the corresponding grade or subject. Such exams must be given at least once a year.

A student in a primary grade is given credit for a grade level, and advanced one grade, if:

- He scores in the ninetieth percentile or above on each section of the exam; and
- The school district representative recommends his advancement; and
- His parent or guardian gives written approval.

A student in the sixth grade or above is given credit for a subject if he scores in the ninetieth percentile or above. If he is given credit, the examination score will be entered in his transcript.

May school districts take part in missing-child prevention and identification programs, even if it means fingerprinting and photographing children?

Yes. They aren't required to do so, but they may. However, a child's parent or guardian must give written consent for such fingerprinting and photography to occur, and the fingerprints and photographs may only be used to identify or locate a missing child, never as evidence in any criminal or juvenile case against the child. Of course, a student's picture may be taken for use in a school yearbook.

May the school give a child medicine?

Each school district develops its own policy about administering medicine to children. With the adoption of such a policy, the school district becomes immune from civil liability for damages or injury resulting from the administration of medicine to a child, provided the parent has given the district written permission to administer medicine and the medicine appears to be in its original container and properly labeled. This doesn't mean the school district is immune from liability for damages or injuries resulting from gross negligence.

What about a student's First Amendment right to freedom of speech?

In one case, a school district's regulation providing for expulsion of students who engaged in major disruptive behavior, such as sit-ins, group violence, or desecration of the American flag, was upheld.

Serious disciplinary action concerning exercise of freedom of speech must be based on the standard that the prohibited speech constitutes substantial interference with normal operation of the school.

Another case held that expulsion of students for producing and distributing a newspaper critical of school officials violated the students' First Amendment rights to freedom of speech. Their conduct didn't substantially interfere with the normal operation of the school; they didn't interrupt class, or distribute the papers during school hours, and they asked fellow students not to take the papers into the school building.

Is hazing legal?

No. It's a criminal offense in any public or private school, college, or university in Texas.

What is hazing?

Any knowing, intentional, or reckless act—directed against a student for the purpose of anything related to membership in an organization having members who are students—that endangers his mental or physical health or safety.

What are some examples of hazing?

- Physical acts such as striking, electrical shocks, or branding;
- Physical activities such as depriving someone of sleep, exposing him to the elements, confining him in a small space, or making him do excessive calisthenics;
- Forcing someone to eat, drink alcohol, or use drugs;
- Activities which threaten the student with ostracism, extreme mental distress, or humiliation; or
- Any activity that induces a student to commit a criminal offense.

Must the student doing the hazing have to intend harm for the hazing to be an offense?

No. He must only knowingly, intentionally, or recklessly commit the act which constitutes hazing.

Can hazing be an act committed by a person acting alone, or must it be committed while acting with others?

It can be either.

If a person knows that hazing is planned, or has already occurred, what is his responsibility?

If he has firsthand knowledge of such hazing, or a plan to engage in hazing, he must report it in writing to school officials. If he doesn't, he has committed a misdemeanor.

Must actual damage to a student's mental or physical health or safety result for hazing to have occurred?

No. An act which carries the risk of such damage is enough.

If the student who was hazed consented to the activity, is it still a criminal offense?

Yes.

Is it ever legal to bring alcoholic beverages into a school, or onto school grounds where a school activity is being held?

No. It's a misdemeanor.

Is it ever lawful for a child to possess a weapon on school grounds?

No. It's a felony.

What if a student brings a weapon to school for self-protection?

Children often say they brought a weapon to school because other students had threatened them and they were afraid. That may be true, but it isn't an acceptable reason for bringing a weapon to school, and the offense is still a felony. Children who are threatened by other students should tell school authorities and their parents and let them handle the problem.

Is it legal for a student to belong to a gang?

In schools below the college level, supported even in part by public funds, it's illegal to belong to a secret society or group, composed wholly or in part of students, which admits members based upon the decision of its existing members rather than the free choice of any student who is qualified by school rules to fulfill the aims of the organization.

For example. Assume there's an organization called the Aryan Knights, formed at a school, which has secret membership rules, meetings, and signs. A student can't be a member of the Aryan Knights unless the membership votes to accept him. Student membership in such an organization is illegal in Texas.

It's also illegal to try to persuade someone to join such an organization.

What can happen to a student who joins, promises to join, or tries to get someone else to join such an organization?

He can be sent to an alternative education institution.

Are there any exceptions in the law?

Yes. If the organization is one dedicated to public welfare, membership is legal. Examples include the Boy Scouts, Girl Scouts, Hi-Y, Girl Reserves, DeMolay, Rainbow Girls, Pan American Clubs, scholarship societies, and other educational organizations sponsored by state or national educational authorities.

When may a school official or teacher legally search a student?

The U.S. Supreme Court has said that two questions must be considered in deciding whether a search violates a student's constitutional right against unreasonable search and seizure.

The court must first determine whether it was reasonable to initiate the search. It was justified if there were reasonable grounds for suspecting the search would turn up evidence the student had violated, or was violating, either the law or the rules of the school.

The court must then decide whether the scope of the search, as actually conducted, was reasonably related to the circumstances which justified the search in the first place. A search is permissible in its scope if the measures used are reasonably related to the objectives of the search and aren't excessively intrusive in view of the age and sex of the student and the nature of the offense. To put it another way, you can't use an elephant gun to kill a mouse.

What is the status of prayer in the public schools?

The First Amendment of the United States Constitution forbids the establishment of religion by the State. For a number of years, the courts have said that prayer as a part of the school day is unconstitutional because it tends to "establish" religion. It isn't allowed.

Is prayer ever allowed at school functions, like sporting events, programs, or graduation ceremonies?

One federal case permitted prayer at a graduation exercise, but under very strict guidelines. Another federal case found a prayer, in the form of a song sung at a football game, to be unconstitutional.

A public school may not endorse one religion over another. It may not support any religion whatever. Some guidelines are:

- There must be a legitimate, nonreligious purpose for the prayer (I'm not certain what a nonreligious reason for prayer might be);
- The primary effect of the prayer must be neither to promote nor hinder religious belief (I'm not making this up); and
- The prayer must not create excessive involvement between the school and religious matters.

It's a difficult situation, trying to determine when and if prayer is okay and when it's not. Expect more cases on the issue soon. Meanwhile, if you want to pray at school, don't move your lips, don't make a sound, and don't tell.

24

Children Who Work

A child's first job is to be a child, to experience and learn the lessons of childhood. So, a child must play and go to school and interact with other people. All of this is a part of her preparation for becoming a happy, productive adult. This is the work a child must do, and it should take precedence over any other job she may be offered.

Work is an important part of our lives as adults. When we meet, one of the first things we ask one another is, "What do you do?" Our work is vital to most of us as a source of income to provide for ourselves and our families. But far more, our jobs build self-esteem, give us a sense of purpose, and engage our interests and abilities. Our culture approves of those who work hard and do their jobs well. We see them as contributing to our society.

One sign of a child's transition to adulthood is her first job. It brings a feeling of pride that may never be exceeded. Whether it's a paper route, baby-sitting, or sacking groceries, it's a signal that the child is growing up. She's trusted to carry out responsibilities. And her services are worth money to someone. How incredible! For a child, just as for anyone else, work can provide a sense of self-worth, being needed, and being a part of the community. The early jobs children have teach important lessons and serve as a dress rehearsal for their careers as adults.

Do you remember your first job? Mine was giving speech lessons to younger children for fifty cents an hour. Now, I know my student's mothers just saw me as a baby-sitter with a twist. But I felt I had an important skill to impart. That first job taught me I loved working with children.

A few years later I had a summer job, selling hats in a department store. A supervisor heard my response one day when a woman asked how a particular hat suited her. My honest reply was that it made her look like a turtle peeking from beneath its shell.

I was fired. But I learned that tact is an important asset when dealing with the public. I also determined that my destiny was not in sales. Certainly not if I had to sell hats.

Yet even work, which is inherently healthy and rewarding, can be damaging under certain circumstances.

Once, very small children were employed as a matter of course, working for pitiful wages in oppressive conditions. Their education was interrupted, and they were robbed of their childhood.

Today we realize that, before they engage in adult work, children must be allowed to be children. Today's child labor laws protect our children from the abuse and exploitation of the past.

Who makes the rules regarding employment of children?

The Child Labor Act is a law passed by the Texas Legislature. That act, and rules set forth by the Texas Workforce Commission, make up our state laws. There may also be local ordinances passed by counties or cities which affect the employment of children.

What is the minimum age at which a child may be legally employed?

Generally speaking, it's an offense to employ a child under fourteen.

Are there laws which govern the number of hours a child may work?

Yes. It's an offense to employ a fourteen- or fifteen-year-old child for more than eight hours a day, or forty-eight hours per week.

Are there laws regarding which hours of the day or night a child may be employed?

Yes. Usually, it's an offense for the employer of a fourteen- or fifteen-year-old who is also enrolled in school to work the child between 10:00 P.M. and 5:00 A.M. on a day followed by a school day or between midnight and 5:00 A.M. on a day not followed by a school day, or, during the summer if the child is not enrolled in school, between midnight and 5:00 A.M. on any day.

Are there any exceptions which would permit a child to work longer hours?

Yes. The Texas Workforce Commission has rules for deciding whether a hardship exists in a particular child's case. If a child's situation falls within those rules, the law about hours explained above doesn't apply.

Does the Texas Workforce Commission have the right to inspect businesses where children may be working, to see that they are in compliance with the law?

Yes.

Are there any types of employment in which the Texas Workforce Commission may prohibit or restrict the employment of children?

Yes. TWC may adopt rules preventing or restricting employment of children fourteen through seventeen in any occupation which has been declared hazardous by an agency of the federal government and which the TWC decides is particularly hazardous to children.

Does this mean that the people who employ all of those cute five- and six-year-old children in movies filmed in Texas are breaking the law?

No. There's a special law permitting children under fourteen to be employed as actors or performers in motion pictures, radio, television, or theatrical productions.

Does the law forbidding employment of children under fourteen, and setting the hours children fourteen and older may work, apply in all situations?

No. The law doesn't apply when the child is:

- Employed in a nonhazardous occupation, under the direct supervision of the child's parent, or an adult having custody of the child, in a business owned or operated by the parent or custodian;
- Delivering newspapers;
- Participating in a work-study program that's supervised by the school and approved by TWC;
- Working in agriculture at a time the child isn't legally required to be in school;
- Employed in a rehabilitation program supervised by a county judge; or
- Engaged in casual, nonhazardous employment which doesn't endanger the health, safety, or well-being of the child, with parental consent.

25

Children and Their Property

Ownership of property is one of the areas where the rights of children differ most significantly from the rights of adults.

A child can't own property in his own name. An adult must hold it in trust for him, and use it in specific ways for his benefit. A child doesn't even own the wages he earns. His parents have the right to that money.

Legislators apparently recognized that children lack the judgment to manage and preserve their property. They also lack the maturity to meet the responsibilities which property ownership imposes. So, for their own benefit, that responsibility was delegated to those responsible for the children themselves. Lawmakers also may have thought that those who must pay to support a child are due reimbursement from money earned by the child or received from his property.

All of that matters when we're talking about inheritance, trust funds, Social Security benefits, or other items that spell relatively big bucks.

That said, never share the awful truth with Mary Lou that her doll isn't really hers, or with Billy that you are the true and lawful owner of his bike.

Can a child ever legally manage his own property?

Not unless his disabilities of minority have been removed by a judge, or he's married. One of the duties of a parent, under the Texas Family Code, is to manage the estate of a child until he's eighteen. So long as parents are married, they have equal rights to manage the child's estate.

Can a child legally execute a contract?

If his disabilities of minority have been removed by a judge or he was ever married, yes. Otherwise, no.

May another person legally bind a child to a contract?

Yes. But this is a touchy area. The person must have been given authority by a court to act in this capacity for the child.

What happens to a child's property when his parents are divorced?

The judge will decide which parent will manage the child's property. We're talking about substantial property, not clothes or toys. Such property is usually described in any lawsuit affecting the child.

Does a child have the right to manage money he earns?

No. His parents have that right.

Is child support paid to a managing conservator on behalf of a child the property of the child or the managing conservator?

The managing conservator has the right to use such money as he believes best. However, the money is supposed to be used for the benefit of the child.

Are Social Security benefits payable to a child his property or the property of his parents or managing conservator?

They're the child's property, but the custodial parent or managing conservator has the right to use the funds as that person sees fit for the child's benefit. If the child is removed from the home of the parent or managing conservator by court order, the benefits are supposed to follow the child to the new managing conservator.

PRS is supposed to inform the Social Security Administration when it removes a child from his home, and the child's benefits are supposed to follow him.

If a child suffers personal injuries as a result of the willful or negligent act of someone else, can he sue for damages?

Yes, through an adult. If he has a legal guardian, appointed by a judge, that person will sue on his behalf. If not, through his parent, who is acting as his "next friend." In most cases, a child can only sue in this manner.

An attorney will be appointed by a judge to represent the child if the parent also has an interest in the case which might differ from the child's.

The attorney must approve any agreed settlement of the child's claim. If the parent has no personal interest in the settlement, it isn't necessary to appoint an attorney for the child.

What happens if a child wins a lawsuit for money damages?

The child can't receive the money directly if he's under eighteen. One of three things can happen to the money he's been awarded.

- A parent or other suitable adult may ask to be appointed guardian of the child's estate.

  If the child is at least fourteen, he can choose his guardian, subject to the court's approval.

  An attorney ad litem will be appointed to represent the child's interests on the question of guardianship.

  Whoever is named guardian of the estate will manage this money, under the court's supervision, until the child turns eighteen.

- If the money awarded the child is not more than $25,000, and no one has asked to be appointed guardian of the estate, the money can be deposited with the county clerk, who will invest the money for the child until he's eighteen.

- A special trust can be established for the child if the child has no guardian and the court decides a trust would be in the child's best interest. A Texas bank or trust company will be named trustee in such an instance.

Can a parent waive or release a child's cause of action against another person?

No. Any attempt by a parent to sign a release or give up a child's right to sue is void.

Can a parent ever sell a child's real property without being appointed guardian of the child's estate?

Yes. But the parent must ask a court for permission to do so, and can receive such permission only if the amount involved is not over $25,000. If it's more than that, the parent must ask to be appointed guardian of the child's estate.

If a parent tries to sell the child's interest in real estate without following these steps, the sale is void, even if the parent is appointed guardian at a later date.

Money received for the child in a valid sale of his property will be deposited with the court and may be withdrawn only as the court permits.

Can a child execute a will?

Only if he's been married, had his disabilities of minority removed for general purposes, or is a member of the armed forces of the United States or the maritime service.

If a child's parent dies without a will, will the child automatically inherit the parent's property?

Texas is a community property state. That means that when two people marry, they will have both separate and community property. His, hers, and theirs.

A person's separate property is:

- That which he owned or claimed to own before the marriage;
- That which he acquired during the marriage as a gift, or through a will or other inheritance; and
- The money he received as damages for personal injuries sustained during the marriage, except for damages awarded for loss of earning capacity.

All property acquired by either or both persons during the marriage, other than separate property as described above, is community property.

When a parent dies without a will, the rules regarding what his children will inherit are different for separate and community property.

The community property of a parent who was married at the time of death and left no will, is distributed as follows:

- One-half of all of the community property, real or personal, will go to the surviving spouse.
- The remaining half of the community property will be distributed equally among the children of the deceased parent. (If a child is deceased, then his share will be divided equally among his children.)

The separate property of a parent is distributed as follows:

- The surviving spouse receives one-third of the personal property and what is called an "estate for life" in one-third of the real property. After the surviving spouse's death, that one-third "estate for life" interest in the real property goes to the children and their descendants.
- All other separate property is divided equally among his children and their descendants. If a deceased child left children of his own, they will divide the share that child would have received had he lived.

All of the property of a parent who was not married at the time of his death, and had no will, will be divided equally among the children. And once again, if a deceased child left children of his own, they will divide the share that child would have received had he lived.

Can a parent execute a will which leaves nothing to a child, or which leaves different percentages of his property to different children?

Yes. If a parent dies without a valid will, the law has rules, written in stone, which define exactly how his property will be divided. A judge can't change those rules. However, when a parent executes a will, he has absolute power over how his property will be distributed. He can leave it all to the children. But he can, if he wishes, leave everything to Linda Sue down at the disco, or the SPCA, or the Society for Intergalactic Travel. The parent can't give away his spouse's one-half of the community property, but otherwise he can do as he pleases.

He can, that is, if:

- The will was executed properly;
- He had testamentary capacity—that is, he wasn't too dotty to know what he was doing; and
- He didn't sign the will because of fraud, duress, or undue influence.

If a parent executes a will leaving everything to his children, and then dies before they reach the age of eighteen, what happens?

Since a child can't legally own property if he's under eighteen, it must be held in trust by a trustee. It's wise to establish a trust, within the parent's will, spelling out who the trustee will be, what powers he will have, and how the property and its income are to be used. If the will doesn't contain such a trust, a judge will have to create one, select a trustee, and decide the trust provisions. As you can imagine, this will be more expensive for the estate and isn't likely to reflect what the parent would have wanted.

If a parent dies without a will, the same thing is true. Property passing to children under such circumstances must be held in trust for them until they're eighteen. Again, this must be handled by a judge. Obviously, it's much wiser and less expensive to execute a will.

May a parent provide that money left to his children in his will be held in trust until they're over eighteen?

Yes. I once prepared a will for a man who insisted that his children's inheritance be held in trust until they reached the age of forty-five! His confidence in their judgment was tentative, at best. But it's common for wills to provide that children won't receive the money from their trusts until they're twenty-one, twenty-five, or even thirty years old.

Is there any other way to protect an inheritance a parent leaves to a minor child?

Yes. Within the trust created in the will, a parent can provide safe-guards against a child's using his inheritance as security for a debt before the child actually receives the inheritance. The funds are protected from the child's creditors by what is called a "spendthrift" provision. In practical terms, the car dealer can't look to the trust fund Junior will receive one day as security for the new Corvette Junior bought before he was entitled to his inheritance.

What rights does a child have to inherit from his parents in Texas?

A parent can execute a will leaving his children part or all or none of his estate. Where there's a valid will, it controls how an estate is distributed. However, where no valid will exists, these are the rights of inheritance which children have regarding their parents:

- A child has the right to inherit from his biological mother;
- A child has the right to inherit from his presumed father; see Chapter 2;
- An adopted child has the right to inherit from his adoptive parents, provided he was adopted as a minor;
- An adopted child keeps the right to inherit from his natural parents, unless a judge rules otherwise, but they have no right to inherit from him;
- A child has the right to inherit from a father whose paternity has been established by a court;
- A child with no presumed father, and whose biological father's paternity has never been established by a court, has the right to inherit from his biological father if the father signed a statement of paternity;
- A child with no presumed father, and no father whose paternity has been established by a court or who has executed a statement of paternity, still has the right to inherit from his biological father.

  The law now provides for such children to share the same rights of inheritance from their biological parents as children whose father's paternity has been established. It's necessary, however, to prove to the judge of a probate court, by clear and convincing evidence, that the deceased was the child's biological father. With DNA testing, that's no longer such a big hill to climb.

May a child be a witness to a will?

Yes, if he's at least fourteen years old.

What happens if a child is born or adopted after his parent executed his final will?

Assume that Mother Jones had two children, Abel and Baker, at the time she signed her will. Later, little Charles is born. Still later, Mother Jones dies in a car wreck without having changed her will to include Charles. Does little Charlie inherit anything?

If Mother Jones didn't leave anything to Abel and Baker when she executed her will, then Charles will take that part of her separate and community property he would have received had she had no will at all when she died.

If any part of the property was left to his father, then Charlie won't receive that portion.

If Mother Jones did make provisions in her will for either or both Abel and Baker, who were living when she signed it, then:

- Charlie's portion of her estate is limited to the same portion she left to Abel and Baker.

- Charlie will receive the share he would have received if she had included him in the will and given him the equal of what she left to the other children.

- If feasible, Charlie's interest will also be of the same character as that of the other children. For example, if Abel and Baker are given absolute title to real estate, or if limitations are put on those titles, Charlie will have that same type of absolute title or limitation on his share of the property.

26

Benefits Available to Children

One of the characteristics of a civilized society is that it provides for the basic needs of those who can't do so themselves. Like children. If their parents, or other adults close to them, can't fulfill a child's requirements for food, clothing, shelter, and medical care, then society must do so. Our conscience demands it.

Debate will probably continue for years to come over the extent that we, through our government, can or should take care of adults who aren't making it on their own.

But few are so callous that they would turn away a hungry child. And so we've made provision in our law to look after children in need.

And will these children grow up to perpetuate the cycle of dependence on public assistance? I don't believe that people want to live off the benevolence of others. I think most people really do want to take care of themselves. As children grow, we must provide them the education and guidance to show them how, and to afford them the opportunity to do so.

What are some of the primary government benefits available to children?

- Supplemental Security Income (SSI);
- Social Security (OASDI);
- Temporary Assistance to Needy Families (TANF), which replaced Aid to Families with Dependent Children (AFDC);
- Food stamps;
- Enforcement of child support;
- Benefits for children with disabilities (see Chapter 21); and
- Medicaid.

What are the requirements to qualify for TANF?

This is a program established by the federal government and administered by the states. It provides money to needy families with children.

Children of families with low income, who lack the financial support of at least one parent due to death, disability, or abandonment, may qualify. The family must apply to the Texas Department of Human Services.

How is the amount of the TANF payment determined?

By looking at the family income and other resources, allowable deductions, and size of the family. The family must have at least one minor child. Contact the Texas Department of Human Services to learn more.

How is TANF affected by a child support order?

A person who applies for TANF must sign over to the state all rights to receive child support. If there's no existing order for child support, the Texas attorney general's office will try to find the absent parent, and establish an order for child support through the court. If there's a valid support order, but the parent isn't current with payments, the attorney general's office will go to court to try to enforce the order.

The support payment will go to reimburse the state and federal government for TANF payments, up to the amount of TANF received by the parent. Currently, the parent does receive the first $50 of any such child support payment.

Is the child's eligibility for TANF affected by who she lives with?

Yes. A child who is living with a nonrelative isn't eligible for TANF, even if she lives there because of a court order. People who are relatives include: parents, grandparents, great- and great-great-grandparents, brothers or sisters, half-brothers or -sisters, first cousins, nephews, nieces, and the spouses or ex-spouses of those persons.

Remember, if the child lives with a relative other than a parent, the attorney general will seek child support from the parent if the relative applies for TANF, unless the parents are already paying at least minimum child support to the relative.

What are food stamps?

They are stamps which may be exchanged at participating stores for food. This is a program established by the federal government to provide help to low-income families. How many stamps a family receives depends on the size of the family and its income.

If the family receives TANF or SSI benefits, there's a presumption that it also qualifies for food stamps. If it doesn't receive these benefits, the family may still qualify for food stamps by falling within poverty-level standards of the federal government.

When is a child eligible for OASDI (Social Security) benefits?

The child must:

- Be the child, stepchild, grandchild, or stepgrandchild of the person insured under OASDI; and
- Be under eighteen, disabled, or a full-time student who has completed the requirements for graduation from high school by age nineteen.

If a child meets these requirements, she's entitled to one-half of the insured's primary insurance amount if the insured is still living, and three-fourths of that amount otherwise.

Neither the size nor income of the child's family is considered.

What is Medicaid?

A federal program providing free medical services to those who qualify. Persons who qualify for SSI qualify for Medicaid, as do those who receive TANF. However, even if children do not receive TANF or SSI, they may still qualify for Medicaid.

What financial assistance is available to disabled children?

Supplemental Security Income (SSI), a federal program handled by the Social Security Administration. The eligibility requirements can be very detailed, and it's best to check with a Social Security office to determine whether eligibility exists in any given case.

The definition of disability for children under SSI requires that a child have a physical or mental condition that can be medically proven and which results in marked and severe functional limitations. It also requires the physical or mental condition to last at least one year or to be expected to cause the child's death. A child may not be considered disabled if she's working at a job considered to be substantial work.

There are specific federal guidelines used to determine whether a child meets that definition.

27

Children and Driving

What fills a child with greater joy, or strikes his parents with more utter terror, than the day the child first gets his driver's license!

And the first time he takes the car out alone? On a date!? At night!!?

His folks age ten years, especially if he's a few minutes late getting home.

And that doesn't even begin to address what his date's parents are thinking.

Never mind. It's another sign they're growing up. And that's necessary.

I had a friend whose daughter was off to the prom under just such circumstances. She'd warned her daughter of every possible danger, given every possible instruction, and then sat back to wait. Anxiously. Turned out the car didn't crash, the boy behaved himself, and none of the disasters she'd imagined came to pass. But the girl was bitten by a poisonous snake as she stepped from the car at her front curb. So help me, it's true. Fortunately, her daughter is fine, now, but it just goes to show that most of the things we worry about never happen.

Who would have ever thought to warn, "Watch out for rattlesnakes!"?

How old must a child be to get a driver's license?

Eighteen.

Is there any way for a child under eighteen to obtain a driver's license?

Yes. If he is sixteen or seventeen. Here's how:

- He enrolls in a driver's training course and receives a passing grade;
- He makes sure he has written proof he's complied with the education requirements;
- He submits the required application with parent or guardian's signature, and his birth certificate or other proof of age and identity; and
- He pays a fee, then takes the required test and passes it.

Are there ever circumstances which would allow someone under sixteen to obtain a driver's license?

Yes. A fifteen-year-old can get a driver's license if:

- He's completed and passed an approved driver's training program;
- He's passed the visual, written, and driving portions of the driver's test; and
- The Department of Public Safety finds that one of the following is true:
  + *Failure to issue the license would work an unusual economic hardship on the child's family; or*
  + *The license should be granted because of sickness or illness in the child's family; or*
  + *The license should be granted because the child is regularly enrolled in a vocational education program which requires a driver's license.*

How old must a child be to take a driver's education course?

Fourteen.

Can the driver's education course requirement ever be waived for someone under the age of eighteen?

Yes, if the Department of Public Safety finds that the child must drive in order to help with family illness, disability, death-related emergency, or economic problems, a sixty-day permit may be issued, subject to renewal every sixty days for so long as the emergency exists.

Is a driver's license required to operate a motorcycle, motorscooter, or moped?

Yes.

How old must a child be to obtain such a license?

Fifteen.

What are the requirements to get a license to operate a motorcycle?

A child must complete and pass an approved motorcycle operator training course and must meet the same educational requirements used for a driver's license application.

What are those educational requirements?

The child must have received a high school diploma or GED, or be currently enrolled in school and have attended school at least eighty days in the semester immediately prior to applying for a license, or have spent the past forty-five days in a GED program.

Is a road test or driving test required for a motorcycle license?

Yes. And the applicant must bring along a car and driver to provide transportation for the examiner observing the test.

Is a road test required to obtain a license to operate a moped?

No, only a written examination on traffic laws applicable to the operation of mopeds.

Do you have to have any kind of license to operate a car while you're in the process of learning to drive?

Yes, a learner's permit.

What can happen to a person under seventeen who violates traffic laws?

He can be fined up to $100 or ordered to perform community service.

This is the one time when a child is eligible for bail, just like an adult, and when he may be locked up for failing to make bond, just like an adult. If he is jailed, he must be held in a facility separate from adult prisoners.

Can a juvenile dispose of his traffic offense by paying a predetermined fine?

No. He must appear in court with his parent or guardian.

When can a child's driver's license be revoked?

When an adult's can. Additionally, if a child appears before a juvenile court judge who finds he committed either a misdemeanor or a felony, his driving privileges can be suspended for up to six months. If the child is placed on probation, and violates his rules of probation, his driving privileges may be suspended up to an additional six months. This means that if he has a driver's license, he loses it for that period of time. If he doesn't have a license, none can be issued to him for that same period of time.

Is there any special law regarding driver's licenses of children who have committed drug-related offenses?

Yes. If a juvenile court judge finds a child was driving while intoxicated, or used, possessed, manufactured, or delivered marijuana or any controlled substance, the judge is required by law to suspend the child's driving privileges until he's seventeen years old, or for one year, whichever is longer.

If a child's driving privileges are suspended for a drug-related offense, can he get a provisional or occupational license for emergency situations or for driving to his job?

Yes, if he would otherwise qualify. He must file a motion with the court.

Is it legal for insurance companies to charge higher rates for liability and collision coverage if the car will be driven by a juvenile?

Yes. And if the car is driven by a juvenile when the insurance policy doesn't cover drivers below a specified age, the insurance policy doesn't provide coverage during the time the car is driven by the child.

When a child driving his parent's car has an accident, is the parent liable?

Yes. See Chapter 5.

28

Children Suspected of Breaking the Law

Children who break the law present unique problems. Whether she's a shoplifter or a killer, you just can't handle a twelve-year-old exactly like you handle someone thirty-eight years old who committed the same crime. At the same time, you certainly can't ignore her actions.

In answer to that dilemma, special laws were enacted regarding children who commit crimes, and special courts, called juvenile courts, were established to administer those laws.

Although all fifty states now have juvenile courts, the first was established in Illinois only about one hundred years ago. They do handle some other types of cases now, but juvenile courts first came into being to address two basic problems: children who break the law, and children who are abused, neglected, or abandoned.

Some jurisdictions with large populations have juvenile courts which hear nothing but juvenile cases. In some other areas, a court which hears many kinds of cases may also be designated a juvenile court.

The majority of our laws which concern children who commit crimes are found in the Juvenile Justice Code, a part of the Texas Family Code.

Our legislators tried to balance two important interests when these laws were drafted. They wanted to ensure the safety of the community at the same time that they provided treatment, training, and rehabilitation for children who break the law.

They attempted to promote the concept of punishment for criminal acts, yet, where appropriate, to remove the taint of criminality from children.

As a practical matter, that's not always easy.

As our society learned and grew, we rejected the harsh punishment and insensitive treatment once directed against children who broke the law. Among those who deal with juvenile offenders, there is now a strong segment throughout the country who believe the pendulum has swung too far toward protection of children. Those who assert that punishment is the proper response to crime, whatever the age of the criminal, are waging a battle with those who favor rehabilitation.

As the serious nature and the sheer volume of juvenile cases have increased, it's easy to understand why there is a "get tough" stance being taken toward juvenile offenders. Yet I believe that you can't give up on all children who commit crimes. You must attempt, wherever possible, to rehabilitate them, not only for their own sake, but also for the safety of society. Otherwise, they and the community are doomed to experience the grim results when they are released to their homes. This emphatically doesn't mean that children should be allowed to escape accountability for their crimes. To the contrary, I don't believe there can be true rehabilitation until a child learns that she's responsible for her actions, that illegal activities result in unpleasant consequences, and that she'll experience those consequences whenever she breaks the law.

Not all youthful lawbreakers can be rehabilitated, and society must be protected from those who cannot. But the majority of such children can be changed.

I also believe a necessary part of rehabilitation is examining, and, where possible, alleviating, the factors which contributed to the child's behavior. Those factors don't excuse the behavior, but they do help explain it. The sad thing is that so little money and effort are spent on prevention, which would be the best solution of all to juvenile crime.

In the past two decades, during which I have worked with delinquent children, the picture has changed dramatically.

In the 1970's, we were mainly concerned with children who were truants or shoplifters. Today, our court dockets routinely include children charged with murder, robbery, and aggravated sexual assault. Where once children stood in court, sorry for what they had done, and worried about what was going to happen to them, today we are often faced with defiance and a chilling lack of remorse.

There is no simple explanation. The emergence of drugs, especially crack cocaine, the advent of gangs, and deep trouble in parts of our economy have played a part. But I believe the greatest contributor to the increase in the incidence and severity of delinquency is the failure of the family. Failure to provide good role models. Failure to provide love, security, and self-esteem to children. Failure to provide the fair, consistently enforced rules children must have to grow into emotionally healthy adults. And the failure of society to find solutions to the grinding poverty that produces such unspeakable hopelessness for so many.

When we address these problems and begin to find solutions for them, we'll begin to deal effectively with juvenile crime. Until we do, we're just putting out brush fires.

We do know of some programs that work. But there simply isn't enough money to offer them to enough children and families for long enough periods of time.

Logic says that, even if we only care about the dollars involved, it's cost-effective to provide these programs to children who need them.

Consider the relative cost to society of counseling for a child, if that counseling helps prevent further criminal behavior throughout her lifetime, as compared to what the same child may cost us all if her life isn't turned around.

What can happen to a child who commits a crime?

If the child is under the age of seventeen, the offense isn't called a crime. In Texas, it's "delinquent conduct." Less serious offenses are referred to as "conduct in need of supervision." Lawmakers tried to spare children the stigma of being labeled criminals.

What happens to a child who breaks the law depends upon two things: the age of the child, and what she did.

If a child is ten through sixteen, she may have to appear in a juvenile court to answer charges filed against her by the State of Texas. If the offense is a minor one, she may go instead to municipal or justice court.

If a child is seventeen, but the offense charged occurred before her seventeenth birthday, she'll still appear in juvenile court rather than stand trial in an adult criminal court.

If a child is nine or younger, she can't be charged with an offense in juvenile court. However, her behavior may indicate that abuse or neglect is present, and law enforcement and PRS can investigate to see if that's the case.

Can anything be done to help children who are at risk of getting into trouble?

Yes. A juvenile court, probation department, law enforcement officer, justice of the peace, or municipal court judge may refer the child and the family to the services to the at-risk youth program.

This program serves children aged seven through sixteen. It is operated by PRS and may include one or more of the following:

Crisis family intervention, emergency short-term residential care for children ten years old or older, family counseling, parenting skills training, youth coping skills training, advocacy training, and mentoring.

If the court rules the child is an at-risk child, the child and the parents may be required to participate in one or more of the above programs.

If the parents fail to comply they can be held in contempt of court.

If a child ten or older fails to do so, she may be sent to juvenile court.

A child isn't eligible if she's charged with a felony other than a state jail felony.

PRS may file a petition asking any county or district court, other than a juvenile court, to find the child is, in fact, at risk.

What must be proven to find that a child is "at risk"?

The court must find that the child has:

- Broken a state, county, or municipal criminal law;
- Been truant from school;
- Run away from home; or
- Been DWI or driving under the influence of drugs.

What rights does a child have if she's questioned by police about a crime?

It depends on whether she's being questioned as a witness or a suspect.

What is a witness?

Someone who may have information that will help police in their investigation of a crime. A witness may be required to go to court for the trial, and what the witness says in court, under oath, is called testimony.

What rights does a witness have?

A witness may leave at any time while police are questioning her. A witness doesn't have to answer any questions unless she chooses to do so. A witness doesn't have the right to an attorney, but she can hire one to advise her if she wants. If she says something that might indicate that she took part in a criminal act, that statement can be used against her later in court.

What is a suspect?

A person who the police believe may have committed a criminal offense.

What rights does a suspect have?

It depends upon whether or not she's in custody.

What does it mean to be in custody?

A child is in custody the moment she's not free to leave, but must remain with the police. "In custody" is the term used rather than "under arrest" when children are involved.

How does a child know whether or not she is in custody?

She asks if she is free to go. If she is permitted to leave the officer's presence and go wherever she wants, at the time she asks the question, she's not in custody. If the officer places any limit on her right to leave at that time, she's in custody. For example, if the officer says "you can leave just as soon as you answer a couple of questions," the child is in custody.

What are the rights of a suspect who is not in custody?

The right to leave at any time. The right to say nothing and to answer no questions. She doesn't have the right to an appointed attorney, but has the right to hire an attorney to advise her. Anything she says or does that would tend to show she had any part in a criminal act can probably be used against her later in court.

What are the rights of a suspect who is in custody?

She doesn't have the right to leave. She must remain with the law enforcement officers and go where and when they tell her to go.

She has the right to call and inform her parents or guardian of her whereabouts.

She has the right to refuse to say anything at all, and not to answer any questions.

She has the right at any time to refuse to say anything further, or answer any more questions, even if she has already answered some questions.

She has the right to have an attorney to advise her and be present both before and during the time she's questioned. If she can't afford to hire an attorney, she has the right to have an attorney selected by the court and paid by the state to represent her.

She has the right to know that anything she says or does while in police custody can be used against her later in court.

She has the right to be told that she has all of these rights before being questioned.

What should a child do when stopped or detained by the police?

She should never run from the police, if they have said they want to talk with her. Evading arrest is itself an offense for which she can be tried in court. She must never strike, struggle with, or offer any physical resistance to a police officer, and she should do as the officer says without argument. If she offers physical resistance, strikes an officer, or inter-feres in any way with the attempt to take her or someone else into cus-tody, she's committing an offense for which she may be tried later in court. Also, physical resistance may cause her or someone else to be injured.

She should be polite. She may be frightened and angry, but anything less than her best behavior is just plain stupid. Consider the fact that, without the police, we would be living in a jungle. Most police officers are decent people, doing a hard job with very little thanks. They know their lives are in danger, every day, all day long. Why make that job any tougher than it already is? Besides, in such a situation, a child can only lose by being anything but respectful.

A child should never lie to the police. She should give them her cor-rect name, address, and age, but nothing else. She should tell them she wants to call her parents, and should talk with them, in private, before answering any questions at all. They should decide together whether to talk to an attorney before the child answers any questions. An attorney can determine whether the child is giving up any of her legal rights by answering questions, and can help her decide what's in her best inter-est. My firm advice is that a child should talk with an attorney before answering questions, whether or not she was involved in the offense. If her parents can't afford an attorney, she should wait to talk with the police until an attorney is appointed.

How much involvement does it take for a child to be charged with an offense?

If she helped hold someone down, even if she didn't strike the person herself, she can be charged with assault, just the same as the person who struck the actual blows.

If she acted as a lookout, or held illegal drugs for someone else, or drove a car she knew was stolen, or helped someone hide stolen items, she can be charged with an offense.

In Texas, the "law of parties" says everyone who takes part in any way is equally responsible for whatever happens during the commission of a crime. For example, imagine that your child and a friend decide to steal a car. Your child has no weapon, and no desire or intention to hurt anyone. Her friend, however, has a gun that your child knew nothing about. They try to steal the car, but the owner attempts to stop them. Your child's friend shoots and kills the man. Your child can be charged with murder, right along with her friend.

It's vitally important for your child to pick her friends carefully, and for you to know who they are. If a child is with someone who starts to break the law, she should leave immediately. She must not do anything whatsoever to help another person who is breaking the law. She must refuse to hold drugs or weapons or stolen items of any kind, because if they're found on her, she can be charged, even if they aren't hers. She must not act as a lookout or help anyone, in any way, to escape from the police. Any person who wants her to do any of these things is simply trying to use her with no concern about what happens to her as a result. Help your child understand that true friends don't get friends into trouble.

Who can take a child into custody for breaking the law?

A law enforcement officer, and sometimes a probation officer.

When can a probation officer take a child into custody?

When a child has already had her case decided by a judge, been placed on probation, and been given rules of probation, and the probation officer has reasonable grounds to believe the child has broken a rule of that probation.

When can a law enforcement officer take a child into custody?

When a court orders it, when a child's conduct would allow the officer to arrest her if she were an adult, or when the officer has reasonable grounds to believe the child has engaged in delinquent conduct or conduct indicating a need for supervision.

What is delinquent conduct?

It is:

- Doing something for which the child could be sent to jail or prison if she were an adult (traffic offenses are an exception, although driving while intoxicated, or while under the influence of alcohol or other drugs, is delinquent conduct);
- Breaking a rule of probation a court has given the child in an earlier case. But here there are some exceptions. Since certain behaviors, like running away from home, not attending school, and minor offenses for which an adult could only be fined are not delinquent conduct, they do not become delinquent conduct even if the child is on probation and those acts violate her rules of probation; or
- Violating an order of a municipal or justice court in a way that constitutes contempt of court.

What does the officer have to do, once the child is in her custody?

Whatever the officer decides to do, she must do it without any detours or undue delay. The officer must do one of the following:

- Dispose of the case without sending it to juvenile court (many very minor offenses are handled in this way);
- Take the child to a hospital if she's seriously ill or injured and needs medical treatment;
- Release the child to her parent or guardian, who must be given prompt notice that the child is in custody;
- Bring the child before a magistrate or judge if there's probable cause to believe the child has engaged in delinquent conduct or conduct indicating a need for supervision. This person must give the child the warnings the law requires before the child's statement about the offense can be taken;
- Deliver the child to a place where her breath and blood may be tested if there are reasonable grounds to think she's been drinking and driving. The child may consent to or refuse the testing. A videotape must be made of the offer of tests and the child's response, and it must be available to the child's attorney. The testing may be done in an adult facility. After the child takes the tests or refuses to take them, she must then be taken directly to one of the other places listed here;
- Take the child to a place designated by the juvenile court as a juvenile processing office, usually a room at the police station. It can't be a cell. A child may only be held at a juvenile processing office for a few purposes. She may be held there until her parent or guardian arrives so that she may be released. She may be detained long enough for the officer to complete necessary paperwork, or to photograph and fingerprint the child in circumstances where it's allowed by law. If the child is to be questioned or to give a statement, she may be held in order to receive the required warnings about her legal rights. The child can't be held at the juvenile processing office over six hours and can't be left alone. She has the right to have her parents and lawyer present; or
- Deliver the child to a juvenile detention facility.

Is there more than one kind of detention facility?

Yes. In addition to the juvenile processing office, where a child may be held only briefly and for limited purposes, there are places of nonsecure custody, certified juvenile detention facilities, and secure detention facilities.

When is a child taken to a nonsecure facility?

If a child is taken into custody for a traffic offense or an offense for which an adult could only be fined (except for public intoxication), she must be released to her parents, taken before a municipal or justice court, or held in a nonsecure facility for no more than six hours.

A nonsecure facility can't be locked, and a child can't be secured to any stationary object.

If a child is taken into custody for truancy or running away, what's to prevent her running from a nonsecure facility?

A child in custody for truancy or running away may be held in a more restrictive juvenile detention center.

Where is a child detained when in custody because of a curfew violation?

If she isn't released to a parent, she'll be taken to municipal or justice court or to a designated juvenile processing office.

When may an officer fingerprint or photograph a child?

Only in the following circumstances:

- If a juvenile court judge consents;
- If the child's parent or guardian gives written consent; or
- If a child is accused of a felony or misdemeanor for which an adult could be sent to jail.

These records can be sent to the Texas Department of Public Safety for inclusion in a statewide juvenile justice information system, once a child is referred to juvenile court.

The records aren't sent if the child isn't referred to juvenile court within ten days, or if she successfully completes a first offender program or what's called an "informal disposition." In such cases the prints and photos are destroyed, and the juvenile court checks to make certain that they are.

When may the officer give a child a polygraph or lie detector examination?

Only if:

- A juvenile court judge consents;
- The child's attorney consents; or

- The juvenile court decides after a hearing to send the child to be tried as an adult in criminal district court.

May a child be tested for HIV, AIDS, or a sexually transmitted disease?

Only if a judge rules that the child has committed one of these offenses: sexual assault, aggravated sexual assault, or indecency with a child. Such test results are confidential, but may be provided to victims of such offenses.

When can a child's statement about her part in an offense be used against her in court?

What the child says at the time the offense was committed, or at the time she was taken into custody, can be used. For example, an officer stops a child, running from a house that has just been burglarized, and, without being asked about the offense, the child says, "I told them we'd get caught; it wasn't my idea to break in there."

The statement must be made at these times, and not later. And it must be a spontaneous statement, not one made in reply to a question from the officer.

Another kind of oral statement that can be used against a child on trial is one where what she says is found to be true. For example, if the child says, "I killed him, and I tossed the gun in the dumpster, right outside his apartment," and a search of the dumpster turns up the gun, the statement can be used.

Oral statements of a child made in court, at a preliminary hearing other than a detention hearing, or before a grand jury are also admissible.

Written statements require that more protection be given to the child in order for the statement to be used in court against her. She must be taken before a magistrate or judge before she makes the statement. The magistrate must be fully convinced that the child is making the statement voluntarily and that she fully understands what the statement says, that the child is suffering no obvious physical or mental condition which would prevent her freely, voluntarily, and knowingly making the statement, and that she understands her legal rights. The magistrate must explain those legal rights to the child. They include the right to:

- Be told that any statement the child makes can be used against her in court;
- Remain silent, and to make no statement whatever;

- Have an attorney to represent her before or during the time she is being questioned;
- Have an attorney appointed for her by the court before she is questioned if she can't afford to hire one, and have her attorney's fees paid by the state; and
- Stop the questioning at any time.

The magistrate must see the child on two separate occasions to go over these rights. Once, before the statement is made, and again, at the time the child signs the statement. No police officer or prosecutor is permitted to be present—unless the magistrate believes herself to be in danger, when an officer or a bailiff may be present to protect her. However, the officer can't carry a weapon into the child's presence.

Another oral statement which is admissible is one which is given while the child is in custody. A magistrate must give the child her warnings before the statement, and the warnings, the child's acknowledgment and voluntary waiver of each right, and the statement itself all must be tape recorded.

Additionally, a child's oral statement is admissible if it wasn't given in response to questioning while she was in custody.

If the statement was given voluntarily and has a bearing on the child's credibility as a witness, it's admissible even if it was given in response to questioning while the child was in custody.

The entire question of whether the statement of a child can be used in court is a tricky one. A lot of arguments between lawyers center around whether or not the circumstances in a given case allow the state to use a statement. Most attorneys would suggest that no statement be made without an attorney's advice, and would caution the child that whatever the child says is probably going to be repeated in court.

Once a child is taken into custody and the police officer has completed the first steps of the investigation, what happens next?

A child may be sent to a first offender program. If that happens, the child won't be referred to the juvenile court, providing the program is completed successfully.

The qualifications for the first offender program are:

- The child hasn't previously been found guilty of delinquent conduct; and
- The present alleged offense is conduct in need of supervision, or
- The offense is delinquent conduct which isn't a felony, or state jail felony, or misdemeanor involving violence to a person, or use or possession of a firearm, illegal knife, club, or prohibited weapon.

The child's parents must consent to participation in the first offender program or she'll be referred to juvenile court.

The first offender program may include restitution, community service, education, training, counseling, and periodic reporting to the office or agency to which the child was referred.

If the child successfully completes the program her case is closed, unless she's taken into custody within ninety days for another offense. If the child fails to complete the program, her case is referred to juvenile court.

No statement the child makes to a person advising or supervising her or participating in the first offender program can be used against her.

If a child doesn't qualify for the first offender program, what then?

The intake officer must determine:

- Whether the person is ten through sixteen years old, or if she's seventeen but the offense in question was committed before her seventeenth birthday; and

- Whether there's probable cause to believe the child committed the offense. "Probable cause" simply means, would a reasonable person, under the circumstances, believe the child probably committed the offense.

If the answer to either of these questions is "no," the child must be released. If the answer to both is "yes," then the case moves to the next step.

Unless they have already been notified, the parents must be told of the child's whereabouts, and why she's in custody.

Whether or not probable cause has been found to exist, if the child is accused of a felony, misdemeanor involving violence to a person, or use or possession of a firearm, illegal knife, club, or prohibited weapon, the case is sent directly to the office of the prosecuting attorney.

The prosecuting attorney reviews the case to decide whether there's enough legal evidence to proceed and whether she should do so.

The prosecuting attorney alone makes the decision whether to file the case. She makes the final decision whether probable cause exists to believe the child committed the offense. If she decides it doesn't, that ends the case. If she finds probable cause, a petition is filed with the juvenile court, or the case is sent back to the juvenile probation department for handling without a court hearing.

What should a child and her parents do if she's released to her parents after questioning by the police?

Nothing further will happen, unless the child is referred by the prosecuting attorney to juvenile court or to the juvenile probation department for participation in various programs, or unless further facts come to light.

If any of the above happens, the parents will receive a letter, telling them to take the child to the juvenile probation department to talk with a juvenile probation officer. Such a letter usually means the prosecuting attorney has decided to file a case, requiring the child to appear in court, or that the prosecuting attorney has referred the case back to the juvenile probation department. It's very important to make, and keep, the appointment with the juvenile probation officer. If you don't, it will probably mean more than one trip to court before the matter is resolved, and you'll be antagonizing the person who will be asked to make recommendations to the judge about what should happen in your child's case.

The probation officer will write a report concerning the child, her family, and the circumstances surrounding the child. You should provide the information requested. If her report cards show good attendance, conduct, and grades, be sure the probation officer receives copies of them. Provide the probation officer with letters from employers, teachers, or ministers in support of the child. If the child takes part in sports, community, or church activities, or has won awards, make sure the probation officer is aware of them.

It's extremely important that the child be attending school, if possible, while awaiting her day in court. It also helps if she has a job of some kind, especially if she isn't in school.

The probation officer will also want to know how the parents plan to supervise the child's behavior. Who will take her to and from school or work? Who will supervise the child when she is not in school or at work?

Other rules should be established by the parents, and the probation officer should be told about them. For example, there should be a curfew. And the earlier everyone can live with, the better. But make it realistic; it may be a while before the case is heard in court.

The child shouldn't have contact of any kind with other children or adults who were involved in the same offense. At the very least, an adult should be present at any such meeting. And the child and her family should stay away from the victim of the offense.

If the victim suffered financial loss, it will help if she's paid the amount of her loss. This should be done voluntarily, as quickly as possible, and receipts should be obtained unless payment is made by check. It's best if the child herself earns the money to pay the victim, even if she must arrange to pay it out over a period of time rather than paying the entire amount at once.

How do you get an appointed attorney?

The probation officer will decide whether the child's parents can afford to hire an attorney for the child. There are guidelines to help. If the parents meet those guidelines, the juvenile probation department will ask the court to appoint an attorney to represent the child. If an attorney is appointed by the court, the state will pay the attorney's fee. That's necessary, because the law requires that every child charged in juvenile court must have her own attorney. It will save time if the parent will bring financial information to the interview.

If the probation officer says you can afford to hire your own attorney, and you disagree, there's still a chance you may be able to have a court-appointed lawyer for your child. You and the child must appear in court on the date set for the hearing. At that time, you'll be permitted to explain to the judge why you should have an appointed attorney. Take financial information with you that will support your claim that you don't have money to hire an attorney. Provide the court with information about unusual expenses, hospital bills, poor health, or other children you are supporting. The judge may appoint an attorney for you at that point. If not, at least you'll probably be given additional time in which to hire one. Tell the judge how much time you need; if it's reasonable, chances are you'll get it.

What should you look for if you have to hire an attorney for your child?

If the judge won't appoint an attorney for your child, the law says you must hire one. Many lawyers don't know a lot about juvenile law. It's a field where specialized rules apply. Observe those lawyers who are handling juvenile cases. They're more likely to be familiar with juvenile law and to know their way around the juvenile court system. See if any of the court staff can tell you the names of attorneys who have been appointed by the court in juvenile cases. Those lawyers are likely to know how to handle your case and are familiar with what's considered a fair fee for their work in such cases. You can also call your local bar association and ask for the names of attorneys experienced in handling juvenile cases.

If a parent pays an attorney to represent a child in juvenile court, what is the attorney's responsibility to the child, and what is the attorney's responsibility to the parent?

Many parents have the mistaken idea that if they're paying the attorney's fees, she must follow their instructions, even if the child wants something entirely different. Not so. What the parent is paying for is the attorney's representation of the child. The child, not the parent, is the attorney's client, and the lawyer's duty and loyalty are to the child. The child has the right to speak with her attorney, without her parents present. Anything the child says to the attorney, or the attorney says to the child, is confidential. The attorney may not tell anyone, including the child's parents, what the child said in private, without the child's specific permission.

What are the attorney's duties to the child?

The attorney must explain the child's legal rights to both the child and her parents, as well as the choices the child will have when she appears in court. The attorney must answer the child's questions about the case and the law, and provide her with as much information as possible so she can make a decision about whether to plead "true" (guilty) or "not true" (not guilty) to the charges.

What if the child says she didn't commit the offense?

If the child tells the attorney she didn't commit the offense, the attorney isn't allowed to let the child plead guilty, even if that's what the child and her parents want her to do.

Must the child plead "true" if she tells the attorney she committed the offense?

No. The child still has a right to make the State prove its case at trial. The attorney must see that the child has a trial if the child wants one, even if the parents want the child to admit she committed the offense.

If the attorney believes a conflict of interest exists between the child and the parents, the attorney is supposed to inform the judge and ask to be appointed the child's guardian ad litem for the duration of her case.

Sometimes, parents find it hard to understand why a child shouldn't be told to plead guilty if she committed the offense, especially if repeated trips to the courthouse result in additional legal fees, threaten the parent's job, and create inconvenience all around.

The reason is simple: The idea behind these rules is that children are individuals, with rights under the law that even their own parents must not prevent them from exercising.

What if the police don't release a child to her parents, but take her to the juvenile detention center?

The probation officer at the juvenile detention center will decide whether to release the child to her parent or to hold her at the detention center. If she's released, she may have to follow certain rules until she goes to court. And her parent must promise to have her in court, on time, on the day of her hearing.

If the child is held at the detention center, she has a right to a hearing by the second working day after being taken into custody, or the first working day if she was taken into custody on a Friday or Saturday.

At that hearing, called a detention hearing, a referee or judge will decide whether to keep the child in detention or release her to a parent or some other person until her court date. The judge first must decide whether there was probable cause to believe the child did commit an offense. If she finds there wasn't, the child is released. If the judge decides there was, the child still must be released unless the judge or referee finds that one of the following five things is true:

- The child is likely to run away before her court date, or someone is likely to take her out of the county;
- The child isn't receiving proper supervision, care, or protection from a responsible adult;
- There is no adult available to see that the child is in court when her presence is required;
- If released, the child might be dangerous to herself or threaten the safety of the public; or
- A court has found at a prior time that she engaged in delinquent conduct or a penal offense punishable by jail or prison, and if released, she's likely to do so again.

Parents must be notified, if possible, of every detention hearing. If they can't be located or don't appear, the hearing will be held anyway and a guardian ad litem or attorney will be appointed for the child.

When, at the first detention hearing, a judge finds probable cause to believe the child committed an offense, it isn't necessary to make that finding at later detention hearings. But the judge has to find one of the five facts listed above is still true at each subsequent hearing to hold the child until the next detention hearing.

A child in detention has a right to a detention hearing every ten working days until a judge makes a final decision in her case. In some smaller counties, a child is due a detention hearing only every fifteen days.

Does a child have the right to an attorney at her detention hearing?

Yes, and if her parents can't afford to hire one, she has the right to have an attorney appointed by the court to represent her without cost.

What other rights does a child have regarding a detention hearing?

She has the right to remain silent regarding any allegations against her.

No statement made by the child at her detention hearing can be used against her at trial.

She has the right to have the detention hearing conducted before a district court judge instead of a juvenile court referee if she prefers to do so.

If a child wants to remain in the detention center, and children occasionally do, she may sign a voluntary request for shelter. That written request must be renewed every ten days. If the child wants to be released sooner than ten days after she signed the request, there must be a hearing the next working day after her request.

Can a child give up her right to a detention hearing if she doesn't want one?

She must have at least one such hearing for the judge to decide whether there was probable cause to believe she committed an offense. After that first hearing, she may sign a written waiver regarding further detention hearings. Her attorney must also sign the waiver. It's only good until the next detention hearing is due and must be signed again every time the child gives up this right.

Do parents have to be present at detention hearings?

No. But if they can come, they probably should, even if they aren't asking for their child's release. A parent who wants a child released to her must attend the hearing.

A child in detention needs to know that she has family members who are interested in her and care about what happens to her. Attending the hearing gives parents a chance to visit with their child, and to be aware of any new circumstances involving her. Additionally, it allows parents to make the probation officer aware of any changes which might improve the child's chances of being released at a later date, if not now.

Sometimes, family members other than parents ask that a child be released to them. If so, they should be present at the hearing.

If no family member will be present, at least the child should be told why. It creates fewer feelings of rejection if a child understands her mother won't be present because she's ill, or her father won't be there because he has to work. A child saves face with her peers at the detention center if she can give them a reason why her parents weren't at her hearing.

If parents want their child released at the detention hearing, what should they do?

They should arrive early enough to talk with the child's attorney before the hearing and let her know that they are asking for the child's release.

The judge will be interested in whether the child may run away before there is a final decision in the case. If the child has never run away, and has a close relationship with her family, be sure the judge knows that.

The judge will need to hear what plan the parents have for supervising their child so she won't get into further trouble. It helps if the child can return to school. Find out if that's possible, and let the judge know if it is. If the child has a job she can go back to, that's a plus, too. It's important for parents to show the judge what adult will be supervising the child during those times she isn't in school or working. The less time the child is left without supervision, the better.

Parents should have established their own set of rules which the child must follow until her court date, and should let the judge know what they are.

The rules should include a curfew; work, school, or both; no association with anyone who was involved with the child in the offense; and no contact with the victim of the offense or the victim's family. Needless to say, the rules should also include no use of alcohol or other drugs, and no further violations of the law.

Often, a child will need to be taken for psychological or other tests before her court date. The parent should assure the judge that the child will be present for such testing. If the child is currently in counseling, or the parents plan to seek counseling for her, they should let the judge know. If the child is taking medication or is under a doctor's care, the judge must be advised.

A final and very important thing to know is this: An adult to whom the child is released can be held in contempt if she can't produce the child at later court hearings.

If parents want to attend the detention hearing, but don't want the child released, what can they do?

They should tell the child's attorney and her juvenile probation officer that they are not seeking the child's release. If they don't want to say that in the child's presence, thoughtful judges and attorneys can sometimes see that it isn't necessary to do so. At least the child knows they cared enough to be present.

If a child's parents won't be present, is it best for her to give up her right to a detention hearing, or should she have one anyway?

After the first detention hearing, which must be held, a child may waive any subsequent detention hearing. But even if no parent is present, she may want to have the hearing. It's a chance to ask for information, learn the date of her court hearing, or find out if her parents have been told of the hearing date. It's also her chance to talk with the judge and the probation officer. She may let the judge know about other relatives who might be willing to have her released to them, and ask that they be contacted before the next detention hearing. If she has a problem, is ill, or simply wants to talk to her probation officer, she can make that known.

If no adult willing to have the child released to her is present, the child must stay in detention. There's no reason she shouldn't give up the right to a hearing if she wants. Even when the child has waived her right to a hearing, if a parent shows up unexpectedly at the last minute, the judge will usually go ahead and hold the hearing.

Is there any reason for a parent to keep coming to detention hearings if the judge has detained the child at previous hearings?

Yes. It matters to the child. She's in a difficult situation, and knowing her parent loves and supports her is important. If work, poor health, a lack of transportation, or other children in the home make it a hardship to attend every hearing, at least try to attend some. And be sure the child knows why you're not there when you can't come. It's easier for a child whose parents don't appear at her detention hearings if they are visiting her at other times when they are able.

Another important reason for being present at detention hearings, even when the judge has already decided not to release the child at earlier hearings, is that things change. If you now have a better plan for supervising the child, or she now has a job waiting which she didn't have before, or she can now return to school, the judge may decide to release the child this time.

Can a child ever be released on a temporary basis?

Yes. Sometimes, judges will let children go home for a short time and then return to the detention center. If there's a death in the family, or serious illness, the child may be permitted to attend the funeral or visit the sick family member.

If the judge doesn't believe there's enough supervision to let the child go home during the week but the parents can show that there's proper supervision on weekends, the child may be released on a weekend pass. That's especially true if she's been in detention for some time.

Holidays often see many children released for a few days to be with their families. Usually, more adult supervision is available then, and judges are human, too.

Is it always best for a parent to seek a child's release from detention?

It depends. If some responsible adult will be available to supervise the child closely, if the child can return to school or work, if the parent has good rapport with the child and the child usually obeys the parent, and if the parent believes the child can be kept away from peers who are a bad influence, release may be a good idea.

If a child is released, follows the rules, and does well at home, her behavior tells the judge the child is likely to succeed on probation. When she goes to court, if she's already attending school regularly, making good grades, participating in school or church activities, and staying out of trouble, it's hard for a judge to decide it would be best to remove her from her home.

On the other hand, if the child doesn't go to school, disobeys the rules, or gets into more trouble, she's in a worse position at the trial than she would have been had she remained in detention. Also, children who have broken the law have often been involved with dangerous people and may not be safe if released.

What kind of visitation is a child permitted while in detention?

She must be allowed visitation "at reasonable times." Individual centers usually have their own rules. Check with the probation officer for local visitation hours and conditions. Usually, the detention center monitors or limits who may visit a child or correspond with her.

May a parent bring gifts, food, or clothing to a child in detention?

Local rules vary. Check with your child's juvenile probation officer first.

Why is a case sometimes filed against one child and not against others who were involved in the same incident?

The attorney for the state must be able to prove the case against each individual charged with the offense. The evidence may be strong against one person, weak or entirely absent against the others, even if each took part in the offense.

For example, if Mike, Scott, and John all broke into a house and stole some money, guns, and stereos, the prosecuting attorney may have a witness who saw Mike break in and can identify him, and a police officer who caught Scott as he ran from the scene, his arms loaded with the stolen firearms. But she may not have any witnesses, or proof, that John was there at all. If that's true, no case will be filed against John. It would be useless to file charges against him if there's no evidence to prove them.

What is "deferred prosecution"?

If the early investigation finds that further proceedings are permissible, the juvenile probation officer may work with the child and her family for not over six months rather than send the case to court for a judge to decide whether the child committed an offense.

This six-month probationary period is voluntary, and the child and parents may end it at any time and ask the court for a hearing.

The prosecuting attorney may approve deferred adjudication for any child. If the law requires that this particular type of case be sent to the prosecuting attorney, or if the child has a prior felony conviction, the probation officer can't grant deferred prosecution without the prosecutor's permission. Any violation of the program must be reported to the juvenile court. This is typically available only for a less serious offense.

How do you know when your child's case is going to court?

A child accused of delinquent conduct or conduct indicating a need for supervision must be given a copy of the document, called a petition, the state has filed with the juvenile court accusing the child of an offense. At least one parent must also be given a copy of that petition. This paper will explain where and when her case will be heard. It must be hand-delivered to the child by a person with the legal authority to do so. This is called service of process.

What does a petition tell the child?

The petition will state specifically what the child is accused of having done, and when and where the act is supposed to have occurred. It will also present the facts that give the court power or authority to hear the case. This power is called jurisdiction. A juvenile court doesn't have jurisdiction unless a child was at least ten and not yet seventeen when the offense occurred. The court also has no jurisdiction unless, at the time of the offense, the child either lived in the county where the case is filed, or the offense occurred there.

29

The Child in Juvenile Court

What are the choices a prosecutor has when filing a case against a child in juvenile court?

Depending upon the kind of case and age of the child, a prosecutor can file a petition requesting:

- Certification for trial as an adult;
- A determinate sentence in juvenile court; or
- Trial before the juvenile court with no determinate sentence.

Who must be present in court when the case is set for hearing?

The child must always be present. Each parent, managing conservator, possessory conservator, court-appointed custodian, and guardian of the child who've been given legal notice are also required to attend.

An exception can be made for anyone, except the child, if the judge finds good cause, if the person lives out of state, or if the parent isn't a conservator of the child.

What happens if a child or parent who has been served doesn't show up for the hearing?

Failing to appear is a bad mistake. The court can order a law enforcement officer to locate and pick up a person who fails to come to court after being properly served and ordered to do so. A child who doesn't come to court can be placed in detention, and a parent who fails to appear can be held in contempt of court. At best, you'll irritate everyone when you should be trying to show how reliable and responsible you and your child are.

For further information on proper behavior in court, see Chapter 1.

May someone who's required to attend hearings in juvenile court be fired for missing work?

No. If that happens to a full-time employee, he has the right to his job back plus damages.

If a child has run away, must the parents still appear in court on the day the hearing is set?

Yes. Only the judge can excuse anyone from a court appearance when the person has been ordered to be present. If the child later returns home, the parents must notify the juvenile probation officer, the child's attorney, and the court. The judge will then issue an order to pick up the child, and will probably place him in the detention center until his new court date.

If a child's parents were served with the papers about the hearing, and they fail to appear, can the hearing be held without them if the child is present?

Yes. If a child's parents fail to appear for any reason after being served, or if it was never possible to serve them because they simply couldn't be found, or if the child's parents are dead and no one else has legal custody of him, the judge can appoint a guardian ad litem for him and the case will be heard. The person appointed may be a relative or the child's attorney. He can't be a law enforcement or probation officer, or a member of the district attorney's office. A parent who was served, and failed to appear, may still face contempt charges.

A guardian ad litem may be appointed for a child, even if a parent is present, when the judge believes the parent is unable or unwilling to make decisions about the case based on the child's best interest.

If the parent hasn't been able to hire an attorney, must the child and parent still come to court on the hearing date?

Yes. A parent may ask the judge for an appointed attorney. If the judge agrees, the case may be reset to allow the attorney time to prepare. If the attorney is appointed during court, the parent and child should get his name and phone number and contact him at once, without waiting for him to reach them. If the judge denies the parent's request, he may give the parent additional time to hire a lawyer. But a parent who shows up, time after time, without an attorney after being ordered to hire one risks being held in contempt.

Who takes part in a court hearing, and what are their jobs?

The juvenile court judge is in charge. He makes certain that the lawyers obey the rules and that the child receives a fair trial. The judge must follow the law just like everyone else. After hearing the evidence, he decides whether or not the child committed an offense, and if so, what should be done to rehabilitate the child and protect society.

Judges also decide whether cases may be reset and rule on various other requests made by attorneys.

The State of Texas is represented at the trial by an assistant district attorney, called a prosecutor or prosecuting attorney, whose job is to present the case against the child.

The attorney for the child makes certain that the child and his parents understand his rights, ensures that the prosecutor proves every necessary part of the case against the child beyond a reasonable doubt, and follows the rules while doing so. The child's attorney must know all of the facts of the case and present every fact in the child's favor. The child's attorney questions the prosecutor's witnesses, trying to expose the weaknesses in their testimony, and calls witnesses for the child to support his claim of innocence, or to show why, even if the child committed the offense, the judge should still consider placing the child at home, or in whatever placement the child desires.

The bailiff maintains order, ensures everyone's safety, and makes certain no one who is in custody escapes.

The clerk of the court keeps the court files, swears in witnesses, and completes all necessary paperwork.

The court reporter is trained to use a special machine to record what witnesses say during the hearing. The reporter is also in charge of all items of physical evidence. The law requires that all trials of children be recorded by a court reporter. If the child wants to appeal his case to a higher court, there must be an exact record of what was said to determine whether the child received a fair trial.

There may also be a representative of the juvenile probation department present to provide reports, give the court information, or tell the court about possible placements for the child.

Some courts also have what are called court coordinators. As the name implies, these people coordinate all of the actions of the court staff to see that things run smoothly.

The other participants are the respondent and witnesses. The complaining witness is the victim of the offense. In a case involving a child accused of breaking the law, the child is called the "respondent," instead of the "defendant," the word used to describe an adult charged with committing a crime.

A juvenile case is a civil suit, not a criminal one, even though the rights of juveniles in such cases resemble the rights granted adult defendants in criminal cases. It's a reflection of the legislature's desire to avoid labeling a child a criminal.

Are there special rules of behavior for the juvenile respondent?

Yes. He should have no contact whatever with the complaining witness. Any such contact could be interpreted as a threat and cause further problems. Tell your attorney if such persons try to initiate a conversation with you or your child.

Neither the child nor his parent should talk with the prosecuting attorney without the child's attorney present.

Address the judge as "your honor" or "judge," and all attorneys as "sir" or "ma'am."

Be careful of clothing displaying slogans or insignias. The judge can read. "Born to Be Bad" on a T-shirt doesn't earn many brownie points with a judge who's trying to decide whether the child is a menace to society.

Judges are also familiar with gang colors and signs. To deliberately exhibit them in court is to forget that wise old adage, "Never tug on Superman's cape."

How does the hearing begin?

All witnesses must be sworn to tell the truth. If a witness doesn't want to swear because of his religious beliefs, he may affirm, or simply promise, to tell the truth.

What happens next?

The attorneys will tell the judge what issues the attorneys are asking the judge to decide that day. Sometimes they agree and sometimes they disagree about what they want the judge to do. The question may be whether to reset the case for another date, or they may be asking the judge to decide certain preliminary matters but to reset the case itself for another day. Or they may be asking the judge to dismiss the case altogether. Or they may be telling the judge that the child has signed a paper admitting that he committed the offense. Or, if the case has been set for trial that day, they may simply be announcing that they are ready for trial, and asking the judge to hold the trial, or to bring in a jury so that the trial may proceed.

There are two kinds of hearings. Issue and nonissue. An issue hearing is a hearing to determine whether the charges are true, and if so, what disposition should be made regarding the child. It is sometimes called a trial on the merits or, when its purpose is to decide what happens to the child, a disposition hearing. Issue hearings are always contested. Nonissue hearings may or may not be.

At a nonissue hearing, a child may ask for a trial setting before either a judge or a jury, unless he is charged with violating an earlier probation, for which there is no right to a jury.

At a nonissue hearing, either side may also file motions asking the judge to enter orders regarding things that must be done before hearing the trial itself. For example, there may be a request for a psychiatric evaluation of the child.

The child may also enter a plea of "true" at a nonissue hearing. In cases before juvenile court, a child does not plead "guilty" or "not guilty." The plea is "true" or "not true." If the child wants to plead true, he and his attorney sign a document, called a Stipulation of Evidence, in which he admits that he committed the offense charged and gives up his right to remain silent, as well as other rights, such as the right to a full trial before a judge or a jury. This may be done at either an issue or nonissue hearing.

What are some of the reasons cases are reset?

One or both sides may want more time to investigate the facts.

An attorney, party to the case, or witness may be ill.

An attorney may already be tied up in another case, and be unable to be present.

Medical or psychological tests may need to be conducted, and their results known, before the case is ready for trial. Even if a child and his parents know in advance their case will be reset, they must be present unless the judge has excused them.

What does the child do if he wants a trial?

He tells his lawyer to request one. Usually, after everyone is sworn in and ordered to return on the trial date, they are excused until then.

If a child pleads true, what happens?

After the child and his attorney sign the Stipulation of Evidence, the admission that he committed the offense, the child must swear that he understood it, and that all the information in it is true and correct. Then the child and his parents will be sworn in as witnesses.

Next, the judge will advise the child of the charges against him, the possible consequences if it is found that he did commit the offenses charged, and the child's rights. The judge will make certain the child understands what specific conduct he's accused of, and where and when it's supposed to have occurred. The judge will explain to the child all of the possible consequences if he is found to have committed the offense, including the law about admission of the record of this case in a criminal case later on. The judge will make certain that the child knows he had a right to remain silent and didn't have to admit that he committed the offense, and that he signed the stipulation voluntarily, without anyone threatening him or promising him anything to get him to do so. The judge will remind the child of his right to a full trial, where the State will have to prove the charges against him beyond a reasonable doubt and his attorney can question the State's witnesses and call his own witnesses. The judge will advise the child of his right to a jury trial.

The judge will tell the child that, if the allegations are found to be true, the judge can suspend the child's driving privileges for a period of six months.

And, if the child is charged with DWI or an offense involving drugs, he should also be told that the law requires the judge to take away his driving privileges for 365 days, or until his seventeenth birthday, whichever is longer.

A judge may suspend or deny a driver's license for commission of any offense, specifically including graffiti writing.

In cases where a sex offense is alleged and the victim was under seventeen, the child should know that if the allegations are found to be true, the judge may order counseling and regular polygraph examinations as a condition of probation. Parents may be ordered to attend instruction.

Once a judge has gone over these rights with the child and his parents, and is sure that they understand and the child still wants to plead true, the stipulation the child has signed will be admitted into evidence.

Based on the child's admission that the charges are true, the judge will find that the child did engage in delinquent conduct or conduct indicating a need for supervision.

That will complete what is called the adjudication phase of the hearing.

Does a child have any choices other than pleading true, or pleading not true and asking for a trial?

Yes. The child can plead no contest to the charges.

What is a no-contest plea?

A "no-contest" plea is one in which the child neither admits nor denies committing the offense. He merely offers no contest to the petition against him. He doesn't sign a Stipulation of Evidence. What happens is this:

The judge explains his rights to him, and asks how he wishes to answer the State's petition. He replies "no contest." Then the attorney for the State tells the judge what his witnesses would say if they testified in court. If the State's witnesses would be able to prove the case by that testimony, then the judge finds the child did engage in the alleged conduct. Although the result is the same, the child has not been required to admit that the charges are true. This is also known as a "nolo contendere" plea.

Is it ever possible to be referred to a Teen Court program instead of being tried in juvenile court?

Yes, sometimes.

If the alleged offense is a misdemeanor, punishable by a fine only, or a violation of a municipal or county ordinance, the judge can send the case to Teen Court. In order for that to happen, the child must waive the privilege against self-incrimination, testify that he or she committed the offense, and ask the court to be allowed to enter the Teen Court program.

The child must not have completed a Teen Court program for the same offense within two years of the time the current offense was committed.

The Teen Court program must be one approved by the judge.

If the child has successfully completed the Teen Court program at the end of ninety days, the juvenile court judge will dismiss the case, and it won't become a part of the child's record.

What if the petition charges the child with several offenses, and he wants to plead true to some, but not others?

The child's attorney should determine if the prosecutor is willing to drop some charges if the child is willing to plead true to others.

Sometimes, the child is willing to admit that he committed the offense, but not everything in the petition is true. Perhaps his name is spelled incorrectly, or his date of birth is wrong, or there's a mistake in the date of the offense. Each detail must be correct before the child signs the stipulation, and he must let his attorney know what changes are needed. Changes the prosecutor makes in the petition are called amendments. Sometimes they're made before the case even comes to court. Each time that happens, however slight the change, the child's attorney has the right to ten days to prepare an answer to the amended petition. The prosecuting attorney can also ask to make changes on the court date. If he does, the child's attorney may still request ten days to prepare his case. Usually, a change made in court on the day of the hearing is a small one, and the child's attorney will probably waive the right to a ten-day delay.

If a child decides he wants a trial, what should he and his parents do to help his attorney prepare for his defense?

What you do during the time your child is awaiting trial is extremely important. It may significantly affect the outcome of the child's case.

- Keep in touch with the attorney. This isn't the time to vanish into the woodwork. Call regularly, and keep your appointments with him.

- Prepare a list of witnesses to the alleged offense, people you believe have information about what really happened.

- Prepare another list of witnesses who will be helpful if the judge or jury decides the child did commit the offense, and the judge has to decide where to place him. This list should include teachers, ministers, or family members who will provide testimony to support the placement you're seeking.

- Get both lists, with addresses and phone numbers, to your attorney as soon as possible. It may be necessary to send out subpoenas to be sure the witnesses appear in court. If you delay too long, your attorney may not be able to talk with the witnesses or have them subpoenaed in time to get them to court when they're needed.

- If there are documents or items which you believe may be helpful, such as report cards, athletic trophies, citizenship awards, or canceled checks for restitution already made, be sure to get them to your attorney and go over them together before court.

- The child should discuss in detail with the attorney exactly what happened. He should always tell his attorney the truth. Otherwise, the attorney can't be properly prepared to defend him. The attorney-client privilege exists between the child and his attorney, which means it's unethical for the attorney to tell anyone what the child has told him in confidence. Even a judge can't force an attorney to disclose what the child said to him. The only time an attorney must tell what the child told him in confidence is when the child has told him of a crime he intends to commit in the future.

- The child must stay out of trouble, with the police, at school, in the neighborhood, and at home. Now, if ever, is the time for him to be a model citizen.

- Neither the child nor his parents should contact the victim or that person's family. If any of those people contact the child, the child's attorney must be informed at once.

- The child should have no contact with any children or adults who were also charged with the offense. These people are known as coactors.

- If the child has a problem with alcohol or other drugs, or needs individual counseling, seek professional help for those problems while awaiting trial. The sooner the child gets such help, the sooner he will be started on the road to rehabilitation. Additionally, a judge is more likely to leave a child in his home if it's apparent that the child's problems are being addressed there. Often, the child's family is experiencing discord and conflict that has nothing to do with the child. Or the child's behavior has caused anger among family members who can't agree what should be done. That is generally a signal that family counseling is needed, too. Seeking counseling in such cases is a very positive move. It doesn't mean anything is "wrong" with those people. But individuals who live together as a family don't exist in a vacuum. What happens to one family member affects the others, and impacts their relationships with each other. Seeking professional help benefits everyone involved.

What takes place if the child has asked to be tried by a judge rather than a jury?

On the day of the trial, the child, parents, and witnesses will be sworn in by the clerk. The attorneys announce they're ready, and the trial begins.

Sometimes, before the trial starts, the attorneys will ask the judge to "place the witnesses under the rule." When attorneys "invoke the rule," the judge will order all of the witnesses in the case to remain outside the courtroom, throughout the trial, until they are called to the witness stand. While they are under the rule, witnesses may not discuss the case with any person except the attorneys involved in the trial. Even after the witness has finished testifying, he is under that same order until the case is concluded or the judge excuses him. The child and his parents may remain in the courtroom throughout the trial. However, they must not discuss the case with anyone other than one of the attorneys.

After the witnesses are sworn and the rule invoked, the judge will explain to the child the charges against him, the possible consequences if those charges are found to be true, and the rights the child is afforded. These remarks are quite similar to those made by the judge when a child has entered a plea of true. Then the judge will ask the child how he pleads, and the child will reply "not true." At this point, the prosecuting attorney begins to present the state's case.

The State of Texas must prove the child's identity, age at the time of the offense, that the offense occurred when and where the petition says it occurred, and every single element required by law to constitute that offense. (Although the state must prove the child's age, if the child doesn't object at the hearing to the state's failure to do so, he waives the right to appeal based on that point.) Each of these points must be proven to be exactly as alleged in the petition.

For example, if the evidence shows that the child's legal name is different than stated in the petition, or his date of birth is incorrect, or the petition says the offense occurred in one county when in fact it occurred in another, or if even the date of the offense is wrong, the state stands to lose its case, because it has failed to prove every essential point of the petition. In addition, every offense has elements which are required to prove that an offense actually occurred. For example, in an assault, if the petition says the child struck the complainant in the eye with his fist and kicked the complainant in the leg with his foot, the prosecuting attorney must prove exactly that. It isn't enough to show the child struck the complaining witness and shoved him a bit.

Further, the judge must find that each one of these points has been proven beyond a reasonable doubt. A child is presumed innocent of all charges against him, until or unless the state proves those charges beyond a reasonable doubt.

A statement made by the child outside of court can't be used against him if it fails to meet all of the requirements of the law. If a child's statement is admitted during the trial, it alone is not enough to justify a finding of delinquent conduct. Other evidence must support it, at least in part. Neither is testimony of an accomplice to the offense enough to sustain a finding of delinquent conduct, unless it is supported by other evidence which tends to connect the child with commission of the offense. And it isn't enough if that supporting evidence just shows that the offense was committed by someone.

Furthermore, any evidence which was illegally obtained can't be used at the trial.

Before the prosecutor begins calling his witnesses, he may inform the judge that attorneys on both sides of the case have agreed on certain elements involved in the case, and want to "stipulate" to them. For example, they may want to stipulate, or agree, that the child's birthday as listed in the petition is correct. Any stipulations entered in the trial record require no further proof. Stipulations save time.

The prosecuting attorney will then begin calling and questioning the State's witnesses, one at a time, trying to prove all the necessary facts of the case. When the prosecutor has finished with a witness, the child's attorney then questions that witness. Each attorney may question each witness more than once. When the prosecuting attorney has questioned all of his witnesses, he'll rest his case.

At this point, if the child's attorney believes the prosecutor has failed to prove the charges beyond a reasonable doubt, he may ask the judge for a "directed verdict." That means he's asking the judge to agree that the state's evidence didn't meet the requirements of proof, and to dismiss the case.

If the judge grants the directed verdict, the case is closed, the child can go, and the state can never again try him for the same offense. To do so would be to place the child in "double jeopardy," putting him at risk of being found guilty twice for the same offense. It isn't allowed.

If the judge denies the motion, the child's attorney will start calling the child's witnesses to the stand. He hopes their testimony will cast doubts upon testimony of the prosecutor's witnesses. When the child's attorney has finished with a witness, it's the prosecutor's turn. This continues until all of the child's witnesses have testified, and been questioned by attorneys on both sides.

Throughout the questioning, you'll hear attorneys say "objection." Sometimes you'll hear them say it a lot. This means that one attorney believes that a question asked by the other attorney doesn't follow the rules of evidence about what kinds of questions may be asked of a witness and how they must be worded. If the judge sustains the objection, the witness is not permitted to answer the question. If the judge overrules the objection, the witness must answer.

If the witness is asked a question, and his answer might cause him to be charged with a crime, he may claim his Fifth Amendment right not to answer. Our Constitution says no one has to incriminate himself.

When the child's attorney has no more witnesses, the judge will ask for rebuttal witnesses. These are witnesses an attorney may call solely for the purpose of disputing the testimony of a witness for the other side.

When there are no more rebuttal witnesses, the judge will ask if there is argument. Each attorney has the right to make statements, called argument, about the evidence. The purpose is to convince the judge to see the evidence in a way most favorable to his side. After arguments, the judge will make a finding. He will either rule that the child did engage in delinquent conduct or conduct indicating a need for supervision, or he will rule that the state failed to prove its case against the child beyond a reasonable doubt. If that's the ruling, the case is dismissed.

Should a child testify in a case in which he is the respondent?

It depends. This is a decision to be discussed with the child's attorney. The prosecutor doesn't have the right to call the child as a witness. The child has a right to testify, but if he does, he must answer questions asked by the prosecutor as well as his own attorney. The state must prove that the child committed the offense; the child isn't required to prove that he didn't. And the child has an absolute right to remain silent.

If the child has admitted to his attorney that he committed the offense, his attorney can't knowingly permit him to lie under oath.

What if a witness who is subpoenaed to testify doesn't appear or refuses to testify?

The person can be picked up and brought to court, held in contempt, and fined or sent to jail.

How does a jury trial differ from a trial before the judge?

A child may decide he'd rather be tried by a jury than a judge. He has that right unless he's charged with violating rules of probation ordered in an earlier case. Even then, he has the right if the alleged violation is an act for which he could be given a determinate sentence. See Chapter 30.

A group of people called a jury panel will be brought to the courtroom. Each attorney will ask questions of them. This examination of the jury panel is called "voir dire," which means "to speak the truth." It gives the attorneys a chance to try to predict who will be most favorable to their side of the case.

When the questioning is finished, each attorney is permitted to strike, or drop, any six jury panel members without giving a reason. They just cross them off the list. These are called "peremptory strikes." The attorneys also may try to strike, or drop, one or more of the panel members "for cause." If the attorney can show the judge that the person might not be fair in this particular case for a specific reason, and the judge agrees, that person is off the list, and the attorney won't have to use one of his six "peremptory strikes" to be sure that particular man or woman is not on the jury. An example of a juror who might be struck "for cause" is a person who is related to the victim of the alleged offense.

After all of the strikes have been made, the first twelve people whose names remain on the list become the jury. The rest of the jury panel is dismissed. The jurors are then required to take an oath promising to do what jurors are supposed to do, and to follow the judge's instructions while doing it. After that, the trial is conducted in pretty much the same way as one tried before the judge.

Sometimes, if the attorneys want the judge to rule on some kind of legal question, the jury will have to leave the courtroom while the attorneys argue their position before the judge.

When the evidence has been heard, the judge will read instructions to the jury about the law, and about questions the jury must answer to decide whether the child engaged in delinquent conduct or conduct indicating a need for supervision. These instructions are called "the charge" to the jury.

Then the attorneys have a chance to make their arguments to the jury. The prosecutor will argue that the evidence proves beyond a reasonable doubt that the child engaged in delinquent conduct or needs supervision. The child's attorney, as you would expect, will argue that the evidence proves no such thing.

The jury then retires to the jury room, where they elect a foreman. Then they set about reaching their decision. All of the jurors must agree in order to find a child's conduct delinquent or in need of supervision.

Usually there are twelve jurors in juvenile cases, although the law permits fewer except in cases where the child has been indicted by a grand jury and could face up to forty years in prison. See Chapter 30.

When the jurors have reached a decision, they return to the courtroom and their verdict is read.

What if the judge or jury decides that a child did engage in delinquent conduct or conduct indicating a need for supervision?

The judge then holds a "disposition" hearing. It may take place that same day or at a later date. If the judge decides the child needs rehabilitation, or that the child poses a threat to himself or others, the judge must then decide where to place the child. There is no right to a jury trial in this disposition phase of the trial unless the child is facing the possibility of a determinate sentence.

How does a judge decide whether a disposition should be made, and what it should be?

By reading reports of probation officers, psychologists, and other professionals, and by listening to witnesses called by both attorneys. The child's attorney must be given copies of all the reports in advance.

What must a judge decide at a disposition hearing?

First, whether or not something further should be done about the child. If the child needs rehabilitation, or if protection of the public or the child requires that some action be taken, then the judge will take such action. If not, the judge will find no disposition is necessary, and the child is free to go.

If some disposition should be made, the judge must first decide whether to allow the child to remain at home, under rules of probation, or to remove the child from his home for placement elsewhere.

The child can't be removed from his home unless the judge finds that the child can't be provided the care and supervision necessary to conditions of probation in his home. In that event, the child may be placed in a foster home, with a relative, in a hospital or other rehabilitation facility, or in any other suitable public or private facility.

The child might be placed in an intermediate sanction facility.

The child may be committed to the Texas Youth Commission if he engaged in delinquent conduct, but not for conduct in need of supervision.

If the child is placed on probation, the judge will give the child rules to be followed.

If the child is removed from his home, the judge must also find the removal was in the child's best interest and reasonable efforts were made to avoid the necessity for removal.

What happens with the child will depend upon what offense he committed. Each offense is assigned a "sanction level." There are seven of them, increasing in severity from one through seven, and it's presumed that these are the appropriate dispositions for each level of offense.

A judge or a probation officer may vary from these sanctions, but if so, must explain why in writing to the juvenile board.

Here are the "sanction levels":

- Conduct indicating a need for supervision (other than an A or B misdemeanor). This level includes counseling, providing information to the child, and release to parents or guardian.

- Class A or B misdemeanor (other than one involving possession or use of a firearm or violating the order of a juvenile, justice, or municipal court). This level includes six months' deferred adjudication.

- Misdemeanor involving the use or possession of a firearm, third-degree felony, or state jail felony. At this level a child may be placed on probation for at least six months, to end when he turns eighteen years of age, or sooner if all the requirements set by the judge have been met. Those requirements may include restitution to the victim, community service, and participation in one or more of a variety of programs. There will also be rules of probation at this level for the child to follow.

- Second-degree felony. This sanction level requires up to fifteen months of probation, with the child under intensive supervision for the first three months or more of that time. In addition, there must be restitution to the child's victim, participation by the child and the parents in a variety of programs, and close monitoring by the probation officer.

- First-degree felony (other than a felony involving the use of a deadly weapon or causing serious bodily injury). At this level, the child will be placed outside the home, on probation, for a period of six to nine months;

he will remain on probation for another six to twelve months after he's allowed to return home. Again, restitution and participation in various programs will be required.

- First-degree felony involving the use of a deadly weapon, or causing serious bodily harm, or an aggravated controlled substance felony. At this level, the child is committed to the Texas Youth Commission. TYC may keep the child in custody until he turns twenty-one. And

- Capital felony, or if the child has been given a determinate sentence after approval of the petition by a grand jury. This level provides for commitment to the Texas Youth Commission. The length of time TYC will keep the child is set when the judge or jury gives the child a sentence of a specific number of years. It is called a determinate sentence.

What kinds of rules of probation are commonly ordered?

The judge can order curfews, require school attendance, forbid contact with coactors or complaining witnesses, and require counseling and participation in various programs offered by the probation department, as well as drug or alcohol treatment and education programs. And those are just a few examples.

The judge can also order that the victim be paid restitution for damages suffered, and usually must require the child to participate in community service as a form of restitution. Parents can also be ordered to perform community service.

Can a parent ask a judge for special help for a child placed on probation?

Yes. Usually, no one knows a child better than his parents, and they are best able to suggest what might help him. Parents should let the child's attorney know if they want to request counseling, tutoring, or testing, and a judge will often grant such requests.

Can the judge issue orders to the child's parents or other persons involved with the child?

Yes. Notice must first be given to anyone affected. Then, after a hearing, the court can order:

- Anyone who contributed to the child's delinquent conduct to do whatever is reasonable and necessary for the child's welfare, or to have no contact with the child;

- Anyone living in the child's household to participate in social or psychological counseling;

- Parents, as well as the child, to pay restitution to a person who suffered damages, injury, or loss as a result of the child's offense;
- Parents to pay court costs and supervisory fees if the child receives probation; and
- Parents to pay child support, if the judge decides to remove the child from the home and place him elsewhere.

What happens if the parents fail to obey such orders?

They can be held in contempt, fined, or sent to jail.

If several children took part in the offense, will the judge order the same disposition for each of them?

Not necessarily. Each case will be examined separately. Some things a judge considers in deciding where to place a child are:

- What part the child actually played in the offense;
- The child's prior record with juvenile authorities;
- Whether the child is in school or working;
- The supervision and support available for the child at home;
- Whether the child's history includes mental or emotional problems;
- Whether the child has ever run away from home;
- The child's relationship with his family; and
- Whether the child might be dangerous to himself or others.

Obviously, the facts are different for each individual, and the judge may decide upon different dispositions concerning several children involved in the same offense.

Does a child have the right to a jury for his disposition hearing?

Only if the prosecutor asks for a determinate sentence.

Is there anything a child can do if he disagrees with the decision of the judge or jury?

Yes. He should discuss with his attorney whether or not to appeal his case to the court of appeals. The child has the right to appeal either or both the determination that he committed the offense charged, and the disposition ordered by the judge. He has the right to be represented by an attorney if he decides to appeal, and to have an attorney appointed for him if he can't afford to hire one.

There's a time limit for filing an appeal, and it's brief. If the child wants to appeal, he must do so quickly.

If the child does appeal, can he go home while he waits for a court of appeals to hear his case?

No. The orders of the court are carried out while the case is being appealed. It's possible for a higher court to allow the child to go free on a personal bond during the appeal, but believe me, that's rare.

Does a child have the right to bail?

Not unless he has been certified for trial as an adult and transferred to the adult criminal court for trial. Then he has the same right to bail as an adult.

What if a child is awaiting trial for one offense, and he commits another offense while he's waiting?

He'll be taken into custody just as he was before. He may be released to his parents, or he may be held at the detention center under the rules and conditions we've discussed earlier.

The new charges may cause a delay of his first case, because the prosecutor may want to change the original petition to include the latest offense and the probation department may want additional time to reconsider its recommendations concerning placement.

If a child has committed offenses with which he hasn't been charged, is there any way to get them taken care of at the same time?

Yes. During the disposition hearing, if the prosecutor consents in writing, a child may admit the other offenses and ask the court to consider them in deciding disposition. The child can then never be tried later for such offenses.

But be careful. If the offense happened in another county, that county's prosecutor must give written consent.

Can a child's juvenile record ever be sealed?

Sometimes. When a child is found not guilty of every offense with which he was charged, his record must be sealed immediately.

Two years after the child is discharged from the juvenile system, his records may be sealed if his was a nonfelony offense. However, a judge can seal these records at any time after the child is out of the system. If the offense was a felony, but the child was not given a determinate sentence, the records can be sealed when the child turns twenty-one.

The records can never be sealed if the child was given a determinate sentence.

May law enforcement agencies gather information on gangs for intelligence purposes, even if there's no reason to believe that any particular gang member has committed a specific offense?

Yes. It may only be kept locally, and only be shared with court or other law enforcement agencies.

What does a juvenile judge do about juvenile respondents who seem to be mentally ill?

The judge must start proceedings to provide temporary or extended mental health services. Nothing further will be done about the child's case until his release.

If the child is released from the hospital before he turns eighteen, the judge can dismiss the case or proceed with a trial.

If a child isn't released before age eighteen, and the offense is one for which he could receive a determinate sentence, the juvenile court judge must transfer the case to adult criminal court. There, a hearing will be held to determine if the person is competent to stand trial.

What if a respondent seems to be mentally retarded?

The judge must start proceedings to determine whether commitment is necessary. Various mental health experts will examine the child and then make recommendations to the court. If the child meets the legal criteria, he will be sent to a residential care facility. Juvenile proceedings will be stayed until the child is released. If the child is released before age eighteen, the court may dismiss the case or proceed to trial. If the offense is one for which he could receive a determinate sentence, and the child hasn't been released by his eighteenth birthday, the case will be transferred to an adult criminal court.

30

Certification: Children in Adult Criminal Court

What does it mean for a child to be "certified"?

She will be tried as an adult in criminal court rather than as a juvenile in juvenile court.

When can a prosecutor ask for a child to be tried as an adult?

The following must be true:

- The child was fourteen or older at the time of the offense and the offense was a capital or first-degree felony or an aggravated controlled substance felony; or
- The child was fifteen or sixteen at the time of the offense and the offense was a first- or second-degree felony or a state jail felony.

The child can't be transferred to adult criminal court for retrial of a case in which a juvenile court has already decided the child's guilt or innocence.

The process for transferring the child is this:

- The child and her parents receive a copy of the petition and written notice advising them that a hearing will decide whether she is to be tried as an adult.
- Before the hearing, the judge will order a complete investigation of the child and her circumstances, and the facts surrounding the offense.
- At the hearing, the sole question the judge will decide is whether the child should be tried as a juvenile or as an adult. This hearing is commonly called a "certification" hearing, because a judge must certify the child for trial as an adult.
- At the certification hearing, the judge will read the report concerning the investigation. The child's attorney must be given copies of all reports at least a day before the hearing. Incidentally, the judge can order the attorney not to give the child or the parent information contained in the report.
- The judge must decide there is probable cause to believe the child committed the offense. If she doesn't find probable cause, the case is dismissed.

- The judge must also find that because of either the seriousness of the alleged offense, or the background of the child, the welfare of the community requires that the child be tried as an adult.
- Factors the judge must consider in reaching a decision include:
  + *Whether the alleged offense was against a person or property (a child is more likely to be certified for an offense against a person);*
  + *The sophistication and maturity of the child;*
  + *The record and previous history of the child;*
  + *The prospects of adequate protection of the public and the likelihood that the child can be rehabilitated by services available to the juvenile court if the child is not certified.*

If a child is charged with several offenses in the same petition, the juvenile court must transfer all or none to the adult court.

Usually, juvenile courts hear cases where a person is accused of committing an offense before turning seventeen, and adult criminal courts hear cases where a person is accused of committing an offense when she was seventeen or older.

But which court tries the case when a person who was under seventeen at the time an offense was committed turns seventeen before being tried, and the prosecutor is not asking for certification?

The juvenile court.

What if the person charged with committing an offense before the age of seventeen turns eighteen before being tried?

If a person turns eighteen or older while an appeal of a juvenile court's decision is pending and the appellate court sends the case back for retrial, the case is retried in the juvenile court.

That's an exception. Otherwise, a juvenile court can send a person eighteen or older to trial in an adult court for any offense committed before the age of seventeen if:

- The person hasn't already been tried for the offense and no decision has been made regarding whether she committed the offense; and
- The court finds from a preponderance of the evidence that for a reason beyond the state's control, it wasn't practical to try the person before she turned eighteen, or
- The state fulfilled its responsibilities but didn't have enough evidence to proceed in juvenile court and new evidence has been found since the person turned eighteen, or

- The person couldn't be found earlier, or
- A previous transfer order was reversed or set aside.

The juvenile court must also find probable cause to believe the child committed the offense.

What if a child has been certified before?

The judge must transfer a child to adult criminal court if she's charged with a felony and has been certified for a previous offense.

There are exceptions. If the child was not indicted after the previous transfer, was acquitted of the charge, the case was dismissed with prejudice, or any conviction was reversed on appeal, this rule doesn't apply.

Is there a right to a jury at a certification hearing?

No.

Does a child have the right to an attorney at a certification hearing?

Yes.

May a child appeal a decision to try her as an adult?

Yes.

If the judge doesn't certify a child, what happens then?

The child will be tried in juvenile court as if a transfer hearing never was held.

Because they don't want the same judge who heard the certification to decide the case, many attorneys ask for a jury in juvenile court.

What happens after a child's case is transferred to the adult criminal court?

At that point she's treated as an adult in every respect except one; no one can receive the death penalty for a crime she committed before she was sixteen, and no one may be executed before the age of seventeen.

She has the same right as an adult to bail, to an attorney, and to a court-appointed attorney if she can't afford to hire her own. However, if she can afford to pay a bail bondsman to get out of jail, the judge is likely to believe she can afford to pay an attorney.

The case will be referred to a grand jury, and if the grand jury believes there is probable cause to think she committed the offense, it will indict her. If the child is indicted, she will stand trial as an adult, and if she isn't, the case will be sent back to juvenile court, where she will be tried as a juvenile.

Are there any offenses for which a child, regardless of age, is never tried by a juvenile court, but always tried in criminal courts as an adult?

Yes, perjury, or lying under oath. A judge must first find that the child understood what it meant to take an oath to tell the truth, and the responsibility it imposed. I've never seen a child tried for perjury. But there it is on the books, bigger than life.

Children, as well as adults, are usually tried in municipal courts for traffic offenses. Municipal courts also try children the first two times they are charged with misdemeanor offenses for which adults can only be fined. After two such convictions, a child will be referred to juvenile court if she's charged with one of these offenses again.

Are boys tried as adults at a different age than girls?

No.

What does it mean when the prosecutor asks the juvenile court judge to give a child a determinate sentence?

The prosecutor is asking the judge to find that the child committed the offense, and to sentence her to serve a specific number of years, first, at the Texas Youth Commission, and then in the state penitentiary.

What is the greatest number of years a juvenile court judge can sentence a child to serve?

For a third-degree felony, not over ten years;
For a second-degree felony, not over twenty years;
For a capital, first-degree, or aggravated controlled substance felony, not over forty years.

How old must a child be to receive a determinate sentence?

Any age from ten through sixteen at the time the offense was committed.

Can a child receive a determinate sentence for any offense, or only for certain ones?

Only certain ones. Among them are:

- Murder;
- Capital murder;

- Aggravated kidnapping;
- Aggravated sexual assault;
- Aggravated assault;
- Aggravated robbery;
- Injury to a child or an elderly or disabled person;
- Felony deadly conduct involving the discharge of a weapon;
- Aggravated controlled substance felony (serious drug offenses);
- Criminal solicitation;
- Indecency with a child;
- Criminal solicitation of a minor;
- Attempted murder or attempted capital murder; and
- Arson, if someone dies or is injured as a result.

Does a child have the right to a jury trial when a determinate sentence has been requested?

Yes. A child always has the right to have a jury decide whether or not she committed the offense, but this is the only instance where a child has the right to have a jury decide what will happen to her if she is found to have committed an offense.

The jury must include twelve people, and all twelve must agree on the verdict.

How does the prosecutor go about seeking a determinate sentence?

The prosecutor files the petition, then sends it to a grand jury of the county where it's filed.

The grand jury may investigate the facts claimed in the petition, and if it "approves" the petition, that approval permits the prosecutor to ask the juvenile court judge or jury to give the child a determinate sentence if she's found guilty. An approval of the petition is like an indictment for an adult.

Nine members of the grand jury must vote to approve the petition.

What if the grand jury doesn't approve the petition?

The child's case goes back to juvenile court, where it is handled as if it had never been sent to the grand jury. The judge can't give the child a determinate sentence, but otherwise may order whatever she could order in any juvenile case.

If a judge or jury gives a child a determinate sentence, what actually happens to the child?

She's committed to the Texas Youth Commission.

She may be paroled by TYC without a court hearing once the child has served ten years for capital murder, three years for first-degree felony, two years for second-degree felony, and one year for third-degree felony.

If that happens before the child turns nineteen, she remains on TYC parole until she's twenty-one.

If the child is nineteen or older, she is transferred to adult parole supervision. If that parole is revoked, she goes directly to the adult prison to serve the remainder of her sentence.

If a child has been sentenced for capital murder and has not been paroled or transferred to adult prison by the time she's twenty-one, she then heads straight to the adult penitentiary.

Can a child be paroled early, or sent early to adult prison?

Yes. TYC can ask the juvenile court to parole a child before she has been in TYC the minimum required length of time for parole. This will be decided at a "release" hearing.

TYC can also request that a child sixteen or older who was given a determinate sentence be transferred to adult prison at any time. This decision will be made at a "transfer" hearing.

What happens at a release hearing?

The judge (there is no jury) can do one of two things.

- Order that the child be released under supervision; or
- Return the child to TYC without approving the child's release.

What happens at a transfer hearing?

The judge can transfer the child to adult prison or return the child to TYC.

Does the right to an attorney apply at a release or transfer hearing?

Yes.

What does a judge consider in deciding whether or not to release the person?

The person's character and experiences before and after commitment to TYC, the nature of the offense, the manner in which it was committed, the person's ability to contribute to society, protection of the victim of the offense or the victim's family, recommendations made by TYC and the prosecutor, the person's best interest, and any other relevant facts.

Does the person have a right to appeal the judge's decision at a transfer hearing?

Only if the judge orders her transferred to the penitentiary.

31

Keeping Your Child out of Trouble

Parenting today is an act of courage. Drive-by shootings, drugs, teenage pregnancy, and gangs are a part of the world we live in. Moms and dads must try to protect their children from those dangers while raising them to be happy, responsible adults. Talk about a challenge.

During twenty-three years of handling juvenile cases as an attorney and a juvenile court judge, I've learned some things that parents can do to keep their children out of trouble.

- Look in the mirror. What you see is what you'll probably get.

  Your child isn't born knowing how to act; he imitates you. Do you use drugs, drink too much, break the law, or participate in an abusive relationship? Your actions, not your words, will be the pattern for his behavior.

- Establish fair rules with fair consequences for breaking them.

  Rules give a child security by telling him what's expected of him and that someone cares enough to provide limits.

  Be sure he understands the rules, then enforce them consistently, not just sometimes, and start when he is very young. Children whose actions have no boundaries are in danger and dangerous to others.

- Show your child how much you love him.

  Tell him so. Hug him. Praise him when he does something that pleases you, and be certain he knows that it's the behavior you dislike, not him, when you correct him. Make it clear to him that you cherish those qualities that make him an individual.

  He'll first learn that he's lovable and worthwhile from you, and that is how development of the self-esteem necessary to healthy emotional growth begins. Some people carry lifelong images of themselves as "bad" or "stupid" because their parents told them they were so as children. Never tell a child he is anything you wouldn't like him to be; such labels may become self-fulfilling.

- Provide adequate supervision for your child.

  A responsible adult must be with small children at all times and nearby or readily accessible by phone to teenagers.

Having a reliable person constantly present is difficult, especially if you work, but consider sharing responsibility for your children with other parents or relatives, or investigate a church or neighborhood day-care program.

An adult should be supervising your child on his way to and from school, because children often become victims or victimize others during that critical time.

Know where your child is and with whom. Give him a curfew.

- Talk to your child about drugs.

Let him know that drugs are not okay with you, and explain why they are such a threat to his future and even his life.

Discover the reason for changes you see in your child. Sometimes parents continue to deny that their child could be on drugs, even when it's obvious to others.

If your child is using drugs, don't accept his assurances that he's quitting; get professional help for him at once.

- Discuss sex with your child.

The answers to your child's first questions about sex should come from you. Be honest and direct, but don't try to tell him everything you know about human sexuality if he just wants to know where babies come from. When he's older, explain that sex is a fulfilling experience at the right time with the right person, but also tell him why sex should be put on hold until he's ready to assume the responsibilities it entails.

Be specific about how AIDS and other sexually transmitted diseases are contracted. Share your information and views about birth control.

- Have fun with your child.

Everyone deserves childhood memories of happy times with family. They help develop a child's values and a sense of his own identity.

Try to be present for any of your child's activities to which parents are invited; it really matters. Find a sports team you can follow together, or develop a hobby you can share.

- Whatever it takes, keep your child in school.

A child who drops out of school is at enormous risk for many kinds of problems, to say nothing of how a lack of education will limit his future opportunities.

Cooperate with your child's teachers and help him to appreciate them.

If your child doesn't want to go to school, find out why. Boredom with classes may indicate a need for greater educational challenges. Talk with his teachers. Difficulty in learning may be a sign of vision or hearing problems or a learning disability. Ask the school or your doctor to evaluate those possibilities. Fear of other children or gangs may be the reason for a child's dislike of school. When that's the case, discuss the problem with school authorities and find a solution.

After all else fails, let him stay with a relative and go to school in another area or enroll him in a GED course.

- Help your child get a part-time job.

Work teaches a child he can earn the cash to buy what he wants. It builds self-esteem and self-reliance and is an effective way to teach respect for the property of others. A child who works to earn the money for a stereo understands what it means for someone to steal it.

- Teach your child to dream.

Help him examine the great variety of choices awaiting him in every area of his life.

Show your child how to set realistic goals and to work toward them. Make sure the goals are his, and not yours for him. No child should grow up to become a doctor or lawyer simply because that's what his father did or would like to have done.

Children need to believe in tomorrow and to plan for their place in it. When a child sees no future for himself, he's a candidate for problems ranging from suicide to violence.

- Tell your child what you believe in.

Expose your child to opportunities to develop religious beliefs. Talk with him about your values. We are all spiritual beings who need to believe in a power greater than ourselves, however we may define it. Sow the seeds to nurture your child's soul.

- Give your child the ability to trust.

A child learns to trust others by finding that his parents meet his basic needs, that they love him, and that they don't hurt him. A child who is neglected or physically, sexually, or emotionally abused by his parents learns early on that he cannot depend upon anyone.

If a child doesn't develop the capacity to trust when he's very small, he may never be able to do so and may lack the ability to form lasting relationships.

- Teach your child how and when to say no.

Children find it especially hard to say no to adults because they have been taught to respect authority. Let your child know when it's right to disobey an adult.

A small child should understand appropriate and inappropriate touching and how to escape someone whose behavior may harm him.

All children should be taught specific things to say and do when they are asked to participate in something dangerous or illegal. Peer pressure is tough to resist, but it's easier to overcome when a child knows exactly how to do so.

- Encourage your child to evaluate others based on their individual qualities.

Hate crimes originate with attitudes toward other groups of people. Teach your child to value the diversity of humanity, and explain why his opinion of others should arise from who they are as individuals rather than what racial, economic, or other group they belong to.

- Be sure your expectations of your child are reasonable.

Asking a child to achieve what is beyond his ability is cruel. Don't compare your child with anyone else; your expectations should be based solely upon his abilities.

If your standards exceed his capabilities, he's likely to become frustrated, angry, and rebellious, or to suffer serious damage to his self-esteem. A child who believes he can never satisfy his parents will stop trying.

Conversely, if you don't require him to conform to rules of behavior and levels of performance which are possible for him, he may believe he doesn't have to follow society's rules, either.

- Never accept or practice violence.

When a child sees one person hit another to win an argument or to exert power, the lesson is that hurting someone else is an acceptable means of settling disputes.

A parent who is either the victim or abuser in a relationship unwittingly provides a child the pattern for conducting his own relationships.

Abused children suffer emotional damage, which affects them long after their physical scars have healed. They often grow into abusers themselves, as do children who witness violence between their parents.

If abuse is occurring in your home, take steps to assure your child's safety and seek counseling.

Teach your child that it sometimes takes more courage to walk away from an explosive situation than to stay and fight.

- Once your child acknowledges a mistake and accepts its consequences, let it go.

Everyone does the wrong thing sometimes. It is counterproductive to dwell upon your child's past misbehavior. Forgive him, and move on.

- Urge your child to join groups for children his age.

  Children need to belong, and they require structure. Participation in organizations such as Scouts, school, church, and civic clubs fulfills those needs and helps divert children from membership in gangs.

- Talk with your child about guns.

  Explain that a gun has no mind of its own and no conscience. When its trigger is pulled, whether accidentally or intentionally, it fires at whatever is in its path.

  Emphasize that there's never a valid reason for a child to touch a handgun, and he must assume that any gun he sees is loaded. Teach him to get away from anyone holding a weapon and to tell an adult.

  If you have a gun in your home, it's your absolute responsibility to be certain that your child doesn't have access to it.

- Admit to your child and yourself that you make mistakes, too.

  Children who believe that their parents are perfect may have problems with their own self-esteem or develop unrealistic expectations of others. Let your child see that you have some flaws, just like everyone else.

Can you prevent your child from getting into trouble? There are no guarantees. However, these steps will tip the scales strongly in your favor, and one day, your grandchildren may be safe because of what your child learned from you.

32

Victims of Juvenile Crime

Rights of individuals who are accused of committing crimes have been carefully examined and protected, while the rights of those who suffered harm at their hands have been largely ignored until recently.

The trend has shifted toward greater concern for the safety and comfort of victims.

The law which established the following rights for victims of children is in the Texas Family Code.

The Texas Code of Criminal Procedure contains similar rights for victims of adult offenders.

Do victims of crimes committed by children have any special legal rights?

Yes. A person who suffered personal injury or harm or financial loss when a child committed an offense has specific legal rights.

Guardians of victims, and spouses, parents, children, or brothers and sisters of deceased victims have the same rights.

What are those rights?

They include the right to:

- Receive from law enforcement agencies adequate protection from harm, or threats of harm, arising from cooperation with prosecution efforts;
- Have the court consider the safety of the victim or her family as an element in deciding whether to detain the child pending her court date;
- Be informed of court proceedings, including appellate proceedings, and be told in a timely manner if they are canceled or reset;
- Be informed, upon request, concerning juvenile justice procedures, including preliminary investigations and deferred prosecutions and appeals;
- Give the judge information during the disposition hearing about the impact of the offense on the victim or the victim's family;

- Receive information about victim's compensation available under the law, and, upon request, to receive referral to social service agencies for additional help;

- Be informed, upon request, of procedures for release of juvenile offenders who have been given determinate sentences to the Texas Youth Commission, or placed in some other facility under supervision;

- Be notified, upon request, of release proceedings concerning the child, to give the Texas Youth Commission information to be considered regarding the child's release, and to be notified, upon request, of the child's release;

- Have safeguards taken to minimize the victim's contact with the child, her family, and her witnesses, before and during the trial, including, if possible, a waiting area separate from those persons;

- Have any property of the victim that is being held as evidence promptly returned once it's no longer needed as evidence;

- Have the state's attorney notify the victim's employer, upon request, that the victim's assistance and testimony may require her absence from work; and

- Be present at all public court proceedings concerning the child, subject to court approval.

How does a victim, guardian of a victim, or a close relative of a deceased victim request such notice of proceedings against a child accused of the offense?

By sending a written request to the court, asking to be notified of all court proceedings, and sending a copy to the prosecuting attorney's office. It must include information concerning the victim's name, the name of the child alleged to have committed the offense, relationship of the person making the request to the victim, and a current address where notices may be sent.

Are there other steps a victim can take to ensure that her rights are protected?

Yes. Let the prosecuting attorney know in advance that you are aware of your rights and intend to exercise them.

Does a victim, or a guardian or relative of the victim, have the right to participate in the case as a third party, along with the State and the juvenile accused of the offense?

No.

What can the victim do if she disagrees with the judge's decision in the case?

Only the actual parties to a case have the right of appeal. The victim and her relatives do not.

Is any agency or individual liable to the victim for failure to provide these rights?

No.

If a child is placed on probation, what protection should the victim request of the court?

First, that a rule of the child's probation be to have no contact with the victim or the victim's family. If she violates a rule of her probation, the child can be returned to court for another hearing, and may be placed outside of her home.

If the victim has suffered financial loss, she should request that the prosecuting attorney ask for repayment of that loss. It's necessary to have written proof of the loss, and it should be provided to the prosecutor before the trial date if possible.

Is any special protection available for children who are victims of other children?

If a child under thirteen is the victim of certain sexual or assaultive offenses, the child's out-of-court statement may be admissible despite the rule against hearsay.

The child's statement to the first adult she told about the offense is admissible if the other side is told in advance, the judge finds the statement is reliable, and the victim is available to testify at the trial.

33

Rights of Unborn Children

Few issues evoke a deeper emotional response today than those concerning the legal rights of fetuses, or unborn children.

Most people have strongly held opinions about abortion. Other issues are being examined which also balance the rights of unborn children with those of their mothers.

As we learn more about the effect of the mother's actions upon fetal development, difficult new questions arise.

As medicine makes advances in treatment of babies prior to their birth, new light is being shed on the subject of viability, that point at which a fetus born alive can survive outside its mother's body.

Typically, when new knowledge becomes available, the law slowly begins to change in response to the new information. For now, here's how it is in Texas.

Is abortion legal in Texas?

Yes. In 1973, the U.S. Supreme Court decided the case of *Roe v. Wade*. The question in that case was whether or not a Texas law that made abortion illegal, except for when it was necessary to save a mother's life, was constitutional. The Supreme Court said it was not. It held that:

- A woman has a constitutional right to privacy, and that includes the right to decide whether or not to have an abortion; and

- A fetus does not have a fundamental right to life, as guaranteed to "persons" under the constitution, because a fetus is not a "person" in the sense contemplated by the Fourteenth Amendment; and

- States have an important interest in protecting potential human life. At a certain point in a woman's pregnancy, that interest becomes strong enough to justify state regulation of abortions; therefore:

  + *States may not regulate or prohibit abortion during the first three months of pregnancy;*

  + *States may establish requirements to protect the health of the pregnant woman during the fourth through the sixth months of pregnancy; and*

+ *States may regulate or prohibit abortion after a fetus becomes viable, except when abortion is necessary to save the mother's life or health. The fetus is presumed to be viable from the start of the seventh month of pregnancy.*

Since *Roe v. Wade*, there have been tremendous advances in neonatal care, and because of that, states may now require physicians to determine the viability of a fetus.

Is it a criminal offense for a woman who has AIDS or is HIV positive to become pregnant?

No. See Chapter 20.

Is it against the law to drink alcoholic beverages while you're pregnant?

No, but there are many who believe it should be.

The mother's use of alcohol can have devastating effects on her unborn child. Even small amounts of alcohol affect the fetus. Excessive alcohol consumption can result in a condition called "fetal alcohol syndrome," or FAS. These babies may suffer from any one or more of the following: low birth weight, small head, speech disorders, hyperactivity, behavioral problems, premature birth, and abnormal facial characteristics. FAS is the third-leading cause of mental retardation in the United States.

A mother who drinks alcohol during her pregnancy increases the risk of spontaneous abortion, and of having her baby stillborn. A mother who quits drinking alcohol during her pregnancy can reduce the chance her baby will be born with these problems.

The earlier she stops, the better her chances of having a normal, healthy child.

Are criminal penalties for drug use any different if the user is pregnant?

No. Some states have charged women whose drug use affected their unborn children with child abuse or injury to a child, but that's quite rare.

Is the use of alcohol or drugs during pregnancy grounds for termination of the mother's parental rights?

It can be if the mother's alcohol or drug consumption during pregnancy causes her child to be born addicted to either. Of course, this doesn't apply if the drugs used by the mother were prescribed for her.

Termination must also be in the child's best interest.

Experts tell us a mother's drug use can affect her unborn child in the following ways:

- Marijuana produces an increased risk of sudden infant death syndrome, a low birth weight, and withdrawal symptoms in the baby;

- Heroin and other narcotics provide an increased risk of spontaneous abortion, stillbirth, low birth weight, small head size, withdrawal symptoms, premature birth, and sudden infant death syndrome;

- Cocaine or crack increases the risk of death, stroke, withdrawal symptoms, damage to internal organs, and severe behavior problems.

Does **Roe v. Wade** *enjoin states from enacting laws to prevent harm to fetuses?*

In my opinion, no. *Roe v. Wade* specifically answers the question of whether or not a state may prohibit abortions. Here, the question is not whether a woman has a right to an abortion. The question is whether a woman who has decided *not* to have an abortion owes a duty to her unborn child not to cause it harm by her actions prior to its birth, and whether a state can enact laws to enforce that duty.

What is the law regarding parental rights if a baby is born alive after an attempted abortion?

Parental rights may be terminated if a child is born alive as the result of an attempted abortion.

A parent can't file a petition to have his own rights terminated in such a situation. I don't know of an instance when this law has been used, but it's the law, nevertheless.

A parent's rights can't be terminated under this provision if the parent either didn't know about the abortion or consented to the abortion only to save the mother's life.

Can a child recover damages in a civil suit against a person for injuries caused to the child by that person before the child was born?

Yes. If a person negligently or intentionally causes injury to a fetus, which is later born alive, the child may recover damages from the person who injured him.

What if the person causing the injury was the baby's own mother or father?

If the child was born alive, the answer may be yes.

I'm not aware of any Texas cases, yet, on this point. In the past, to protect family solidarity, the doctrine of parental tort immunity prevailed. That means children couldn't sue their parents for civil wrongs of which children were the victims. But the trend appears to be toward holding parents responsible, just as any other person would be, for injuries to a child before he is born. A few courts in other states have already done so.

Can a child inherit from a father who died before the child was born?

Yes. See Chapter 25.

What if a person's negligent or intentional act causes a fetus to die before birth?

It may be possible for the baby's parents to bring a wrongful death suit against the person who caused the fetus's death.

Index

abandonment of child, 81–83, 105, 110.
    See also termination of parent-
    child relationship
abortion, 147, 161, 262–264
abuse. *See* physical abuse and neglect;
    sexual abuse
address-change notification, 55
ad litem, 5. *See also* attorney ad litem;
    guardian ad litem
adoption
    advertisements for, 26
    appeal of adoption case, 33
    and attorney representing child, 32
    Bill of Review for, 34
    children who may be adopted, 23–
        24, 28–29
    child's consent for, 30, 31, 123
    criminal background check of adop-
        tive parents, 32
    and death of adoptive parent, 34
    Decree of Adoption, 11, 33, 34
    definition of, 23
    and divorce of adoptive parents, 34
    fees involved in, 25–26
    finalization of, 33
    happiness associated with, 22
    hearing on, 33
    information on child for adoptive
        parents, 34
    and inheritance issues, 34–35, 122,
        196
    legal documents necessary for, 31
    and locating birth family and
        adopted children, 35
    methods of securing placement of
        child for, 25–27
    more than one couple asking to
        adopt same child, 33
    name change petition in suit for, 135
    and out-of-state child placement
        agency, 27–28

parent-child relationship in cases
    of, 11
persons able to adopt, 24–25
Petition for Adoption of a Child,
    28–30
Petition to Terminate the Parent-
    Child Relationship, 29, 32–33
through private, licensed child place-
    ment agency, 25–28
private placement by child's mother
    or managing conservator, 27
problems associated with, 22–23
professionals as go-betweens for, 25
proof of parentage in cases of, 11
through PRS, 25, 26–27
rights of adopted child in relation to
    birth family, 34–35, 132
rights of birth family toward, 34–35,
    122
setting aside of, through Bill of Re-
    view, 34
six-month requirement for child liv-
    ing in adoptive home, 30
social study for, 31–32
by stepparent, 23, 80, 123, 135
telling children they're adopted, 35
trial date for, 32
adoption registry, 35
adult criminal trials. *See* criminal trials
Affidavit of Relinquishment, 31, 80, 82,
    85–86, 124
Affidavit of Waiver of Interest, 86
Affidavits of Status, 31
age requirements
    for adoptive parents, 24
    for alcohol use, 138, 165–166
    for child leaving home without par-
        ent's permission, 125
    for determinate sentence, 250
    for driver's education course, 202
    for driving, 132, 138, 201

for employment of children, 189
for juvenile court, 207, 228, 248
for legal contracts, 132
for majority, 137
for marriage, 129
for motorcycle, motorscooter, or
    moped license, 202
for school attendance, 138, 140
for voting, 132, 138
Agreed Motion to Modify, 68
AIDS, 141–143, 148, 216, 255
alcohol use. *See also* drug abuse
    age for start of, 164
    age requirements for, 138, 165–166
    by children, 163–168
    consequences of minor's drinking,
        166–167, 180, 204, 234
    counseling for child, 237
    driving under influence of alcohol,
        164, 204, 214, 234
    expunging conviction of, 168
    and hazing, 184
    hotline on, 172
    parental consent for minor's drink-
        ing, 166
    by parents, 164–165
    physical effects of, 165
    during pregnancy, 83, 141, 162, 263–
        264
    prevalence of, among minors, 163,
        164
    prevention of bar opening near
        school, 168
    and removal of disabilities of mi-
        nority, 138
    risk of addiction to alcohol, 164
    sale of alcoholic beverages to under-
        age persons, 167
    sources of help for and information
        on, 171–172
    and suicide, 145
alternative dispute resolution, 44–45
alternative education program, 179, 181
annulment of marriage of child, 130–32
appeals
    of adoption case, 33
    of certification for trial as adult, 249
    of child support order, 64
    of juvenile court decisions, 244–245,
        248

of transfer to prison, 253
by victims of juvenile crime, 261
arbitration. *See* alternative dispute
    resolution
ARD committee, 154–155, 156, 157, 158
arrests. *See* law enforcement officers
artificial insemination, 11
Association for the Advancement of
    Mexican-Americans, 172
athletes' steroid use, 169
at-risk youth program, 207–208, 212
attorney ad litem, 5–8, 96, 193
attorney general's office, 30, 119
attorneys. *See also* prosecuting attorneys
    and appeal of juvenile court deci-
        sion, 244–245
    and ARD meetings, 158
    behavior toward, in court, 232
    being on time for appointments, 5
    at certification hearing, 249
    for child in adoption trial, 32
    and confidentiality, 4, 113, 221, 236
    contract of, 4
    court-appointed attorneys, 85, 96,
        220, 230, 231
    at detention hearings, 223–225
    fees of, 3–4
    as go-betweens in adoptions, 25
    for interference with possession of
        children, 72–73
    for juvenile court hearings, 230, 231,
        232–233
    for juvenile court jury trial, 240–241
    for juvenile court trial by judge, 237–
        238
    lawsuit for damages for personal in-
        juries to child, 192
    objections to questions during testi-
        mony, 3, 239
    and preparation for trial in juvenile
        court, 236
    and private placement of child by
        birth mother or managing con-
        servator, 27
    and removal of disabilities of mi-
        nority, 139
    responsibilities of, toward client and
        parent, 3–5, 221
    role of, versus guardian ad litem's
        role, 6

selection of, 3–5, 220
suspect's right to attorney, 209, 210
witness guidelines for questioning by, 2–3
automobile driving. *See* driving

bail, 245, 249
bailiffs, 231
bars, 167, 168
benefits, 127, 161, 192, 198–200
best interest of child, 6
bilingual education, 176–178
Bill of Review for adoption cases, 34
birth certificate, 11, 15–16, 134, 136, 173
blood tests of paternity, 18–19

CASA (Court-appointed Special Advocate), 6
Centers for Disease Control, 142, 143
Center to Prevent Handgun Violence, 145
certification for trial as adult, 216, 245, 247–249
child abuse. *See* physical abuse and neglect; sexual abuse
Child Labor Act, 189–190
child placement agencies, 25–28, 45, 80, 86, 119
Children. *See also* adoption; child support; juvenile offenders; parent-child relationship; unborn children
of alcoholics, 164–165
definition of child with no living parent, 23, 28–29
guidelines for parents on keeping child out of trouble, 254–258
legal definition of, 9
as property, 79, 87
rights, duties, and powers of, relative to parents, 10
as witnesses, 115–116
Children's Protective Services, 88
child support
and adoption, 30
amount determination for, 59–64
appeal of support order, 64
for children living in more than one household, 62–63

and college expenses, 57
and death of parent, 57
for disabled child, 57
end of, 57, 64
extension of, 57
gender considerations in, 56
and health insurance, 64–65
and joint managing conservators, 48
and legal definition of child, 9
management of, by managing conservator, 192
after marriage of child, 132
and medical expenses, 65
modification of, 68–69
for more than one child in divorce decree, 64
past-due child support, 58
and paternity suit, 20
payment of, 57
persons responsible for, 49, 56
and remarriage of either parent, 56, 68–69
retroactive child support, 57
by self-employed person, 63
and TANF payments, 199
time limit on, 57, 64
and visitation, 53, 56
wage withholding of, 57–59
withholding of, as weapon, 38
cigarette smoking, 168
civil suits. *See also* juvenile court
of child against parent, 37
for injuries caused to child before birth, 264–265
for interference with possession of children, 71, 74–75
juvenile case as, 231
for personal injuries to child, 192–193
for property damages caused by their child, 37
for removal of disabilities of minority, 138–139
wrongful death suit against person causing fetus's death, 265
clerks of court, 231
clothing for court appearance, 2, 232
coactors, 236
cocaine, 168, 169, 172, 264. *See also* drug abuse

college expenses, 57
complaining witness, 231, 232
conduct in need of supervision, 126, 207, 212
confidentiality
    attorney-client privilege, 4, 113, 221, 236
    and child abuse reporting, 90, 113
    of National Runaway Switchboard, 126
conservatorship. *See* managing conservators; possessory conservators
contracts, 4, 132, 138, 191
controlled substances. *See* drug abuse
counseling
    for abused children, 102, 147–148
    at-risk youth program, 207
    child's consent for, 147–148
    following removal of child from home, 94, 99
    for juvenile offenders, 207, 224, 234, 237
    for parents, 91–92, 97, 243
    for pregnant students and teen parents, 176
court-appointed attorneys, 85, 96, 220, 230, 231
Court-appointed Special Advocate (CASA), 6
court coordinators, 231
court reporters, 231
courtroom. *See* juvenile court
crack cocaine, 169, 264. *See also* drug abuse
crime. *See* delinquent conduct; felonies; juvenile court; juvenile offenders; misdemeanors; victims of juvenile crime
crimes against children. *See* physical abuse and neglect; sexual abuse
criminal background check of adoptive parents, 32
criminal trials
    certification of child for adult criminal court, 247–253
    for child abuse, 115–116, 261
    child witnesses in, 115
    district attorney's decision not to try a case, 114
    and grand jury, 241, 249–250, 251
    for perjury, 250

curfew violation, 215
custody. *See also* managing conservators; possessory conservators
    child's interview with judge on, 47–48
    child's preference for, 39–40
    and interference with possession of children, 71
    modification of, 66–70

deadly force used by police, 213
death
    of managing conservator, 69–70
    of parents, 31, 34, 57, 80, 122–123
    suicide by teens, 143–145
    wrongful death suit on fetus's death, 265
death certificates, 31
Decree of Adoption, 11, 33, 34
defense attorneys. *See* attorneys
deferred prosecution, 227
delinquent conduct, 207, 211. *See also* juvenile offenders; suspects
depression, 144
designer drugs, 169. *See also* drug abuse
detention facilities. *See* juvenile detention facilities
detention hearings, 223–226
determinate sentence, 243, 244, 246, 250–252
directed verdict, 238–239
disabilities of minority. *See* removal of disabilities of minority
disabled children
    child support for, 57
    discipline of, by school, 156
    financial assistance for, 161
    legislation on, 150–151
    in private school, 152
    special education for, 152–160, 175
    sterilization of, 160
disabled parents, 84, 150–151
discipline, 107–109, 156
disposition hearing, 241–243, 244
dispute resolution. *See* alternative dispute resolution
divorce. *See also* child support; custody; managing conservators; visitation
    of adoptive parents before Decree of Adoption, 34
    alternative dispute resolution in, 44–45

and child support payment, 38, 56–65
and court-ordered counseling, 51
and denial and/or sabotage of visitation, 39
and denial of husband as biological father, 13
guidelines on children and, 38–40
managing and possessory conservatorship in, 41–49
of minors, 132–133
and Motion to Modify, 66–70
and parent-child relationship, 40
and paternity establishment, 17
and property of child, 192
remarriage of minor following, 133
and Suit to Affect the Parent-Child Relationship, 118
temporary orders in, 53–54
and visitation, 50–55
DNA tests of paternity, 18
doctors. *See* health
domestic violence, 46–47, 50. *See also* physical abuse and neglect
double jeopardy, 239
DPS. *See* Texas Department of Public Safety (DPS)
dress for court appearance, 2, 232
drinking. *See* alcohol use
driver's education course, 176, 201, 202
driver's license. *See* driving
driving, 132, 138, 174, 176, 201–204, 234
driving under influence of alcohol, 164, 204, 214, 234
dropping out of school, 140, 174
drug abuse. *See also* alcohol use
  age for start of, 163
  commonly used drugs, 163–164, 168–169
  as conduct indicating need for supervision, 212
  consequences of, 172, 180, 204, 234
  and hazing, 184
  high-risk factors for, 171
  and juvenile offenders, 206
  by parents, 83, 107, 141, 162
  during pregnancy, 83, 141, 162, 263–264
  prevalence of, among children, 141, 162–163
  prevention of, 255
  signs of, 170–171
  sources of help for and information on, 171–172
  and suicide, 145
  treatment for, 147, 172, 237
DWI, 164, 204, 214, 234

Ecstasy, 169
education. *See* schools; special education
Education for All Handicapped Act of 1975, 150
electronic pager on school property, 182
emergency shelters, 126–127
emotional illness. *See* mentally/emotionally ill children and parents
employment of children, 188–190, 256
English-as-a-second-language courses, 176–178
ethics rules. *See* confidentiality
ethnic background and adoption, 24
expulsion from school, 157, 180–182

failure to appear in court, 1, 229–230
failure to report child abuse, 114
failure-to-thrive children, 105
false reports of child abuse, 47, 69, 114
family failure and delinquency, 206
family violence. *See* domestic violence
fathers. *See also* parent-child relationship
  and artificial insemination, 11
  biological father defined, 13
  child bearing surname of, 136
  civil suit against, for injuries caused to child before birth, 264–265
  legal definition of, 9, 11, 13
  legal father defined, 11, 13
  Original Suit to Affect the Parent-Child Relationship by, 119
  parental rights of, compared with mother, 11
  paternity establishment for, 15–21
  presumed biological father, 9, 11, 12–13, 17, 21
  rights of biological father who may not be presumed father, 20–21
  termination of rights of, 84, 86
  versus mother as managing conservator, 47
felonies, 212–213, 242–243, 247, 250–251

fetuses. *See* unborn children
Fifth Amendment rights, 239
final exams, exemption from, 183
financial assistance. *See* benefits
fingerprinting, 183, 215
First Amendment rights, 184
first offender program, 215, 217–218
flight with child, 90, 91
food stamps, 198, 199
foster care, 81, 88, 94, 99, 100, 119, 158, 173, 242
freedom of speech at school, 184

gangs, 186, 206, 232, 246, 256
GED, 174, 203
gifted and talented program, 182–183
graduation requirements, 157
grand jury, 241, 249–250, 251
grandparents, 48, 74, 75, 77, 117–124, 146, 199
group homes, 99
guardian ad litem, 5–8, 32, 96, 139, 230
guardians, 13–14
guilty/not guilty pleas. *See* true/not true pleas
guns. *See* weapons

habeas corpus. *See* Writ of Habeas Corpus
habitual felony conduct, 213
hallucinogens, 163. *See also* drug abuse
handicapped children. *See* disabled children
hashish, 163
hazing, 184–185
health
    AIDS and HIV infection, 141–143, 148, 216, 255
    child's consent for own medical treatment, 147
    doctor's information to parents on child's health, 147
    expenses for medical care not covered by insurance, 65
    failure to provide medical care, 110, 111, 112
    immunizations, 146, 148–149
    and Medicaid benefits, 198, 200
    medical examination in child abuse investigations, 91, 148
    medical examinations for juvenile court case, 233

    medicine administered by schools, 183–184
    minor's right to consent to abortion, 147
    parent's right to refuse medical care based on religion, 112, 148
    power to consent to treatment for child, 145–148
    pregnancy of teens, 145
    problems faced by children, 141–145
    suicide, 143–145
health insurance, 64–65
heroin, 163, 264. *See also* drug abuse
HIV infection, 141–143, 148, 216, 255
homosexuals, 25
hotlines, 113, 143, 158, 172
Hurst, E. Hunter, 164

"illegitimate" label, 15
immunizations, 146, 148–149
informal disposition, 215
inhalants, 163, 169, 212. *See also* drug abuse
inheritance, 34–35, 122, 194–196, 265
insurance for teen drivers, 204
interference with possession of children
    acceptable reasons for, 72, 76, 78
    child's consent to, 78
    child's refusal to go on visitation, 78
    legal responses to, 71–75
    protection against, 73
    and temporary orders, 71, 76, 77
    and visitation orders, 71
    and Writ of Habeas Corpus, 71, 75–78
    wrongful removal of child from U.S., 73
intermediate sanction facilities, 242
international child abduction, 73
Interstate Compact on the Placement of Children, 27–28
intervenors, 46, 48
issue hearings, 232

J. W. T., In the Interest of, 17
jobs for children. *See* employment of children
joint managing conservatorship, 43–44, 47, 48, 52, 67–68
judges. *See also* juvenile court
    and adoption, 31–33
    and certification for trial as adult, 247–248

and custody battles, 47–48
and detention hearings, 222–225
and disposition hearing, 241–243,
    244
jury trial in juvenile court, 240–241
and juvenile court hearings, 232–233
and no-contest plea, 234–235
order to child's parents or others in-
    volved with child, 243–244
proper behavior toward, 1–2, 3, 232
responsibilities of, 230–231
and transfer hearings, 252–253
trial by judge in juvenile court, 237–
    239
and witnesses, 3
jury panel, 240
jury trials
    for adoption, 32–33
    for annulment of marriage of child,
        131
    charge to jury, 240–241
    and determinate sentence, 251
    for disposition hearing, 244
    oath for jurors, 240
    for paternity establishment, 20
    proper behavior for, 1–3
    for removal of child from the home,
        99
    selection of jury for, 240
    size of jury, 241
    for termination of parent-child rela-
        tionship, 32–33, 86, 115–116
    versus trial before judge in juvenile
        court, 240–241, 249
juvenile court. *See also* juvenile offend-
    ers; law enforcement officers;
    probation
    age requirements for, 207, 228, 248
    appeal of court's decision, 244–245,
        248
    attorney for child in, 230–233, 237–
        239
    and child's admission to other of-
        fenses, 245
    child's right to testify in, 239–240
    child's statement as part of evidence
        in, 216–217
    and crime committed while child
        awaiting trial for another offense,
        245
    and determinate sentence, 243, 244,
        246, 250–252

different dispositions for children
    taking part in same offense, 227,
    244
directed verdict in trial by judge,
    238–239
disposition hearing in, 241–243, 244
failure to appear in, 1, 229–230, 240
historical development of, 205
issue hearings in, 232
judge's order to child's parents or
    others involved with child, 243–
    244
jurisdiction of, 205, 207, 228, 248
jury trial versus trial before judge,
    240–241, 249
and mentally/emotionally impaired
    respondents, 246
no-contest plea in, 234–235
nonissue hearings in, 232–233
persons participating in hearing,
    229–231
petition indicating court case, 227–
    228
preparation for trial in, 219–220,
    236–237
and probation, 243
proper behavior in, 1–2, 232
prosecuting attorney in, 229, 232,
    237–239
removal of child from home by, 241–
    242
for repeat misdemeanors, 250
respondent in, 231, 236, 239–240
rules of behavior for, 1–2, 232
and sealing of juvenile record, 245–
    246
Teen Court program versus, 235
trial by judge in, 233, 237–239
true/not true pleas in, 221–222, 233–
    234, 253
witnesses in, 2–3, 231, 232, 236,
    237–239, 240
juvenile detention facilities, 214, 215,
    222–226
Juvenile Justice Code, 205
juvenile justice information system
    (DPS), 215
juvenile offenders. *See also* felonies;
    juvenile court; juvenile deten-
    tion facilities; law enforcement
    officers; misdemeanors; pro-
    bation

age of, and what happens to offender, 207
AIDS and HIV testing for, 216
amount of involvement needed to be
charged with offense, 210–211
counseling for, 207
in custody, 208–209, 211, 213–214,
217–218
deadly force used against, by police,
213
and deferred prosecution, 227
and delinquent conduct, 207, 211
and detention hearings, 222–225
determinate sentence for, 243, 244,
246, 250–252
different dispositions for children
taking part in same offense, 227,
244
and drug abuse, 206
expulsion of, from school, 180
and failure of family, 206
fingerprinting or photographing of,
215
and first offender program, 215, 217–
218
"get tough" stance toward, 205–206
and habitual felony conduct, 213
and law of parties, 210
options for, if child not qualified for
first offender program, 218
options of police officers, once in
custody, 214, 222
and petition indicating court case,
227–228
polygraph examinations for, 215–
216
and probable cause, 218
rehabilitation of, 206
rights of, 208–209, 216–217
search of, by police, 213
and seriousness of offense and what
happens to offender, 207
statements made by, used in court,
216–217
juvenile probation officers. *See* probation officers
juvenile processing office, 214
juvenile record, sealing of, 245–246

Kempe, C. Henry, 87
kidnapping, 74
kindergarten, 175

law enforcement officers
behavior if stopped or detained by,
209–210
child in custody of, 208–209, 211,
213–214, 217–218
and crimes against children, 114
deadly force used by, 213
lying to, 210
questioning of witnesses and suspects by, 208–210
and release of child to parents, 219–
220
and removal of child from the home,
88, 90
and runaway children, 126–127
search of child by, 213
law of parties, 210
lawsuits. *See* civil suits
lawyers. *See* attorneys
learner's permit for driving, 203
legal guardians. *See* guardians
liability insurance for teen drivers, 204
liability of parents for their children's
acts, 36–37, 204
licensed child placement agencies. *See*
child placement agencies
lie detector examinations, 215–216, 234
lying
to law enforcement officers, 210
under oath, 2, 250

majority, definition of, 137
managing conservators
for abused child, 109
and adoption of child, 27, 29, 30,
31, 32
and alternative dispute resolution,
44–45
and child abuse, 46–47
child placement agency as, 45, 46
child's input on, 47–48, 123
and child support, 48, 56–65, 192
compared with guardians, 13–14
death of, 69–70
definition of, 41
following removal of child from
home, 93, 95, 99–100
intervenor appointed as, 46, 48
joint managing conservatorship, 43–
44, 47, 48
judge's decision on, 45–47
modifications of, 66–68

mother versus father as, 47
non-parent appointed as, 45, 46, 47, 77, 124
number of, for one child, 46
paternity suit filed by, 16
Protective and Regulatory Services (RPS) Department as, 46, 56, 86, 93, 95, 99–100
refusal of visitation by, 52, 53
responsibility for pick up and delivery of child, 54–55
rights and duties of, 41–43
and sexual abuse in family, 46–47
versus placement, 95
marijuana, 163, 168, 172, 204, 264. *See also* drug abuse
marriage license, 129
marriage of child, 129–133, 191
Mary Ellen, Case of, 87
McDonald, Donald Ian, 164
MDMA, 169
mediation. *See* alternative dispute resolution
Medicaid, 198, 200
medical care. *See* health
Mental Health and Mental Retardation Department, 158
mentally/emotionally ill children and parents, 84, 246
mentally impaired children and parents, 84, 160, 161, 246
minority
 definition of, 137
 removal of disabilities of minority, 137–140
misdemeanors, 212, 235, 242, 250
missing children, 173, 183
money. *See* property of children
mothers. *See also* parent-child relationship
 artificial insemination of, 11
 civil suit against, for injuries caused to child before birth, 264–265
 and donor embryo, 11
 legal definition of, 9
 as managing conservator, 47
 placement of child for adoption by, 27
 proof of parentage, 11
 rights of, compared with father, 11
 shelter for minor mother, 126–127
Motion to Modify for divorce orders, 66–70

motorcycle, motorscooter, or moped license, 202–203
movies, 190
municipal courts, 250

name change of child, 134–136
narcotics, 163, 172, 264. *See also* drug abuse
neglect. *See* physical abuse and neglect
net resources, 61–62
no-contest (nolo contendere) plea, 234–235
nonissue hearings, 232–233
non-parents. *See also* grandparents; relatives; siblings
 as managing conservators, 45, 46, 47, 77, 124
 neglect by, 110–111
 rights of, 117–124, 123–124
 TANF payments for child living with, 199
 and termination of parent-child relationship, 77, 118–120, 122–123
Notice of Intent to claim paternity, 20

OASDI (Social Security) benefits, 192, 198, 200
objections to questions during testimony, 3, 239
offenders. *See* juvenile offenders
Office for Civil Rights, 151, 160
office of attorney general. *See* attorney general's office
Original Suit to Affect the Parent-Child Relationship, 118–20, 121
overtime pay and child support, 62

pager. *See* electronic pager on school property
Palmer Drug Abuse Program, 172
parent-child relationship. *See also* fathers; mothers
 birth parents versus adoptive parents, 11, 34
 child's lawsuit against parent, 37
 and conservatorship versus guardianship, 13–14, 41–49
 and divorce, 40
 legal definition of parent and child, 9
 legal duties of parents toward children, 10

legal rights of parents regarding
    child, 10, 34–35, 48, 49
and liability of parents for their chil-
    dren's acts, 36–37
modification of rights of parents,
    69–70
mother's proof of parentage, 11
paternity establishment, 11, 15–21
rights, duties, and powers of children
    relative to parents, 10
termination of, 6, 7, 29, 32–33, 79–
    86
parole, 252–253
past-due child support, 58
paternity establishment, 11, 15–21
paternity registry, 7, 20
paternity tests, 18–19
peace officers. *See* law enforcement
    officers
peremptory strikes of jury panel mem-
    bers, 240
perjury, 2, 250
Petition for Adoption of a Child, 28–30
Petition to Terminate the Parent-Child
    Relationship, 29, 32
physical abuse and neglect
    consequences to child of, 101–102,
        257
    counseling for abused child, 102,
        147–148
    definition of and facts on, 101–102,
        104–106, 109–112
    failure to report, 114
    false report of, 47, 69, 114
    and implausible explanations for
        child's injuries, 107
    legal consequences if parent found
        guilty of, 82–83, 109
    and nonabusive parent, 109
    and parents as managing conserva-
        tors, 46–47, 69
    PRS investigation of, 90–92
    recorded testimony of child abuse
        victims for trial, 115–116
    removal of child from home due to,
        89, 90, 93–94, 109
    removal of person who abused child
        from the home, 92
    reporting of, 90, 113–14
    versus discipline, 108–109
physical disabilities. *See* disabled chil-
    dren; disabled parents

physicians. *See* health
police. *See* law enforcement officers
polygraph examinations, 215–216, 234
possession of children. *See* interference
    with possession of children
possessory conservators
    access versus, 120
    child's move to home of, 68
    and child support, 53, 56–65, 68
    conviction of, for child abuse, 69
    definition of, 41
    and failure to appear for visitation,
        52
    grandparents as, 48, 120
    intervenor as, 48
    judge's decision on, 48
    more than one person appointed
        as, 48
    and phone calls to child, 54
    and pick up and delivery of child,
        54–55
    rights and duties of, 41–42, 48
    and Standard Possession Order, 50–
        54
    and visitation, 50–55
prayer in school, 187
pregnancy. *See also* abortion
    and AIDS/HIV positive mother, 148,
        263
    alcohol and drug abuse by mother
        during, 83, 141, 162, 263–264
    consent for treatment related to, 147
    problem of teen pregnancy, 145
    and schools, 176
prekindergarten, 175, 178
presumed biological father, 9, 11, 12–13,
    17, 21
pretrial conference for paternity estab-
    lishment, 19
prisons, 252–253. *See also* juvenile de-
    tention facilities
probable cause, 218
probation, 203, 211, 219, 227, 242–243,
    261
probation officers, 88, 89, 211, 219, 220,
    222, 225, 227, 231
property damage by child, 36–37
property of children
    child's management of, 191
    child support payments, 192
    damages for personal injuries to
        child, 192–193

after divorce of parents, 192
inheritance by child, 34–35, 122, 194–197, 265
and married child, 132, 191
money earned by child, 192
and removal of disabilities of minority, 191
sale of real property by parents, 193
Social Security benefits as, 192
prosecuting attorneys. *See also* attorneys
and child's admission to other offenses with which he/she hasn't been charged, 245
and crime committed while child awaits trial for another offense, 245
and decision of probable cause, 218
and decision to file/not file case, 114, 218
and determinate sentence, 244, 251
in juvenile court, 232, 237–241
and victims of juvenile crime, 260
Protective and Regulatory Services (PRS) Department
Abuse Hotline of, 113
and adoptions, 25, 26–27, 35
and ARD meetings, 158
and children whose parents refuse to let them live at home, 126
investigations of abuse and neglect by, 90–92
and juvenile offenders, 207
as managing conservator, 45, 46, 56, 86, 93, 95, 99–100
and removal of child from the home, 88, 89–98
reporting of child abuse to, 90, 113–114
and runaway children, 126
termination suits by, 6, 7, 80, 82, 83, 84, 93
psychological examinations, 91, 224, 233

race and adoption, 24
recorded testimony of child abuse victims, 115–116
Rehabilitation Act of 1973, 150
relatives. *See also* grandparents; siblings
biological relatives of adopted child, 122
and death of parent, 122–123

juvenile court placement of child with, 242
as managing conservators, 124
placement of child with, following removal of child from home, 94, 98, 99
and power to consent to treatment for child, 146
rights of aunts and uncles, 122, 124
and shelter for runaway children, 126
TANF payments to child living with, 199
religion and medical treatment for child, 112, 148
remarriage
and child support, 56, 68–69
of minor, 133
removal of child from the home
child's right to representation at show cause hearing, 96
conditions for, 89–90, 91, 92
conditions for return of child to home, 97
events following second (show cause) hearing, 99
final decisions regarding, 99–100
first (emergency) hearing following, 93–94
guidelines for parent's regaining possession of child, 96–97
historical perspectives on, 87
jury trial for, 99
by juvenile court, 241–242
notifications of parent about, 92, 94–95
parents at hearings on, 94–95, 96
problems associated with, 87–88
and property ownership, 191
and PRS investigation of child abuse report, 91–92
representatives of State who may remove child, 88
second (show cause) hearing following, 94–98
steps taken by PRS after, 92–96
temporary restraining order for, 90
Writ of Attachment for, 90
removal of disabilities of minority, 137–140, 191, 193
reporting requirements for child abuse, 90, 113–114

Resource Center on Substance Abuse, 145
respondents in juvenile court, 231, 236, 239–240
restitution, payment of, 220, 244
retainers for attorneys, 4
retroactive child support, 57
Revocation Statement, 32
Roe v. Wade, 262–263, 264
runaway children, 74, 83, 89, 125–127, 212, 215, 230

sanction levels of crime, 242–243
schools
    absences from, 174, 212
    age requirements for attendance, 138, 140
    alcohol use in, 185
    alternative education program in, 179, 181
    attendance requirements to receive credit for classes, 175
    bars opening near, 168
    and bilingual education, 176–178
    and disabled children's rights, 151–160
    driver's education and traffic safety course, 176
    electronic pager in, 182
    English-as-a-second-language courses in, 176–178
    excused absences from, 179, 212
    expulsion from, 157, 180–182
    extracurricular activities in, 152, 177
    final exams, 183
    and freedom of speech, 184
    gangs in, 186
    gifted and talented program in, 182–183
    hair-length requirements by, 180
    hazing in, 184–185
    identification required for enrollment in, 173
    immunizations for, 148–149
    importance of attendance, 255–256
    kindergarten, 175
    legal excuses for missing school, 174
    and married students, 175
    medicine administered by, 183–184
    missing-child programs, 183
    and parent's inability to make child attend, 174
    parent's refusal to enroll child in, 83
    and power to consent to treatment for child, 146
    prayer in, 187
    and pregnant students and teen parents, 176
    prekindergarten, 175, 178
    and removal of disabilities of minority, 138, 140
    removal of student from class by teacher, 179–180
    residence of child and enrollment in, 173
    search of student in, 186
    "skipping" students to next grade, 183
    special education in, 152–160, 175
    students organizations in, 186
    summer school for children with limited English skills, 178
    suspension of student by, 178–179, 180
    tardiness to, 174, 179
    truancy from, 173–174, 212
    and tutorial services, 176
    unexcused absences from, 212
    weapons in, 180–181, 185
sealing of juvenile record, 245–246
search of child
    by police, 213
    by schools, 186
sedatives, 163
self-employment and child support payments, 63
service of citation for Petition for Adoption, 30
sex education, 255
sex offenses by minors, 216, 234
sexual abuse
    and consent by child to sexual behavior, 109
    counseling for abused child, 102, 147–148
    definition of and facts on, 102–104, 106–107
    failure to report, 114
    false report of, 47, 69, 114
    legal consequences if parent found guilty of, 82–83, 109

by managing or possessory conservators, 69

and nonabusive parent, 109

out-of-court statements admissible in cases of, 261

and parents as managing conservators, 46–47

physical harm from, 109

PRS investigation of, 90–92

recorded testimony of child abuse victims for trial, 115–116

removal of child from home due to, 89–90, 93–94, 109

removal of person who abused child from the home, 92

reporting of, 90, 113–114

symptoms of, 102–103

sexual activities of teens, 142–143

sexually transmitted diseases, 143, 216

siblings, 35, 122, 124, 146

single people, adoption by, 24

"skipping" students to next grade, 183

smoking by minors, 168

Social Security Administration, 161, 192

Social Security (OASDI) benefits, 192, 198, 200

social study for adoption, 31–32

special education

ARD committee in, 154–158

assessment and testing for placement in, 153–154

discipline of children in, 156

due process in, 154, 158–160

expulsion of student in, 157

goal of, 157

and graduation requirements, 157

hotline on, 158

information sources on, 158

legislation on, 150, 175

options of educational settings in, 156

and preparation for adult living, 157

qualifying disabilities for, 153

requirements for, 152–153

services beyond regular school year, 156

transfer to new school district, 158

speech, freedom of, 184

SSI. *See* Supplemental Security Income (SSI)

Standard Possession Order, 50–54

stepparents

adoption by, 23, 80, 123, 135

rights of, 123

and termination of parent-child relationship, 81, 119, 123

sterilization of disabled children, 160

steroids, 169

stimulants, 163. *See also* drug abuse

striking of jury panel members for cause, 240

sudden infant death syndrome, 264

suicide and suicide attempts, 111, 143–145

suits. *See* civil suits

Suit to Affect the Parent-Child Relationship, 77, 118, 122–123

supervision of child, 110, 254–255

Supplemental Security Income (SSI), 161, 198, 199

suspects. *See also* juvenile offenders

amount of involvement needed to be charged with offense, 210–211

attorney for, 209, 210

behavior if stopped or detained by police, 209–210

in custody, 208–209, 211, 213–214, 217–218

definition of, 208

release of child to parents after questioning by police, 219–220

rights of, 208–209, 216–217

suspension of student, 178–179, 180

TANF. *See* Temporary Aid to Needy Families (TANF)

tardiness to school, 174, 179

TEA. *See* Texas Education Agency (TEA)

Teen Court program, 235

Temporary Aid to Needy Families (TANF), 61, 127, 198–199

temporary orders

in divorce petition, 53–54

and interference with possession of children, 71, 76, 77

temporary restraining order, for removal of child from the home, 90

termination of parent-child relationship

and adoption, 29, 32–33, 80, 86

and Affidavit of Relinquishment, 80, 82, 85–86

and Affidavit of Waiver of Interest, 86

for alleged or probable father, 84, 86
and child abuse and neglect, 82–83, 109
and child's right to court-appointed attorney, 85
child's testimony in suit for, 115–116
definition of, 29, 80
dismissal of petition, 86
evidence needed for, 81
filing of petition before birth of child, 83
finality of, 81
and grandparents, 121
granting of, by court, 86
grounds for, 81–83, 84, 263–264
and guardian ad litem, 6
jury trial for, 32–33, 86, 115–116
and minor parent, 85
parent's request for, 80, 81, 85
and parent's right to court-appointed attorney, 85, 96
persons who may file petition to terminate, 6, 7, 80–81
Petition to Terminate the Parent-Child Relationship, 29, 32
and PRS, 6, 7, 80, 82–84, 86, 93
tests of paternity, 18–19
Texas Bureau of Vital Statistics, 20
Texas Department of Health, 148
Texas Department of Human Services, 199
Texas Department of Mental Health and Mental Retardation, 158
Texas Department of Protective and Regulatory Services (PRS). *See* Protective and Regulatory Services (PRS) Department
Texas Department of Public Safety (DPS), 202, 215
Texas Education Agency (TEA), 151, 158–160
Texas Healthy Kids Corporation, 64–65
Texas School for the Blind and Visually Impaired, 155
Texas School for the Deaf, 155
Texas Workforce Commission (TWC), 189
Texas Youth Commission (TYC), 126, 146, 242–244, 246, 250–253
tobacco use, 168
traffic offenses, 203, 250
tranquilizers, 163

travel arrangements for visitation, 53
trials. *See* criminal trials; judges; jury trials; juvenile court
truancy, 173–174, 212, 215
true/not true pleas, 221–222, 233–234, 253
tutorial services, 176
TWC. *See* Texas Workforce Commission (TWC)
TYC. *See* Texas Youth Commission (TYC)

unborn children, 83, 141, 148, 162, 262–265
U.S. Department of Education, 154, 159–160
U.S. Department of Health and Human Services, 150–151
U.S. Department of Justice, 163

victims of abuse and neglect. *See* physical abuse and neglect; sexual abuse
victims of juvenile crime, 259–261
videotaped testimony of child abuse victims, 116
violations of possession orders. *See* interference with possession of children
visitation, 39, 50–55, 66–70, 71, 78
voir dire, 240
voluntary adoption registry, 35
voting, 132, 138

wage withholding, 57–59, 65
Waivers of Citation, 31
Waivers of Interest, 31
weapons
    expulsion from school for carrying, 180–181
    misdemeanors with, 242
    parent's talking with child about, 258
    in schools or on school grounds, 180–181, 185
    for self-protection, 185
    suicide and guns, 145
weekend visitation, 51
wills, 193–197. *See also* inheritance
witnesses
    and attorney objections to questions, 3, 239
    attorneys' questioning of, 238–239
    children as, 115–116

child's list of and subpoenas for, 236
complaining witness, 231, 232
definition of, 208
failure of, to appear, 240
Fifth Amendment rights of, 239
guidelines for, 2–3
placing witness under the rule, 237
police questioning of, 208
recorded testimony of child abuse victims, 115–116

refusal of, to testify, 240
swearing in of, 232
work and children. *See* employment of children
Writ of Attachment, for removal of child from the home, 90
Writ of Habeas Corpus, 71, 75–78

XTC, 169

Youth Suicide National Center, 145